Robert Frost: Modern Poetics and the Landscapes of Self

For Amy and Rachel

Robert Frost: Modern Poetics and the Landscapes of Self

Frank Lentricchia

Duke University Press   Durham, N.C.   1975

Contents

Acknowledgments

I am pleased to acknowledge the advice, encouragement, and criticisms of my friends and colleagues near and far. Among the many who helped over the past five years, I'd like to single out David Ferry of Wellesley College and Brom Weber of the University of California, Davis, who were the generous and insightful readers for the Duke University Press. Roy Harvey Pearce of the University of California, San Diego; Blake Nevius of the University of California, Los Angeles; James Breslin of the University of California, Berkeley; Gerald Graff of Northwestern University, and Bernard Duffey of Duke University all gave unselfishly at moments inconvenient to themselves. They made a difference. The kindness and wit of Ashbel G. Brice, director of the Duke University Press, made the period of waiting and worrying easier to bear.

My thanks also to two shrewd editors: Jac L. Tharpe who allowed me to reprint in somewhat altered form my introductory chapter ("Robert Frost and Modern Poetics") which appeared in *Frost: Centennial Essays*; Earle Labor who granted me permission to reprint some pages (again in altered form) on "Mending Wall" which appeared in the *CEA Critic* for May, 1972 under the title "Experience as Meaning: Robert Frost's 'Mending Wall'."

Gratitude stipulates that I protect with anonymity my colleagues in the Department of English and Comparative Literature at the University of California, Irvine. They know well what they have contributed. I must, however, thank Howard Babb, an unfailing source of confidence and optimism, and Myron Simon who subtly and patiently encouraged my most crucial revisions.

There is one dear person, whose spirit hovers about this book—but her meaning and role cannot be said by my words.

At some level I'd like this study to be taken as a full-length response to George Nitchie, whose tough attack on Frost (*Human Values in the*

Poetry of Robert Frost, Durham: 1960) energized me at an early stage. I have not engaged Nitchie point by point; the total argument I offer is simply an alternative to his, which concludes that Frost is not up to Yeats, Stevens, and Eliot. (My view that Frost's theory of poetry is indebted to the organicist tradition, for example, is an alternative to Nitchie's argument because his is rooted in a Horatian view of the poem as a kind of repository for philosophical precepts, metaphorically ornamented. I don't think Frost believed that.) The last chapter of John Lynen's book, *The Pastoral Art of Robert Frost* (New Haven, 1960), is an eloquent plea for Frost's modernity, and also a persuasive alternative to Nitchie's view. Lastly, among the critical books, no one interested in Frost's modernity can afford to ignore Reuben Brower's *The Poetry of Robert Frost: Constellations of Intention* (New York, 1963). Brower has done some things so well that it would be superfluous to do them again. Several of his readings buttress my arguments in important places. I did not think it necessary to repeat what he has said.

Among other full-length critical studies several have been of value to me. Lawrance Thompson's *Fire and Ice: The Art and Thought of Robert Frost* (New York, 1942), pp. 3–61, Reginald Cook's *The Dimensions of Robert Frost* (New York, 1958), chapter 2, and Elizabeth Isaacs's *An Introduction to Robert Frost* (Denver, 1962), pp. 39–102, have all broken theoretical ground before me. Although my approach to theoretical problems and my conclusions are different from theirs, their scholarship improved mine.

The critical literature on Frost of essay-length is vast. Of the several pieces that bear significantly on what I do, the following are especially outstanding: M. L. Rosenthal's pages in *The Modern Poets: A Critical Introduction* (New York, 1960); W. H. Auden's "Robert Frost," reprinted in *The Dyer's Hand and Other Essays* (New York, 1962); James M. Cox's "Introduction" to *Robert Frost: A Collection of Critical Essays* (Englewood Cliffs, 1962); Robert Penn Warren's "The Themes of Robert Frost," reprinted in *Selected Essays* (New York, 1966); Clark Griffith's "Frost and the American View of Nature," *American Quarterly,* XX (Spring, 1968), 21–37; Harry Berger's "Poetry as Revision: Interpreting Robert Frost," *Criticism,* X (Winter, 1968), 1–22. Many other articles were helpful in my preparation. I learned particularly from those critics with whom I disagreed, for, often, I found a sharp focus for my own ideas because of the clarity and precision with which they put their opposing positions. The following is a list of shorter pieces that I found useful in the earlier stages of my work: J. McBride Dabbs, "Robert Frost and the Dark Woods," *The Yale Review*, XXIII (March, 1934), 514–520; Hyatt H. Waggoner, "The Humanistic Idealism of Robert Frost," *American Literature*, XIII (November, 1941), 207–223; C. H. Foster, "Robert Frost and the New England Tradition," *University of Colorado Studies*, II (October, 1945), 370–381; W. G. O'Donnell, "Robert Frost and New England: A Revaluation," *The Yale Review*, XXXVII (Summer, 1948), 698–712; Randall Jarrell, "The Other Robert Frost" and "To the Laodiceans," in *Poetry and the Age* (New York, 1953), pp. 28–36, 37–69; Reginald Cook, "Emerson and Frost: A Parallel of Seers," *New England Quarterly*, XXXXI (June, 1958), 200–217; Marion Montgomery, "Robert Frost and His Use of Barriers: Man vs. Nature toward God," *South Atlantic Quarterly*, LVII (Summer, 1958) 339–353; Lionel Trilling, "A Speech on Robert Frost: A Cultural Episode," *Partisan Review*, XXVI (Summer, 1959), 445–452; John T. Ogilvie, "From Woods to Stars: A Pattern of Imagery in Robert Frost's Poetry," *South Atlantic Quarterly*, LVII (Winter, 1959), 64–76; Lloyd N. Dendinger, "The Irrational Appeal of Frost's Dark Deep Woods," *Southern Review*, n.s., II (October, 1966), 822–829; Reginald Cook, "Frost the Diversionist," *New England Quarterly*, XL (September, 1967), 323–338.

F. L.

University of California, Irvine
July 1, 1974

A Polemical Preface

Among the most impressive literary critics published in America in the last two decades none are more provocative than those who attempt to articulate theories of the whole of American literature. The preeminent theoretical books in this area are Charles Feidelson's *Symbolism and American Literature* (1953); R. W. B. Lewis's *The American Adam* (1955); Richard Chase's *The American Novel and Its Tradition* (1957); Roy Harvey Pearce's *The Continuity of American Poetry* (1961); Leo Marx's *The Machine in the Garden* (1964); and Richard Poirier's *A World Elsewhere* (1966). With the exception of Feidelson, these critics share the fundamental assumption—rooted in the literary superpatriotism of the 1820s and 1830s—that there are (however elusive) peculiarly American cultural forces energizing our literature. The shared thesis of these recent theorists of American literature is that ours is a culture uniquely characterized by irreconcilable contradictions and tensions to which major American writers hold up the aesthetic mirror.

The frequency and intensity with which various dualisms appear in our literature do seem to be special to the American scene, but they are not uniquely American (as Marx and Pearce acknowledge). Rather, they are variant expressions of a wider international cultural scene—romantic, post-romantic, and modern—and have their origins in the broadly Kantian notion which places a creative self (as the source of all freedom, hope, and redemption) against an alien, resistant environment (as the disabling ground of convention, memory, and inhibiting communal structures and values). A recent collection of theories of American literature shrewdly puts the theorists of duality side by side, but excludes Feidelson, not because he doesn't posit a dualism (he does), but, I gather, because his controlling perspective draws so heavily on continental and English sources. Feidelson's work is generally regarded as ground-breaking, essential, and brilliant, but also as unsound ("by intention" as Stephen Whicher put it), eccentric, and "arid," in the words of one reviewer.

I am aware that what I am about to say may be regarded as an attempt to forestall the criticism of aridity and eccentricity, and aware, too, that some may take it as a mark of pretension that I should compare my methods with Feidelson's. First of all, I do not wish to put myself in league with Feidelson against the others. He may not care for my company, for one thing; nor do I know, for another, that he has an adversary view of his relationship with other leading Americanists. Secondly, I believe that anyone familiar with the critics named above will know that I owe a debt to them all. I mean only to say that the conclusions of those who speak for the "Americanness" of American literature are not incompatible with the "unAmerican" views that I hold. I admit to a mild polemical intention because I find the most important theoretical books on American literature somewhat (and unnecessarily) parochial. Surely American literature needs no defending against those English critics (and American anglophiles) who still take their cues from the nineteenth-century Englishman who asked (nastily), "Who reads an American book?"

In my view Robert Frost has been too much identified with his American tradition by those who care most about his poetry; and, as if in tacit agreement with Frost's interpreters, too much ignored by cross-cultural scholars of romanticism, modernism, and literary theory. The argument I pursue is typologically close to the Americanist arguments of Marx, Poirier, and Pearce: the primary *agon* in Robert Frost, a dramatic tension that emerges in his earliest poems, can be felt as a struggle between the fiction-making imagination and the antifictive of the given environment, social and natural. That this sort of point of view can be worked out—through the mediation of William James—within an international, modernist philosophical context does not weaken the case for Frost and American literature; on the contrary, I think it urges its human centrality. An important lesson of Frost is that the great liberated place of imagination celebrated by Poirier, Marx, and many romanticists (poets and critics) sometimes offers us no liberation at all. Frost is an ironist in the profoundest sense who teaches us that the dreaded antifictive—the real thing —is often to be preferred to what we make in the imagination, because the fictive "world elsewhere" may be a place of madness.

We have not had a broad-ranging critical study of Robert Frost since 1963. What that means precisely I am not sure. (Only a few since Jonson and Herrick have been more unobtrusively subtle and complex, have better integrated wit with high seriousness.) What is certain, however, is that at one time or another Frost managed to alienate major American critics. Cleanth Brooks once dismissed him on aesthetic grounds; Malcolm Cowley on political grounds; Yvor Winters on moral grounds. Though it is true, it is also irrelevant that Frost's figurative ways do not resemble those of Donne; irrelevant that he was not enamored of Rooseveltian liberalism; irrelevant that he did not deliver an image of a rational universe in his poems. But the views of Brooks, Cowley, and Winters have unquestionably shaped the views of many of us. For too many the question of Robert Frost has long been closed. In this book I intend to open that question again in basic ways. Frost is a major poet, and what that means, among other things, is that he has written in enduring language about our enduring conflicts. The price of not knowing him intimately may be our own self-diminishment.

Robert Frost: Modern Poetics and the Landscapes of Self

Introduction: Robert Frost and Modern Poetics

I offer this opening chapter as a theoretical prologue to the study of Robert Frost's poetry and poetics. My key figures and terms are familiar to students of post-Kantian literary theory, but their presence in a study of Frost is likely to appear odd not only to Americanists but also to the many who tend to think that Robert Frost, where ever else he may be located, must definitely be excluded from the company of the great modern poets (as J. Hillis Miller has so excluded him from *Poets of Reality*). The single most damaging and question-begging critical opinion about Frost today has not been rigorously formulated; it is simply a widespread and casual assumption among the *cognoscenti* of literary theory that Frost cannot bear sustained theoretical contemplation. I am urging, on the contrary, that the difficulty in Frost's poetics is not absence of depth and modernist sophistication, but too much subtlety. Thus far (and surely to his credit) he has successfully eluded the easy generalizations of the schools.

The most striking feature of Frost's thought is that it unifies what at the surface appear to be mutually exclusive dimensions of the modern literary mind. At the center of Frost's theory is the idea we find everywhere in Kant and the romantics that our mental acts constitute the world of our experience. Such a notion of mind leads to the romantic insistence that the poet's imagination is creative; that poems do not imitate a fully structured, antecedent reality, but rather inform a disordered world with value and meaning. But, curiously, snugly alongside this romanticism in Frost stands the philosophy of common sense realism which posits a world "out there," independent of our acts of perception. What I take as the principle of coherence in Frost's thinking has its basis in the pragmatism of William James. It is peculiarly the strength of James, that great philosophical mediator, to recognize a difficult real world which plays some determinative role in our lives, while also allowing for the possibility of the active consciousness to carve out, to a certain extent, the world of its desire.

I have made considerable use throughout, with special emphasis in this introductory chapter, of the conception of "landscape," both in its phenomenological and in its ordinary sense, because I believe that the notion may help us to contemplate the opposing forces in Frost's poetics not as a contradiction within a philosophical system but as twin impulses issuing out of the needs of a unified human consciousness. "Landscape" suggests both a configuration of objects really there in nature and, as well, the phenomenological notion that any particular landscape is coherent because the mind of the artist makes it so. The following passage from J. H. Van Den Berg's *The Phenomenological Approach to Psychiatry* helps to summarize the salient intention of Martin Heidegger's definition of human being and to explain my usage of both "phenomenology" and "landscape":

> The relationship of man and world is so profound, that it is an error to separate them. If we do, then man ceases to be man and the world to be the world. The world is no conglomeration of mere objects to be described in the language of physical science. The world is our home, our habitat, the materialization of our subjectivity. Who wants to become acquainted with man, should listen to the language spoken by the things in his existence. Who wants to describe man should make an analysis of the "landscape" within which he demonstrates, explains and reveals himself.[1]

In extension of Van Den Berg's remarks I shall urge that the special qualities of coherence and the peculiar dominance of this or that object in the landscape are reflections of the primordial ground of Frost's creative acts: the poet's subjectivity, his deepest inclinations and interests as a person.

1

As my point of departure I choose Frost's strange and surprising poem, "All Revelation"[2]:

> A head thrusts in as for the view,
> But where it is it thrusts in from
> Or what it is it thrusts into
> By that Cyb'laean avenue,
> And what can of its coming come,

And whither it will be withdrawn,
And what take hence or leave behind,
These things the mind has pondered on
A moment and still asking gone.
Strange apparition of the mind!

But the impervious geode
Was entered, and its inner crust
Of crystals with a ray cathode
At every point and facet glowed
In answer to the mental thrust.

Eyes seeking the response of eyes
Bring out the stars, bring out the flowers,
Thus concentrating earth and skies
So none need be afraid of size.
All revelation has been ours.

Frost's subject in "All Revelation" is a common poetic and philosophical subject after Kant and the romantics; it is strange and surprising only
within the context of most traditional thought about Robert Frost. His
subject is the act of the mind, the dynamic thrust of consciousness which
he evokes in his metaphor of the cathode ray. Because the glowing effect
inside the dark cavity of the geode originates from the action of the
cathode ray itself, our vision of the geode's interior is inescapably mediated
by our very instrument of scientific cognition. Frost shrewdly manages,
however, with the first four words of the poem ("A head thrusts in") to
suggest that the action of the cathode ray is figurative of human perception in general. In the third stanza the cathode ray emerges as a metaphor
for the tendency of human consciousness to be excursive, to reach out,
grasp, and shape its world. Frost's metaphoric expansion of the cathode
ray is paralleled by his metaphoric expansion of the geode itself. Initially
only a "stone nodule," the dictionary signification, Frost makes it mean by
the end of the poem something like "our world," "external reality in
general." In *The Poetry of Robert Frost: Constellations of Intention*
Reuben Brower points out how precise Frost's metaphor is: "geode," in
its etymological derivation, means "earth-like"; and this meaning is
solidly reinforced in the phrase "Cyb'laean avenue" (from Cybele, goddess of earth).

One way of reading "All Revelation," then, is to see it as a poet's confrontation with the leading idea of post-Kantian epistemology: that the

mind is in some part constructive of the world. But there are other, complicating philosophical features in the poem which once perceived make a simple Kantian reading impossible to sustain. In the first stanza, for example, a number of questions are bracketed that many traditional philosophers make the central concern of their quests. For Frost, though, the question of the origins of mind ("where it is it thrusts in from"); the question of the nature of the objective world considered as a thing in itself ("what it is it thrusts into"); the question of the final and enduring value of the constitutive acts of mind ("what can of its coming come")— all of these are questions that can be answered only provisionally, if at all. The suggestion is fairly strong that when such questions are taken to the metaphysical level they have little pragmatic value for Frost: "These things the mind has pondered on / A moment and still asking gone."

The third and fourth stanzas particularize a philosophical paradox which is crucial to Frost's poems and poetics. By affirming contrary philosophical perspectives—by insisting, on the one hand, that consciousness insinuates itself into the world, in part constituting that world (the geode *was* entered, the crystals do "answer" to the "mental thrust"), and by insisting as well (with realists) that the object is there, independent of the mind (the geode is "impervious," to use Frost's word, and resists flagrant transformation) Frost asks us to accept a poetic stance which (logically) is impure and ambiguous. But for a neoromantic in pursuit of the complicated feel of his experience in the world—a world *now* open to human imperative and wish (a shapeable place); a world *now* repressive and intractable in its thereness—it is a stance far more adequate than what we are generally given in philosophical traditions since Kant. When in the last stanza Frost does question the value of this peculiar meeting of mind and object (this "strange apparition"), his answer is pragmatic. Stars and flowers, earth and skies are there, but his consciousness shapes its environment in order to concentrate "the immensities" ("So none need be afraid of size"), make them manageable for the self and thereby supply a psychic need to feel in our confrontations with nature that we are not hopelessly lost and adrift in a world that engulfs and drowns us. The constructive acts of consciousness make the world answer, as Nietzsche reminds us in his extension of Kant, to the desires of our emotional nature; and, specifically, in this poem, to the desire for human mutuality—"Eyes seeking the response of eyes"—within an inhuman environment.

"All revelation has been ours," reads the last line. It is we who reveal the world—as we desire to see it revealed—and by so doing we reveal the revealing self. It is characteristic of Frost's poetic stance that he is generally able to maintain the perilous balance which he achieves in "All Revelation," where he moves in and out of the constituting mind. From the "inside" he achieves the kind of imaginative vision of a "better nature" demanded by his psychic needs—a vision which I shall be locating within his "redemptive" act of consciousness. From the "outside" he achieves an ironic self-consciousness which tells him that constitutive visions of a better nature are "apparitions" in the sense of "illusions." The act of ironic consciousness enables Frost to maintain his double vision, his skepticism, and his common sense which let nature be as it is; it is an act which often turns out to be as psychically health-giving as his more romantic acts of redemption.

2

On the American intellectual scene at the turn of the century there were basically three philosophical alternatives open to the young Robert Frost: the way of naturalism, which denied creativity and autonomy to human consciousness; the way of Josiah Royce's idealism which guaranteed creative freedom but only within the context of a metaphysics that a young, emerging modern mind could not accept; or the *via media* of William James's pragmatism which saved the autonomy of consciousness without asking, at the same time, for an acceptance of the early Emerson's view of nature and self. Those "redemptive" and "ironic" thrusts of consciousness embedded in "All Revelation" and repeatedly revealed in Frost's poems and urged by his poetics are illuminated by the philosophy and psychology of James, who provided Frost with the chief intellectual adventure of his brief Harvard experience at the end of the 1890s.

What was basic to the appeal of James for Frost, and for a number of minds that came to maturity at the turn of our century, was that naturalistic toughness which kept James from floating out of time in search for resolutions to human dilemmas. Yet for all his storied hostility toward his Harvard colleague, Josiah Royce, and toward various idealistic positions, James showed a faith—usually associated with a post-Kantian view of mind—in the creative potential of human consciousness which would establish the priority of the human act even in time. James's concept of the freedom of the human act of mind liberates the self from the subjection to the shaping dictates of material reality that seemed demanded by later nineteenth-century naturalism. Joseph Blau has put it this way: James "was a man whose training in the hard-headedness of science never completely subdued his soft-hearted belief that men are not merely automata, strictly determined in a mechanical world, but are, at least to some degree, the makers and shapers of their world."[3] I would characterize the principle of James's philosophical mediation between the tough-mindedness of naturalism and the tender-mindedness of Royce's idealism as "aesthetic": a term which I hope suggests that he predicates a freely creative activity of mind. It is doubtful that James's frequent recourse to metaphors which characterize the molding power of consciousness as an artistic process could have failed to catch the eye of the young Robert Frost, then in his formative poetic years.

We might imagine that James's reconciliation of scientific naturalism and Royce's idealism saved for Frost the truths of two distinct but not utterly incompatible philosophical traditions. From Royce's Kantian tradition James could accept the proposition that mind actively participates in the constitution of the world of fact without also accepting Royce's idealistic theory of timeless mental categories, or his theory of the Absolute, or his theory that evil is a privation, or his notion that the eternal and temporal orders are continuous. In James's modernism such issues were dead. And certainly they were dead for Frost. From those of tough-minded persuasion, James could accept the skeptical and common sense view of the world of objects as indeed "out there," as hard, dense, and often dangerous. It is a fundamental postulate of his famous discussion of the "stream of consciousness" that the objects of consciousness belong to a sharable and independent order.[4] By putting together the Kantian and realist views James could posit an objective world that is yet always caressed and bathed in human consciousness, receiving its final touches from the excursive (or "intentional") tendency of consciousness to reach out beyond itself and by so doing insinuate its needs and shapes into the given world.

Though the full philosophical context of his existential phenomenology is not relevant to Frost's poems, Jean-Paul Sartre has described a peculiar duality within human experience which points us to the very center of Frost's poems, James's pragmatism, and Sartre's own vision:

Each of our perceptions is accompanied by the consciousness that human reality is a "revealer," that is, it is through human reality that "there is" being, or, to put it differently, that man is the means by which things are manifested. It is our presence in the world which multiplies relations. It is we who set up a relationship between this tree and that bit of sky. Thanks to us, that star which has been dead for millennia, that quarter moon, and that dark river are disclosed in the unity of a landscape. . . . With each of our acts, the world reveals to us a new face. But, if we know that we are directors of being, we also know that we are not its producers. If we turn away from this landscape, it will sink back; there is no one mad enough to think that it is going to be annihilated. It is we who shall be annihilated, and the earth will remain in its lethargy until another consciousness comes along to awaken it. Thus, to our inner certainty of being "revealers" is added that of being inessential in relation to the thing revealed.[5]

The epistemological emphasis in James which places a premium on the power of human subjectivity to "reveal" and "build out" the world of experience was consistently articulated in his various books. In the first volume of *The Principles of Psychology* (1890) he put it this way:

Out of what is in itself an indistinguishable, swarming *continuum*, devoid of distinction or emphasis, our senses make for us, by attending to this notion and ignoring that, a world full of contrasts, of sharp accents, of abrupt changes, of picturesque light and shade.[6]

In another attempt to explain the nature of our perception of the world he said: "if we pass to its aesthetic department, our law is still more obvious. . . . The mind, in short, works on the data it receives very much as a sculptor works on his block of stone."[7] Still, even as he puts forth a view post-Kantian in its suggestion of a creative function for consciousness, James, in his proto-existentialism, refused to accept Kant's importation, into the act of knowledge, of timeless intersubjective categories of perception because he believed that prereflective consciousness was not transpersonal but irreducibly private and that its various constructions of the world flowed from a contingent subjectivity, the interests of an embodied self evolving through time and pressured by place. James separated himself from neo-Kantianism once and for all when he refused to take the notion of the constitutive power of consciousness to what he called the solipsistic conclusion of Kant and the neo-Kantians. Aligning himself with the tough-minded, he wrote that, for Kant, "Reality becomes a mere empty locus, or unknowable, the so-called Noumenon, the manifold of phenomenon is in the mind. We, on the contrary, put the Multiplicity with the Reality outside. . . ."[8] Without slighting the creative self, James affirms an insight of philosophical realism which the mainstream of post-Kantian idealism cannot affirm: that the pluralistic richness and particularity of the world stands recalcitrantly there, independent of mind, coercing our attention. Though his philosophical realism is recurrent throughout his career, James's formulation of it in his later work takes on this shrewd, phenomenological cast: "There may or may not be an extra-experiential *ding an sich* that keeps the ball rolling, or an 'absolute' that lies eternally behind all the successive determinations which thought has made. But within our experience *itself*. . . . some determinations show themselves as being independent of others . . . ."[9] The basic Kantian insight that man brings meaning into the world in a creative act has been transferred from a static idealistic setting—the eternal geometry of consciousness—to an existential one: the empirical self in a real world.

James envisions the drama of consciousness beginning when mind is confronted by a world which in its destructive unintelligibility seems to call out for a creative intelligence: "the visible surfaces of heaven and earth refuse to be brought by us into any intelligible unity at all. Every phenomenon that we would praise there exists cheek by jowl with some contrary phenomenon. . . ."[10] Such a vision of the face of reality is "poisonous,"[11] James concluded—ultimately fatal to psychological serenity —and intolerable. The preservation of our "mental sanity"[12] is directly dependent upon the mind's power to transform its environment, to create for itself something not already there, to take that romantic leap beyond the function that traditional empiricism normally assigned to it. In short, the creative act of mind in James's philosophy defines the self as the redeemer of brute fact and chaos into human value, pattern, and significance.

3

The crucial metaphor for the creative act of mind in James, that of the process of the sculptor,[13] is strikingly reflected in passages in Frost's letters: "My object is true form—is and always will be. . . . I fight to be allowed to sit cross-legged on the old flint pile and flake a lump into an artifact."[14] Or, more explicitly still: "I thank the Lord for crudity which is rawness, which is raw material. . . . A real artist delights in roughness for what he can do to it. He's the brute who can knock the corners off the marble block. . . ."[15]

This sculpting act of consciousness becomes literary in character as it avails itself to the poet's technique. Given our modern fascination with the amalgamatory, ordering powers of metaphor we cannot help recalling Johnson on Cowley, Coleridge on imagination, Eliot on Marvell, and on to the dearest concerns of New Critics and neo-New Critics when we meet with this in James: "Purely objective truth, truth in whose establishment the function of giving human satisfaction in marrying previous parts of experience with newer parts played no role whatsoever, is nowhere to be found. . . . 'to be true' *means* only to perform this marriage-function."[16]

When James spoke of the "marriage-function" of consciousness he implicitly analogized the creative act of mind to the dynamic, integrative process of metaphoric activity. For Frost, the metaphoric act of the mind, one of his favorite philosophical themes,[17] is basically a shaping and order-making process. "The only materialist," as he put it, "is the man who gets lost in his material without a gathering metaphor to throw it into shape and order. He is the lost soul."[18] Metaphoric activity is indigenous, Frost frequently suggested, not only to poetic thinking but to all thinking:[19] "Poetry is simply made of metaphor. So also is philosophy—and science, too, for that matter. . . ."[20] One of his more extensive remarks on metaphor occurs in a letter to Louis Untermeyer:

> . . . isn't it a poetical strangeness that while the world was going full blast on the Darwinian metaphors of evolution, survival values and the Devil take the hindmost, a polemical Jew in exile was working up the metaphor of the state's being like a family to displace them from mind and give us a new figure to live by. Marx had the strength not to be overawed by the metaphor in vogue. Life is like a battle. But so is it also like shelter. . . . We are all toadies to the fashionable metaphor of the hour. Great is he who imposes the metaphor. . . . There are no logical steps from one to the other. There is no logical connection.[21]

So, in Frost's view, and in Nietzsche's and Hans Vaihinger's before him, the metaphoric integrations of powerful thinkers become (for ordinary men) the structures—the "world hypotheses," as Stephen Pepper put it—which condition and frame our understanding of human experience. The integrations of metaphor have immediate consequences for our lives because the shapes of our worldly experience may be traced to the play of linguistic figuration.

In a suggestive passage from *Pragmatism*, James evokes his sense of human experience as "intolerably confused and gothic," "multitudinous beyond imagination, tangled, muddy, painful and perplexed."[22] The proper response to such a situation, his epistemological principles suggest, is a creative act. In what is probably his fullest single statement on the nature and value of creative activity, the "Letter to *The Amherst Student*," Frost evokes a sense of reality close to what James had evoked in the passage just quoted. Reality in Frost is often projected in psychological language as a place of "excruciations," of "hugeness and confusion," of "black and utter chaos."[23] And the proper response to it is the "figure of order," the "little form which I assert upon it."[24] The order created by any act of consciousness for James and the order created by a specifically artistic act of consciousness for Frost yield similarly therapeutic values. James calls it an inner "ease, peace," and "rest," while Frost sees the process of aesthetic composition as "composing to the spirit,"[25] as a release from "excruciations." It is finally a quality of Frost's tough-mindedness—he places the chaos and the confusion outside the mind, as James had in his criticism of Kant—which underscores the existential urgency of composition, the need for the form-making power of artistic consciousness to come into play.

For all its value this redemptive act of consciousness has its terrible moments when, impelled by a disturbed psyche, it shapes out a "lesser" (not a "better") world destructive to self. "We build out the flux inevitably," James wrote. "The great question is: does it, with our additions, *rise or fall in value?* Are the additions *worthy or unworthy?*"[26] Or, as Frost put it in "The Oven Bird," what are we to make of a "diminished thing?" The "diminished thing" is the fallen, postromantic world of the moderns, and the question we confront over and over again in Frost's poetry is: have our human additions to reality enhanced or further diminished the "diminished thing?" Do our "additions," our various acts of consciousness, enhance or diminish our selves? Such questions presuppose that an ironic, realistic awareness is possible, even necessary, as a therapeutic corrective to what the idealist sees as the constitutive power of consciousness. We can stand outside our projections (though good neo-Kantians seem to doubt it) and our very doing so becomes the basis of our mental stability. A number of Frost's unfortunate female characters, inescapably housed in their obsessions, never do understand the truth of these words of James: "There is a push, an urgency, within our very experience, against which we on the whole are powerless, and which drives us in a direction that is the destiny of our belief."[27]

4

In the limited post-Kantianism of James and Frost ("limited" because injected with a powerful dose of common sense), consciousness confronts objects which sit out there in a sharable public world. Those objects are not created by the poet's imagination or by the mind of any other human being. We would not be shocked to find in the poems of a man who, say, spent most of his formative and mature years in the countryside of New Hampshire and Vermont, as did Robert Frost, and who shared Frost's literary and philosophical predilections, a recognizably common landscape. The consciousness of our hypothetical poet could have focused, presumably, upon a similar set of objects; his poetic landscape would likely be marked by similar fixed features. So far the tenets of literary realism supply all of the critical procedures that we need. But if we assume that each consciousness is at some level distinct and private—and that is a chief point of the psychology of James and of common sense—then we must assume, as well, that the objects of the perceived world will radiate a different, special subjective presence; will cohere in ways contingent upon the particular consciousness which has apprehended those objects, and, in apprehending them, enveloped them with the interiority of the perceiving self. The act of perception which represents the landscape is affectively suffused. James supplies a good example for this point. The phenomenon of the "eternal recurrence of the common order," he says, "which so fills a Whitman with mystic satisfaction, is to a Schopenhauer . . . the feeling of an 'awful inner emptiness' from out of which he views it all."[28]

If the world's furniture is partially shaped and revealed by consciousness, then we can expect to find in the world evoked by a particular writer's *oeuvre* that the phenomena of his imagined reality will reveal, or radiate, his revealing consciousness, to extend the theoretical implications of the last line of "All Revelation." And now we have taken a considerable step beyond literary realism because we need a method which can help us grasp the intersection of literature's objective (or mimetic) dimension with its radically subjective (or expressive) one. Georges Poulet has summarized this matter quite clearly:

Every thought, to be sure, is a thought *of* something. It is turned invincibly towards the somewhere else, toward the outside. Issuing from itself, it appears to leap over a void, meet certain obstacles, explore certain surfaces, and envelop or invade certain objects. It describes and recounts to itself all these objects, and these accounts or these descriptions constitute the inexhaustible objective aspect of literature. But every thought is also simply a thought. It is that which exists in itself, isolatedly, mentally. Whatever its objects may be, thought can never place them, think them, except in the interior of itself.[29]

The following passage from James on the privacy of personal consciousness tells us that the leap from Frost to Poulet is really no leap at all:

Each of these minds keeps its own thoughts to itself. There is no giving or bartering between them. No thought even comes into direct *sight* of a thought in another personal consciousness than its own. Absolute insulation, irreducible pluralism, is the law. It seems as if the elementary psychic fact were not *thought* or *this thought* or *that thought*, but *my thought*, every thought being *owned*. Neither contemporaneity, nor proximity in space, nor similarity of quality and content are able to fuse thoughts together which are sundered by this barrier of belonging to different personal minds. The breaches between such thoughts are the most absolute breaches in nature.[30]

5

The literary critic may cull from William James three suggestions to help him close the chasm between the poetry and the self of Robert Frost. First, the objects of the perceiver's world are marked by the privacy of his apprehending consciousness; as Van Den Berg puts it, the world is the "materialization of our subjectivity." Second, the various objects marked by consciousness are also ordered or arranged by consciousness, and those very arrangements or "landscapes" will be revelations of the poet's needs, his way of looking at things, his personal identity. The constituted landscapes of consciousness thus become keys to interior landscapes, the unique psychological structures of Frost's experience. Finally, because consciousness is continuous, the self maintains its identity through time, thereby insuring that the individual poems in the Frost canon, though spread out through the poet's private and public history, are enveloped by a guiding presence which guarantees the wholeness of the poetic corpus.

Studying Robert Frost's interior self as pure interiority is impossible. But we have his poems, and within them those dominant, fixed objects, transferred from the real world, and transformed in the poetic medium where they have become objects in a poetic landscape. Whether the object is mediated by the consciousness of the lyric "I," or whether the object is mediated by Frost's more fully dramatized selves—the personae of his longer dialogues and monologues—the psychic life of Robert Frost himself is what is ultimately evoked by the fixed objects in his poetic landscape. Philosophically rooted in America in William James, this neo-romantic expressive poetic that I am urging for Frost is elaborately detailed in the European phenomenological tradition and by several recent American critics. Its basic assumption is that the unique subjectivity *behind* the poem invades the poem itself despite the conventionalizing social and aesthetic forces—the various determinations of his culture at work to dissolve the poet's individual identity as a person.

In the first part of this study I sketch out the poetic landscape by attending to its fixed features, to what critics have traditionally called "recurrent symbols." I have identified dominant features in the poetic landscape and have explored them within the linguistic networks in which they appear. As a critical concept "landscape" becomes synonymous with the poem itself and carries always this double meaning: not a simple configuration of objects, "out there" in inhuman otherness, but a configuration of objects intermeshed with the poet's self. In the pages ahead, then, for "poem" read: a linguistic preservation of a landscape-engaging act of consciousness.

"Tree at My Window"[31] is Frost's most self-conscious treatment of landscapes, interior and exterior:

> Tree at my window, window tree,
> My sash is lowered when night comes on;
> But let there never be curtain drawn
> Between you and me.
>
> Vague dream-head lifted out of the ground,
> And thing next most diffuse to cloud,
> Not all your light tongues talking aloud
> Could be profound.

But, tree, I have seen you taken and tossed,
And if you have seen me when I slept,
You have seen me when I was taken and swept
And all but lost.

That day she put our heads together,
Fate had her imagination about her,
Your head so much concerned with outer,
Mine with inner, weather.

Something in Frost wants to distinguish landscapes, to mark off "inner" from "outer," subject from object, human from nonhuman; perhaps it is because Frost feels so strongly that the outer landscape is not congenial to the self: the sash, at night, must be lowered, we must stay enclosed for our own good. All of which is to say that this poem, like so many poems by Frost, is grounded in a tough realist's view of things. Yet Frost gives us no unnavigable gulf between subject and object. The sash must be lowered, but the curtain must never be drawn across the window. Thus, between self and not-self Frost places a transparency which allows for an interaction of sorts, as enclosed self and weathered tree take creative looks at one another. The tree, self-like, dreams and speaks; the self, tree-like, is swept and tossed. The intentional, other-directed subjectivity of the poet marks the exterior landscape by naming it "window tree" and "dream-head." In so naming it he reveals not a deeper "something" interfused with the landscape and with the self, as Wordsworth believed, but only the character of his excursive subjectivity, a subjectivity constituted in the very interaction, the naturalizing of "inner" and the humanizing of "outer."

Frost's subjectivity is, in an important (though not metaphysical) sense, romantic: his consciousness expresses itself dominantly as a dream-energy which wants to transform (by entering) the landscape it encounters. It tends to be redemptive, though it may be counter-redemptive; it desires that all objects become subjects, but only to a point. For the essential Frost is also comic and ironic, and he will allow redemption to go only so far. The "dream-head" is, after all, "vague"; the "light tongues" speak meaninglessly because they "utter" nonhuman sound. The poet of ironic consciousness insists, in a direct thrust at his own redemptive self and at the noumenal confidence of the early romantics, on the pure objecthood of nature, and in so insisting preserves the integrity of the single, simple subject against the big world beyond self. And that, too, in Frost's poetry, is a lesson derived from the interaction of subjectivity with its environment. The flowing of subject into object is presented by Frost modestly and cautiously—i.e., humorously—as a datum of consciousness (this is the way it feels sometimes) and not as evidence for a metaphysical monism (this is the way it really is with the universe). So, objects will remain objects, even when they are enclosed in subjectivity; subjects will remain subjects, even when they are weathered.

Frost's complex sense of the interrelations and distinctions of interior and exterior landscapes in "Tree at My Window" urges us to modify the Cartesianism that we find in the statements of Poulet and James on the nature of a personal consciousness. If James, anticipating Poulet, appears to appeal to Descartes' sense of personal consciousness as pure, fully constituted spiritual substance, utterly self-contained and forever inaccessible to the outside and all spatio-temporal definition, then we must correct James with James. For it is one of James's first principles of psychology that consciousness is an out-going, pragmatic energy that acts upon its environment, and defines itself by its acts. Attempting to mediate extremes, to formulate a position between the Cartesian sense of a subjectivity which is never related, or relatable to an outer environment, and the naturalistic sense of a subjectivity which is nothing but a derivative form of the objective environment, James suggests that the inner citadel of selfhood, the unique subjective character of a personal consciousness, has a real status, but that it can be grasped and known only as it expresses itself, as it is impelled outward to interaction with objective conditions by the pragmatic energy at the very core of consciousness. John Dewey, an admirer of James, would come to say that selfhood is a mere potentiality until it is "both formed and brought to consciousness through interaction with an environment."[32]

In the second part of this study I explore the aesthetic and philosophical dimensions of Frost's poems within the more inclusive context of post-Kantian literary theory in order to define the modern intellectual environment of those poems. In recent organicist theories the stress is heavily on the shaping force of the poetic medium, on the idea that the discourse of poetry is a special mode of language which reveals a unique world. Extending the range of organicist aesthetic theory with the insights of the phenomenological tradition, the poem becomes a preservation—i.e., a "preserve"—which sustains for our contemplative pleasure the distinctive world—the very life—of the poet's consciousness. If, as James would insist, ordinary consciousness, or mere perception, shapes out the self's world, then for Frost, who is decidedly organicist in his bias, the shaping instrument is decisively language itself which discloses the "inner weather" of his subjective universe in the intersection of self and landscape.

Frost's Jamesian view of self and his organicist tendency in poetics pose a difficult and fascinating question. The question is this: what is the nature and value of that self-sufficient poetic world, which is shaped in language by a constitutive act of his consciousness, vis-à-vis the real world which James and Frost accept as stubbornly there, independent of consciousness? Guided by Frost's Jamesian sympathies and by the several theoretical problems implicitly posed by the poems, I have attempted to isolate his response to this key question of modern aesthetics while placing him against the background of some typical modernist answers. At every important theoretical juncture the significant measurement of Frost's participation in and dissent from major modern theories of imagination is his Jamesian commitment to the powers and limits of human consciousness to recreate its world in accordance with the needs and desires of self. Frost's poetics, his conceptual landscape, as it were, is congruent with the patterns of experience, the interior landscape that I find revealed in his poems; such congruency seems to me to be convincing evidence that, the important negative criticism of Yvor Winters and George Nitchie to the contrary, Frost's sensibility is profoundly unified.[33]

Let there be no confusion about the particular relationship that I claim for Frost and the modern tradition. Though Frost read William James, and through James came into contact with a number of the salient themes of modernist philosophy and aesthetics, I doubt that Frost was "influenced" in the sense that historicists used to say that imaginative writers were influenced or "shaped" by the "intellectual backgrounds of the times." My understanding is that writers are rarely influenced in that way; they learn almost nothing from philosophers, aestheticians, and literary critics. What happens is that they sometimes read a philosopher (or even a literary critic) and find their own intuitions about things reflected discursively, and hence in that sense confirmed. Modernism becomes the historical ambience of Frost's work in the sense that it is what one comes to conceptually if one moves outward from his poems in an attempt to define the intellectual milieu of the kinds of experience found there.

Frost is not modernist because he holds self-consciously to certain ideas which we identify with this or that modern philosopher because there are few ideas as such in his poetry (modernist or otherwise). Properly speaking his poems do not "belong" to the intellectual environment we call "the modern mind" because "the modern mind" does not have independent, Platonic existence. It is a thing that the poems themselves have helped to create. The perspectives of modern philosophy and aesthetics are conceptual abstractions from that dense, pre-ideational, primary data of human experience which Frost renders from the inside, as lived.

More than most modern poets Frost needs to have some sort of historical context deliberately constructed for him. Unlike Wallace Stevens, Frost rarely deals directly with the issues of post-Kantian epistemology; unlike Hart Crane, William Carlos Williams, and W. H. Auden, he rarely situates us in the modern urban environment; unlike Ezra Pound and T. S. Eliot he does not measure in any richly allusive way the modern moment against tradition and the past. And, from the point of view of language and metrical experiment, Frost looks very traditional. In two of the best books about him, he is presented as inhabiting a sort of timeless world. John Lynen sees Frost in the venerable tradition of pastoralism. Reuben Brower, drawing his comparisons from the range of world literature, relates him to the tradition of tough-minded, unflinching writers who see things as they are and do not hesitate to tell the score. Lynen and Brower are both persuasive. Frost inhabits a timeless world as do all poets of high quality. Yet Frost did not exist in a vacuum, and his poems do not present an ahistorical consciousness. What I would call his "implicit poetics" is one way of entering history, of locating the poet in time. "Implicit poetics" is a regulative principle which does not help much in explicating the poems, but which does help us to "generalize" the experiential patterns of those poems, and hence to extend their significance for our times.

Part One: Landscapes of Self

1. Invitations

These were poems of youth, written separately, between 1892 and 1912, not in a design to be together. . . . They represented a sort of clinical curve. I . . . realized they had a unity, could be a book. (R. F. to Elizabeth Sergeant, Robert Frost: The Trial by Existence, p. 97)

In 1913 when Robert Frost published A Boy's Will, his first book of poems, it was not then prefaced by the two quatrains he called "The Pasture." But in later years "The Pasture" became the prefatory poem to a number of his volumes, and when he decided to make his collection of 1949 it stood prominently as prologue to Complete Poems of Robert Frost. Whatever the personal experiences which may have motivated the writing of this poem (there is evidence suggesting that it was intended initially as a gesture of reconciliation to his wife Elinor[1]), I believe it is appropriate to read it allegorically, at some level, as an invitation to the pastoral experience evoked in the poetry of Robert Frost, and as an implicit and unconscious revelation, as he himself came to decide, of some of his basic poetic strategies and intentions.

> I'm going out to clean the pasture spring;
> I'll only stop to rake the leaves away
> (And wait to watch the water clear, I may):
> I shan't be gone long.—You come too.
>
> I'm going out to fetch the little calf
> That's standing by the mother. It's so young
> It totters when she licks it with her tongue.
> I shan't be gone long.—You come too.[2]

By assuming the voice of the poet who introduces his readers to a book of poems, as well as the voice of the farmer who invites someone to participate in a common event of the farm life, Frost encourages us to understand that, as poet-farmer he is asking us to enter his pastoral world—a world which he makes, and makes accessible in and through the literary medium. The experiences on the farm, the person who undergoes such experiences, the major features of a particular landscape, the way it is living outside the city—these are the subjects for Frost's imagination—his dramatic images unveil that rural sort of human experience. But the farmer is also writer and his poems repeatedly dramatize the entrance into the pastoral world of a self-conscious poet who meditates over his own created fictions of the pastoral life.

The poet-farmer in "The Pasture" performs two acts: one of cleansing (which becomes an act of clarification); the other of fetching, with a metaphoric suggestion that this act of fetching is also an act of preservation, for the sense of danger is genuine—the calf is not capable of staying out there very long. From the wider perspective that Frost imposed upon this poem by his very placing of it as introduction to *Complete Poems*, the farmer's two acts become allegorical reflections of the double action of the poet's imaginative consciousness, and those acts of imagination may suggest fundamental attitudes toward both nature and poetry.

Our invitation to enter the pastoral world is hedged. We must not bring to the experience a passive heart that watches and receives, as Wordsworth would have it, but an active imagination that clarifies (to echo one of Frost's key definitions of poetry[3]), because experience wants the cleansing imagination of the poet. In his act of fetching, the imaginative man must take the vulnerable things of this world (often even himself) and bring them into protective enclosure. From the perspective of Frost's canon these acts of clearing and protecting tend to merge with other poetic acts: those of staying confusion, or making forms out of chaos. Enclosures, forms, clarifications, stays—controlling metaphors for the poem itself—maintain their value from a sense of opposition—they need confusion, chaos and threats from without. Though not a dominant quality of "The Pasture," there is a dialectical sense of experience in the twice-repeated refrain, "I shan't be gone long." The journey "out," from farmhouse to "pasture spring" is what is emphasized in "The Pasture." But just as often in Frost the journey is concluded with an abrupt return to the farmhouse as the threatened self seeks enclosure once more. I find that a characteristic movement of the imaginative man in Frost's poetry is one of advance and retreat: out to confrontation with the confusions of experience; back inside to enclosure before it is too late.

To speak of a dialectical sense of experience in Frost's canon is to speak implicitly of an ironic consciousness that characterizes a significant number of his major poems. Thus, the retreat to enclosure evoked at the periphery of "The Pasture" can be seen (with proper hindsight) as a guide to the confusing, dangerous, and tension-creating qualities of experience that Frost dramatizes consistently in his poetic world. And yet there is a certain sense in which the ironic undertone of "The Pasture," which we grasp from the perspective of the poetic *corpus*, is countered by another level of experience, this one beyond the ironic dimension, and we grasp it by confronting the poem in isolation, for itself, as a song poem. If we can balance the two readings we may come to a sense of the range of experience that Frost's poetry reveals.

The biographical clue cited in the opening paragraph (and then too quickly dismissed) is a surer guide to the intrinsic mood of "The Pasture." More than a poem of ironic irresolution, it is a poem spawned in the precious fragility of love's redemptive moment. Gentle and conciliatory in tone, it sings (with sexual implication) for human union, for a coming together: "You come too." Seen from this perspective, the poem's twice-repeated refrain is an expression of an urge to redeem the painful separateness of self; to become as open, as transparent as the cleared pasture spring; as innocent and accepting as the little calf. The invitation is not to an ironic experience foreshadowed at the poem's fringes, but rather to a type of salvation that is expressed at the poem's core. And salvation means, in Frost's world, that particular moment when "mature," self-conscious, and complex awareness is suppressed, and when single, naive vision—a return to the Edenic innocence of unself-consciousness within a psychically soothing pastoral scene—is encouraged. In the redemptive moment—and in Frost it is often not much more than a moment—we transcend our isolation and the perplexities of our human condition, as we are released from the "seige of hateful contraries."

1

The first poem in A *Boy's Will,* "Into My Own,"[4] evokes a self who seems to court pure destructive engulfment, not protective enclosure; not the redemption of isolation through love, but the intensification of isolation:

> One of my wishes is that those dark trees,
> So old and firm they scarcely show the breeze,
> Were not, as 'twere, the merest mask of gloom,
> But stretched away unto the edge of doom.
> I should not be withheld but that someday
> Into their vastness I should steal away,
> Fearless of ever finding open land,
> Or highway where the slow wheel pours the sand.

The image of the "dark trees" is obsessive: it turns up again and again in Frost's poems and, as it does, gathers to itself and organizes a complex area of meaning. It becomes a "constitutive symbol"[5] which reveals the meaning of a significant feature of Frost's landscape. Here, in this particular poem, however, the meaning of the trees is simple enough: in his counterpointing of the image with those of "open land," "highway," and the embedded image of the horsedrawn carriage, Frost endows the trees with pre- and even antihuman meaning. The quest for self-identity ("They would not find me changed from him they knew / Only more sure of all I thought was true") appears to necessitate, for the self in the poem, radical severance from the human community and immersion in darkness. Ultimately (and I believe later poems support this reading) the journey into the immense dark wood becomes a metaphor for a journey into interior space, a journey into the dark immensity of the self's wilderness which will finally stimulate, once again, the need for community.

The image of the trees is handled again in "Ghost House,"[6] the poem immediately following. While sustaining the basic mood of "Into My Own" in "Ghost House," Frost probes the image this time in its relations with a second major feature in his landscape—the deserted, crumbling house. There is only a cellar hole left, "a vanished abode" where, paradoxically, the poet "dwells"—in the mind's home, if not in the actual physical place. More explicitly, now, Frost celebrates the antihuman ("The woods come back to the mowing field"), with misanthropic suggestion ("The footpath down to the well is healed"). The human imagination and what it can make, or hack out of nature, is opposed by nature itself, always trespassing against imagination's clearings. The vastness of the dark wood, the sureness with which it will come back to reclaim and to extinguish the human scene is, in the dialectical sense, what creates the tension between self and nature; what underscores the value of the self's creations, be they homes, poems, or mowing fields. In celebrating the antihuman—time's destructive element and the menacing advance of the woods—Frost celebrates, in a sense, the anticreative. Lines from W. B. Yeats's "Lapis Lazuli" help to explicate this point:

> All things fall and are built again,
> And those that build them again are gay.[7]

There is no gaiety in Frost's poem, at this point, because it is not the building, creative spirit that he celebrates, but the destructive one.

But he will not conclude with a hymn to the ultimate in anticreativity —death, or more specifically, the death wish. The "unlit place"—the images of darkness and of light evoking, traditionally, chaos and created order respectively—this unlit place cannot suffice. Disengagement from the human scene, though deliberately sought, is finally unbearable:

> It is under the small, dim, summer star.
> I know not who these mute folk are
>   Who share the unlit place with me—
>   Those stones out under the low-limbed tree
> Doubtless bear names that the mosses mar.

In the logic of this poem, if footpaths can be "healed," then creeping mosses ought not to "mar." But mar they do and with this verb the desolated scene begins to come back to life as, ironically, the poet meditates on the little family graveyard: "They are tireless folk, but slow and sad— / Though two, close keeping, are lass and lad. . ." —lass and lad only because the lonely, isolated mind delights in imagining them so; the names cannot be read, the poet cannot know, in fact, who lies under the adjacent stones. As the life-force of imagination begins to revitalize the "unlit place," to build anew upon the overgrown cellar hole, the pressure of the anticreative, "the woods come back," is released. And it seems a welcome release.

So the cellar hole which had initially captured the death-dwelling meditation of the poet and seemed a perfect emblem of the inevitable destruction of the human world, nurtures as well a longing for the house that used to be; motivates the meditating mind toward the exercise of its own constructive powers. The destroyed enclosure encourages the self in the poem to seek again the felicities of protected space and to re-establish for itself the repose and stability that enclosed space promises in the face of time's flux and contingencies. Later poems suggest that as a place especially hospitable to reverie, dream, imagining, and hence poetic creativity, the house cradles uniquely human values.

The philosophical problem suggested by "Ghost House"—to what extent is the mind responsible for the shape and feel of the world it experiences?—is a dominant postromantic concern that we generally trace to Kant's "Copernican" revolution in epistemology. Too often when we make literary application of the Kantian insight we tend to see the brighter side of his idea: poets project the harmony of their visions onto a disordered universe and thereby redeem it by supplying it with form and value. But poets may also project their own interior disorders, their sufferings, and their warped consciousness onto a world which, though it may be in sad need of redemption, is much better than they sometimes construct it. We approach what I would call the darker psychological extensions of the Kantian theory. By placing Kant in psychological perspective—by switching the focus from his intersubjective epistemological categories to the irreducibly personal psyche—I purposely violate his epistemology; he could not allow for anything but form and order to be projected in the mind's constitutive action. Reading Kant through William James or Sigmund Freud it is clear that the character of the various acts of the mind will be determined by the psychological constitution of the particular, private self engaging in those acts. The crippled self is thus likely to experience a world that reflects its own disturbed psyche. Frost is usually aware of the difference between his own projections and the thing itself. His unobtrusive "as 'twere," in "Into My Own," suggests that the somber darkness of the woods is in part a reflection of his interior, even as the fanciful entertaining of romantic illusion in "Ghost House" is a reflection of the poet's need to transmute an inhumanly barren world. The gap between things as they are and the poet's fictions—dark or bright —and the poet's acute awareness and manipulation of this epistemological problem is a familiar feature of modern poetry: Frost was often as self-conscious about his projected fictions as Wallace Stevens.

It was primarily because of Stevens's brilliant advocacy that an imagination wholly human, with no access to a transcendental reality, became characterized as our last, best source of psychological redemption in a world in which it is no longer fashionable to believe in theological relief. One of the difficult lessons of Robert Frost, and of Wallace Stevens as well, is that an imagination wholly human is a powerful source of damnation—it is psychological death-force as well as life-force, since it alone creates our private hells. Stevens located the cold modern version of hell within the "snow man" self whose discovery of the beauty of a winter landscape is simultaneously a discovery of an inhuman nothingness. With a ferocious wit that Frost would later come to duplicate, Stevens reveals that the nothingness "out there" flows from the nothingness within, from what Frost called our "desert places"—those moments of perception when we objectivize our humanness and become snow men, diminished men who make a diminished world.

The winter landscape as it is evoked in Joyce, Stevens, Eliot, Mann, and others, is a recurrent modern symbol of the experience of self-diminishment and self-desolation, of an isolated ego cut off from all contact, and it plays a critical role in the psychological drama of two superb poems from Frost's middle and later career, "Stopping By Woods on a Snowy Evening" and "Desert Places." We encounter this landscape in Frost first, however, in two lesser poems from *A Boy's Will*, "Stars" and "Storm Fear." In "Stars"[8] the wanderer lost in a snow storm finds himself trapped in a self-destructive fiction as he links his perceptions of whiteness in such a way that he casts the world into malevolently anthropomorphic form— in spite of his rational affirmation of an indifferent universe.

> How countlessly they congregate
>   O'er our tumultuous snow,
> Which flows in shapes as tall as trees
>   When wintry winds do blow!—
>
> As if with keenness for our fate,
>   Our faltering few steps on
> To white rest, and a place of rest
>   Invisible at dawn—
>
> And yet with neither love nor hate,
>   Those stars like some snow-white
> Minerva's snow-white marble eyes
>   Without the gift of sight.

Though indifference is calmly asserted, a desperate voice at the heart of "Stars" breaks through the poem's veneer of rational tone by evoking Minerva as a cruel goddess of nature; the imagistic blendings of snow, stars, suffocation and freezing in the drifts "tall as trees" are the prelude to a loss of control. Often in Frost a perception of trees keys the self's panic moment, the caving-in of our rational powers, and the seeing of malicious intention in an inhumanly indifferent world.

In "Storm Fear"[9]—the poem immediately following "Stars" in *A Boy's Will*—a coolly stoical man caught in his farmhouse in a blizzard of terrible intensity cannot escape the betrayal of his own metaphorical habits of reflection. As he projects the world in storm as a protean kind of monster that is possessed with the single desire of getting those within the house, he is drawn to the hysterical edge:

> When the wind works against us in the dark,
> And pelts with snow
> The lower-chamber window on the east,
> And whispers with a sort of stifled bark,
> The beast,
> 'Come out! Come out!'—
> It costs no inward struggle not to go,
> Ah, no!
> I count our strength,
> Two and a child,
> Those of us not asleep subdued to mark
> How the cold creeps as the fire dies at length—
> How drifts are piled,
> Dooryard and road ungraded,
> Till even the comforting barn grows far away,
> And my heart owns a doubt
> Whether 'tis in us to arise with day
> And save ourselves unaided.

The swing from "Ghost House" to "Storm Fear" is a swing to a dramatically opposed state of consciousness: from a pleasurable dwelling on the swallowing of the human scene by nature, to the terror of envisioning what is essentially the same obliteration of the enclosures that the human will has constructed—the fading of the "comforting" barn in the thick of the storm, the awful blending of road and dooryard with uncultivated field and wood under blankets of snow.

After concluding an analysis of some passages from Baudelaire and Rimbaud, Gaston Bachelard makes a general comment on the psychological and metaphysical dimensions of enclosed space that is precisely illuminative of what I have been suggesting here about the symbolism of houses in Frost and a foreshadowing of one of the central themes in his poetics:

> outside the occupied house, the winter cosmos is a simplified cosmos. It is a non-house in the same way that metaphysicians speak of a non-I, and between the house and the non-house it is easy to establish all sorts of contradictions. . . . The house derives reserves and refinements of intimacy from winter; while in the outside world, snow covers all tracks, blurs the road, muffles every sound, conceals all colors. As a result of this universal whiteness, we feel a form of cosmic negation in action. The dreamer of houses knows and senses this, and because of the diminished entity of the outside world, experiences all the qualities of intimacy with increased intensity.[10]

2

Nature's cycle of seasons is often reflective in Frost of a parallel cyclical movement within his emotive life. With almost no transition we move, in *A Boy's Will,* from the self's phases of enclosed dark moodiness and willed alienation, from the autumnal decay and wintry paralysis of poems such as "My November Guest," "A Late Walk," and "Storm Fear," to the exuberance of vital flow and the rebirth of a more open, expansive self, a self beyond estrangement:

> Come with rain, O loud Southwester!
> Bring the singer, bring the nester;
> Give the buried flower a dream;
> Make the settled snowbank steam;
> Find the brown beneath the white;
> But whate'er you do tonight,
> Bathe my window, make it flow,
> Melt it as the ice will go;
> Melt the glass and leave the sticks
> Like a hermit's crucifix;
> Burst into my narrow stall;
> Swing the picture on the wall;
> Run the rattling pages o'er;
> Scatter poems on the floor;
> Turn the poet out of door.[11]

Here, in "To the Thawing Wind," is another hymn to the forces of nature; this one, however, does not mask wishes for self-obliteration. Nature's processes are no longer seen as a source of death, a burying of human endeavor, but as a source of life. From the romantic perspective, nature's dynamism is the creative, living principle and it rightfully displaces the anticreative principle, manifested in the arrogant impositions of human artifice—those poems scattered on the floor. One does not want or need to lodge his fictions between the self and a threatening world because the setting of our lives does not now cry out for redemption, as in "Ghost House"; nor, as in "Stars" and "Storm Fear" does its dangerous places draw out of the self even more dangerous fictions of an active evil loosed in the world. Enclosures become irrelevant when we feel ourselves "at home" in the natural world. The important detail in the poem is "Melt the glass." Things as they are seem paradise enough and the poet is on the verge of returning to the pure springs of romantic poetry, since he would leave the deadening artificial structures of houses and poems—hoping, perhaps, even for their destruction—in an effort to bathe and merge himself in nature's currents of life. In Spring the self, as well as nature, is "thawed," and so flows again.

The poem following "To the Thawing Wind" in *A Boy's Will* is "A Prayer in Spring."[12] Recognizing in a rare moment that in spring the given facts of nature are their own poetry—they do not need the shaping spirit of imagination—the poet thereby discovers a plentitude of value that is purely there. The prayer, then—"give us pleasure in the flowers today" . . . "make us happy in the happy bees" . . . "make us happy in the darting bird"—is that the self will extinguish its mediating presence by eliminating its projected structures; that it will approach nature as Thou, not It; that it will cherish things in themselves, not transmute them, or use them for further ends. But it is a very rare moment, indeed—transcience seems to hover about the edges of this celebration of nature's facts—and that, I believe, is why the poem is cast in the form of prayer: let this be so because I know that this is only an isolated spot in time. The precariousness of the pastoral moment in "A Prayer in Spring" helps us to hear the poem's supplicatory tone and to prepare the inevitable return of the fictionalizing imagination in "Rose Pogonias."[13]

A saturated meadow,
Sun-shaped and jewel-small,

A circle scarcely wider
  Than the trees around were tall;
Where winds were quite excluded,
  And the air was stifling sweet
With the breath of many flowers—
  A temple of the heat.

There we bowed us in the burning,
  As the sun's right worship is,
To pick where none could miss them
  A thousand orchises;
For though the grass was scattered,
  Yet every second spear
Seemed tipped with wings of color
  That tinged the atmosphere.

We raised a simple prayer
  Before we left the spot,
That in the general mowing
  That place might be forgot;
Or if not all so favored,
  Obtain such grace of hours,
That none should mow the grass there
  While so confused with flowers.

This poem's tone of unabashed wonder and celebration links it firmly with "A Prayer in Spring" and excludes the impositions of imagination's fictive structures. But I believe that the sense of wonder which is communicated by "Rose Pogonias" flows from the poet's discovery of a place of rest within nature itself and the imaginative journey spurred by that discovery. What he celebrates (besides rose pogonias) is the intimation of form that he has felt in the world. Nature's suggestion of enclosed physical space becomes a figure for a sanctuary of self; a protected place where the self can rest in freedom, cut loose from the ties and pressures of social reality. There is nothing so composing to the spirit as composition itself, Frost once told Sidney Cox,[14] implying that formal structures and the process of making formal structures serve as sanctuaries for the mind weary of the instability of a moving, ever-changing world. The dimensional detail in "Rose Pogonias" is therefore extraordinarily important: the meadow full of flowers is encircled by a dense growth of trees, dense enough to cut off wind. The place is tiny—the diameter of the meadow not much greater than the height of the trees. This description of physical place, which is so suggestive of a self-contained world of enclosed space free from the pressures of the everyday world, is also a figuration for a psychological "place," for a mental enclosure that frees the poet from the penetrations of dangerous psychic experience. The threatened self seeks sanctuary—a "temple" is as fine a sanctuary as it can create. What physical nature does in "Rose Pogonias," in a spirit of cooperation with self, is to encourage the imagination to exert its constructive powers and to make from the material that actual nature supplies—in this instance a tree-encircled, flower-laden meadow—a fictive world which, in turn, would both sanctify the materials of which it is made and compose the self who engages in the process of making. The metaphoric linkages come so easily and so modestly—"naturally" is perhaps a better word—that they tend to slip by us unnoticed. The basic metaphor is sacramental: the physical enclosure is transformed into a "temple," where "we bowed us in the burning," and, "in our worship," "raised a simple prayer," pleading for the "grace of hours." Even in this homage of imagination to nature, where in the act of homage nature is changed—not transmuted, but quietly changed by being bathed in a redeeming consciousness—the rhetoric of prayer reminds us, as it did once before, of the precariousness and preciousness ("jewel-small") of enclosures, natural or imaginative—and reminds us that the destructive element will not be excluded. In the "general mowing" the cocoon-like spot might not be forgot and the implication is that the temples of imagination will be razed with those of reality. The lovely flowers may be cut; those not cut will surely fade, and seasonal change will strip the trees of their heavy shielding foliage.

3

"The Vantage Point,"[15] which is often praised for its virtuosity in the sonnet form, is a nodal poem; for the series of oppositions which it suggests, which it looks back upon, and which it looks forward to. The actual vantage point is a strategically located spot where the self can remain in isolation—"Myself unseen"—and meditate on the opposition of human society and nature. From his hiding place on the slope of a hill the speaker can brood upon the life and death of man—"the homes of men" and "the graves of men"—and all of those entangled considerations in between. When such meditation becomes "too much," he can turn on his arm, from his reclining position, and, face flat on the earth, partake of non-human refreshment. Human society comes to represent for Frost very often the engagement demanded by community, a mooring in confusion, while nature can figure for him a state of isolation and simplicity that catapults one into an absolute freedom from the quotidian and restraint placed on self by community. Immersion in nature, as Leo Marx notes in *The Machine in The Garden,* yields values similar to those yielded by the imagination since both nature and imagination can offer release and resolution. But as I describe the opposition of community and nature I have done what Frost has not: emphasized the idea of opposition too much and in the process lost touch with the interlocking relationship of the contraries. The self in the poem suggests that nothing will, by itself, suffice; that he needs the values represented by both ends of his antinomy, even as one set of values would appear to negate the other.

The point of vantage is itself a place where the self can hide, and while hiding maintain its isolation—and hence satisfy its desire for isolating autonomy even as it meditates upon community. "The Tuft of Flowers,"[16] one of Frost's more maligned early poems, dramatizes the urge of self to move out of isolation and toward community. The problem with the poem is that its concluding, moralizing couplet seems to glitter with the "casy gold" of imagination that Frost generally scorned. The lines " 'Men work together,' I told him from the heart, / 'Whether they work together or apart' " seem unearned in the context of loneliness established immediately in the poem's opening lines. A single figure moves across a meadow "to turn the grass once after one / Who mowed it in the dew before the sun." Unable to find the mower, he is led to a meditation on essential alienation:

> But he had gone his way, the grass all mown,
> And I must be, as he had been—alone,
>
> "As all must be," I said within my heart,
> "Whether they work together or apart."

The critic who believes in the genuineness of the experience rendered in this poem has the task of explaining just how the speaker can move from a statement of aloneness as the essential feature of the human condition to a statement of community as the deeper truth, without, of course, appealing to the sentimentality of the speaker, which might or might not explain his character but which would surely not save the poem. What makes the critic's task doubly difficult is the easy way in which "The Tuft of Flowers" may be located within a popular eighteenth-century genre of moral-descriptive poetry. The poem's interior logic appears to rest on the doctrine that occurrences in the natural world have moral correspondence in the human world. There is one poem in particular, in American literature, written in the English moral-descriptive mode, that Frost's "The Tuft of Flowers" echoes very strongly: William Cullen Bryant's "To a Waterfowl." This poem was read so often to young Robert by his mother that he had it by heart.[17] The phrase from "The Tuft of Flowers," "a spirit kindred," may have even been a conscious echo of *Kindred Spirits*, the title of Asher B. Durand's romantic painting of Bryant and Thomas Cole, the allegorizing Hudson River School artist. Bryant's "To a Waterfowl" and Frost's "The Tuft of Flowers" are similar in structure and theme, but there is a crucial difference which, once perceived, tells us a great deal about the differences between the Age of Frost and the Age of Bryant; about the nature of a modern imaginative consciousness, and about the way a genuine poet can take the received patterns and conventions of a traditional poetry and transform them in his creative act.

The problematic lines of the poem occur after the chance flight of a butterfly

> led my eye to look
> At a tall tuft of flowers beside a brook,
>
> A leaping tongue of bloom the scythe had spared
> Beside a reedy brook the scythe had bared.
>
> The mower in the dew had loved them thus,
> By leaving them to flourish, not for us,
>
> Nor yet to draw one thought of ours to him,
> But from sheer morning gladness at the brim.
>
> The butterfly and I had lit upon,
> Nevertheless, a message from the dawn,
>
> That made me hear the wakening birds around,
> And hear his long scythe whispering to the ground,
>
> And feel a spirit kindred to my own;
> So that henceforth I worked no more alone; . . .

When Bryant's lonely waterfowl, winging over hostile territory, completes his flight south safely, Bryant is led to the comforting, analogical conclusion that some greater Power guides him on his journey through a difficult land. Frost's discovery of the single tuft of flowers by the brook—helped in part by nature herself, by the flight of the butterfly which directs the poet's perception—delivers up a purely humanistic message: the flowers become, somehow, or so it would seem, a fraternal symbol, a vehicle of communication. The poem concludes:

> But glad with him, I worked as with his aid,
> And weary, sought at noon with him the shade;
>
> And dreaming, as it were, held brotherly speech
> With one whose thought I had not hoped to reach.
>
> "Men work together," I told him from the heart,
> "Whether they work together or apart."

The figurative "I worked *as* with his aid" ought to brake didactic readings of the poem and lead us back to consider once again the tuft of flowers. But let me use Frost's phrase because it is far more interesting: "A leaping tongue of bloom." Now, perhaps, we can be more comfortable with messages from the dawn because we know who speaks them.

Frost once made the extravagant statement that each of his poems had a hidden metaphoric base. It is an accurate description of "The Tuft of Flowers." What is revealed in the poem is the poet's process of creative discovery in language. We watch him mine the gold of meaning from a dead metaphor, and the revitalization of a dead metaphor pushes him toward further discoveries of "messages" from the dawn and helps him to hear "whispering scythes." The entire didactic burden of the heretofore embarrassing last lines of the poem now takes its proper place within a metaphoric structure. We are in the country of "as if." The signs of a creative self, spurred by the need of a responsive human environment, have been there all along—so openly, in fact, that we tend to miss them. There is first the speaker's explicit denial that the mower left the flowers so that someone else might enjoy them; there is, as well, the explicit denial that the mower intended the flowers to be a binding symbol between men. So we cannot really be sure of the mower's motivation. He does not necessarily "spare" the flowers (as the speaker tells us) because of some need to stay the utilitarian process of the work of mowing; it may be only by accident, after all, that the flowers stand uncut. What we can be certain of is the speaker himself, whose point of view filters all that we can know, and who reveals his psychological needs to us more than he reveals any external reality. The speaker must believe that the mower acted self-consciously out of more-than-utilitarian motivation and is therefore willing to attribute to him an aesthetic sensitivity; he is willing to say to himself: "I shall respond to the flowers *as if* they were spared in an act of aesthetic cherishing."

The insistent willfulness of tone in the line "Nevertheless, a message from the dawn" surfaces in the metaphoric context, and the victory over isolation is seen for what it is—not an objective fact of moral experience, but a privately won triumph of the imaginative man who understands very well the difference between spiritual satisfaction (which is all Bryant's) and imaginative need (which is all Frost can assuage). The tuft of flowers becomes a sign of communication only because, in his isolation, the will of a lonely man declares it to be so. The modern imaginative man who finds himself cut loose from the comforts of shared, communal belief—religious, ethical, or epistemological—is faced with the problem of living his life in the most soothing way that he can. The best single critical sentence ever written about Frost deserves to be quoted here: "In the sense that for Frost 'revealing' is 'making,' all revelation has been his."[18] Yet Frost's complex position would encourage us to qualify even this insightful statement. In his realism he recognizes external control over the creative impulse to shape out the world of his desire. The flight of the butterfly is only *apparently* erratic. Frost's image of the searching butterfly is an image of teleological activity outside himself, and (if I sense correctly his implication) a proper prelude to a parallel, inner teleological process, the desired end of which is an imaginative revelation that will release the speaker from his alienation. When the speaker's eye is "led"—an important word in a realist's vocabulary—to the flowers by the butterfly, his imagination is triggered, *his* search assumes meditative direction. The actual, desolate scene is subtly transformed as the speaker "leads" himself out of bewilderment and loneliness to a special kind of community. And this is Frost's way of acknowledging that nature itself, in its independence from human will, provides the guidance and designed context out of which a lonely imaginative man may spin his vision of a much-needed mutuality.

In the brilliant poem "Mowing"[19] Frost dramatizes once again his theme of the isolated self as he blends the roles of poet and farmer (as player and worker)—the demands of imaginative vision and the demands of fact. Without compromising either fact or the necessary pleasures of vision, Frost has it both ways at once:

There was never a sound beside the wood but one,
And that was my long scythe whispering to the ground.
What was it it whispered? I knew not well myself;
Perhaps it was something about the heat of the sun,
Something, perhaps, about the lack of sound—
And that was why it whispered and did not speak.
It was no dream of the gift of idle hours,
Or easy gold at the hand of fay or elf:
Anything more than the truth would have seemed too weak
To the earnest love that laid the swale in rows,
Not without feeble-pointed spikes of flowers
(Pale orchises), and scared a bright green snake.
The fact is the sweetest dream that labor knows.
My long scythe whispered and left the hay to make.

The dramatic scene (recalling "The Tuft of Flowers") is a field beside a woods, with a lonesome figure walking slowly along, working his scythe, which is making a swooshing sound. I emphasize the loneliness of the figure in the landscape and the sound of his scythe because I think the poem is about the silence and the isolation endured in labor—"Perhaps it was something . . . about the lack of sound"—and the human response to it. The isolated, homeless self is recurrent in the poetry of Frost; another one of his major, obsessive images. Though the figure in "Mowing" is not nearly as destitute as some of the selves projected in other poems, he is a variation on the archetype, sharing in his loneliness. I wish to suggest here (and believe that later chapters will bear me out in my contentions) that Frost probes the role of imagination in "Mowing" in its primitive, universal phase. By "primitive" and "universal" I mean that he is not only concerned with imagination as a power of mind unique to the poet—though in places he does seem to mean only that—but also as an indispensable and basic mode of human response to the world.

It is a given in "Mowing" that the scythe whispers, from the first to the last line. It becomes, as it whispers, something more than pure object, though obviously something also a good deal less than human. It is only because of his open, self-conscious confrontation with his metaphor that Frost can get away with his game. The need to break out of silence is balanced by the ironic awareness that imaginative solutions—such as those which have scythes whispering—often have a delicate status. Frost playfully creates mystery with his coyness: "What was it it whispered? I knew not well myself." Then he makes up a witty explanation about why

the scythe whispered: "Something, perhaps, about the lack of sound— /
And that was why it whispered and did not speak."

Frost's wit has touched a serious subject ("the lack of sound"), and the
tone of this very irregular sonnet shifts abruptly in the last eight lines:
"It was no dream of the gift of idle hours." His imaginative play is engaged in as something more than sheer play. Paradoxically, the "play" of
imagination is embedded, in this poem, in a context of "work," the concept of which in formal aesthetics after Kant is always the diametrical
opposite of the concept of play. By insisting that he is not engaged in an
excessive (because irresponsible) kind of imaginative play (no "easy
gold" here), an imaginative play which, in its radical autonomy, gives off
no exhalations of reality, Frost asserts that his playfulness is bounded;
that he has carried self-consciousness into the play world; that his imaginative scythe does not violate the facts of work. Yet, though the Yankee
realist insinuates his humorous and ironic presence into the poem when he
asks that curious question about what the scythe was whispering, the
scythe *does* continue to whisper; work itself takes on an aesthetic dimension, and facts *are* violated, despite the line "The fact is the sweetest
dream that labor knows." The statement in the poem's penultimate line
might be glossed in this way: the poet's homage to fact, to the antifictive,
is paid in the admission of fact into the play world of his whispering
scythe as we glimpse the real thing, the actual scythe, cutting his be-
loved flowers as "it laid the swale in rows," and nearly slashing "a bright
green snake." (Note how Frost details the delicacy of the severed flowers,
how he lingers parenthetically over the "pale orchises".) The poet may
transcend his isolation in an imaginative act by allowing his scythe to
speak. But, as in "The Tuft of Flowers," the resolution is a subtly qualified one, for in the imaginative process he must make a realist's gesture
and acknowledge the utilitarian process of work which spares him no
natural loveliness.

4

I can think of no more appropriate poem to complete this introduction
to Frost's poetic landscape and themes than the rarely noticed "Going
For Water."[20] It is a fragile, perfect piece and in it we find the major
fixed features of Frost's world and a dramatic rendering of the trans-

muting, fictionalizing role of imagination, in a holiday mood, displaying its exuberant, playful energies:

> The well was dry beside the door,
>   And so we went with pail and can
> Across the fields behind the house
>   To seek the brook if still it ran;
>
> Not loth to have excuse to go,
>   Because the autumn eve was fair
> (Though chill), because the fields were ours,
>   And by the brook our woods were there.
>
> We ran as if to meet the moon
>   That slowly dawned behind the trees,
> The barren boughs without the leaves,
>   Without the birds, without the breeze.
>
> But once within the wood, we paused
>   Like gnomes that hid us from the moon,
> Ready to run to hiding new
>   With laughter when she found us soon.
>
> Each laid on other a staying hand
>   To listen ere we dared to look,
> And in the hush we joined to make
>   We heard, we knew we heard the brook.
>
> A note as from a single place,
>   A slender tinkling fall that made
> Now drops that floated on the pool
>   Like pearls, and now a silver blade.

The task of going for water forms the realistic base from which the play imagination, fueled by the transformative magic of "as if," takes off. The physical journey to the brook beside the woods parallels a journey to the gay play-world in the mind where freedom and psychic wholeness are regained. "Not loth to have excuse to go," the speaker says, suggesting that perhaps the search for water is subordinated in his perspective (or perhaps I should say *their* perspective) to the quest for something that is as powerful a sustainer of the psychological self as water is a sustainer of the physical self. The scene in which the quest is taken has become a familiar one, even at this early point in Frost's career: the farmhouse and the woods, and, now, particularly after the experience of "The Tuft of Flowers," (the "tongue of bloom" grew beside the brook) we begin to sense that the brook, too, has magnetized the poet's mind. But there is something special about the landscape in "Going For Water." Frost does not simply create an archetypal landscape and then tap it in poem after poem. The obsessive images in his poems suggest complex areas of experience: in his best poems the image carries experiences from other poems, but it is fashioned anew, structured into a slightly different context. In "Going For Water" the quest is taken at night, and the dark woods are entered. This is a poem, however, without fear at its core because the dark wood is not bathed in nightmare (as it so often is in Frost) but in the spirit of freedom, of play, and of harmonious integration. (Note how the imaginative way of experiencing dominates as the auditory and the visual are blended in the last stanza.) We are close to "Rose Pogonias" and the sense of benevolent enclosure in a soothing, pastoral scene: The woods are ours, and so are the fields.

From the beginning, this is a poem of "we," not "I," and so perhaps with the problem of isolation no problem at all—the self is freed for gayer tasks. Are the two in the poem husband and wife? brother and sister? adults or children? These questions cannot be answered on internal grounds. What is clear is that there are two together, close together, and that they are probably adults, but adults who are loosed from the grimmer realities of the adult world. Having dared to imagine, they now roam, playing hide and seek with the moon, in the land of the child ("Ready to run to hiding new / With laughter when she found us soon"), a land populated by elves, where the adult self is sloughed off, and where lovely mystery is common occurrence. If we ignore his transcendental philosophy, Emerson provides the perfect gloss for the experience rendered in the poem: "In the woods . . . a man casts off his years, as the snake his slough, and at what period soever of life is always a child." The qualifying hand of the post-Emersonian mind is felt, however, in the key figures of "like gnomes," "like pearls," which, though they project the magic world, suggest as well that metaphoric identification is not to be insisted upon in such a context of fantasy; that there are two worlds present always in the poem (high-lighted perfectly by simile which insists openly on differences as well as likenesses), and that the excursion into the land of fairy is only an excursion—a lovely, but brief holiday. The qualification, however, is gently made; the vision is all of tranquility. When the quest is completed the religious tone of the awe-filled lines

"And in the hush we joined to make / We heard, we knew we heard the brook" hints at something like finding the grail of pleasure. And the grail, Frost seems to say, is recovered only by those of us who, still knowing how to engage in creative play, can transcend adult self-consciousness. In the last stanza of the poem the adverbial modification "now"—crucially repeated—suggests that the magical time of play has been fully recaptured for the present in a moment of intense affective memory.

5

While sketching out Frost's landscape in *A Boy's Will* I have let a number of important questions go begging about the dialectic of "I" and "We," self and community, isolation and integration; about the dialectic of nature as threatening to self and nature as receptive to self; about the value of imaginative acts of the mind; about the role of figurative language in the creative process; about the nature of poetic fictions and of poetic play; and, most importantly, I have let go begging the question of the relationship of Frost's person to the selves projected in his poems by freely interchanging "poet" and "self in the poem." My object in this chapter was neither to answer these questions, nor to press a monolithic argument, but only to introduce a series of perspectives in practical and theoretical criticism. I would hope that this chapter would invite the reader to undertake with me further explorations in Frost's poetic landscape and in his aesthetics in the chapters that follow, even as "The Pasture" and, as I see it, *A Boy's Will* in general, are invitations from Robert Frost to pursue his personal quests in *Complete Poems*.

2. The Brook

The hope with
water is that it
will conceal nothing,

that a clearness
will follow upon it
like the clearness
after much rain,

or the clearness
where the air
reaches to the river
and touches it,

where the rain
falls from the trees
into the river.

(James McMichael, "Celery")

There is nothing mysterious about the origins of Robert Frost's symbolism. Because the brook, the farmhouse, and the woods often form the dominant configuration on the land of a New England farmer, it would be remarkable if Frost's poems were not laden with such images. One of his characters in "The House Keeper"[1] says,

> "I hate to think of the old place when we're gone,
> With the brook going by below the yard,
> And no one here but hens blowing about."

A reader of Frost ought not to become excited by this particular brook—its casual appearance indicates that it is a fixture of the country experience; that it could be anybody's brook. And yet this image and others recur again and again in the poems, often in structurally and thematically crucial places. In "Going For Water" the brook was sought and approached as a sacred object of quest; in "The Tuft of Flowers" it marked the spot of discovery of that strange "tongue of bloom" which touched off an imaginative vision of human communion. These brooks belong personally to Robert Frost—by bathing them in his consciousness he has created them as metaphors of self. Frost's brook stands as an objective feature in a landscape that sometimes appeases, sometimes threatens the self. But as cherished object of his consciousness the brook encourages a flowing of self, as it were, as it signals a desire for openness—a thrust of self toward the experience of integration with itself and with others—a desire for the peace that follows upon the resolution of interior and exterior tensions. The brook links Frost, though with very strong qualifications, to that romantic vision, often articulated by Emerson and Whitman in America, which projects the self as an unbounded, dynamic process—a flowing into a world of mutuality. Contrarily, the house as metaphor of self will link Frost to the bleakest emphases in romantic and postromantic poetry and thought; to a vision of self as fixed, alienated, and hidden in a world which makes hiding an urgent psychic necessity.

1

There are several poems in which the image of the brook dominates the scene almost totally, thereby becoming the controlling symbol out of which the poem's profoundest experiences are generated. The earliest of these is "The Mountain,"[2] which was published in Frost's brilliant second volume, *North of Boston*. It begins in a tone of quiet disturbance, with a description of a river about which hovers an ominous sense of the destructive:

> The river at the time was fallen away,
> And made a widespread brawl on cobblestones;
> But the signs showed what it had done in spring:
> Good grassland gullied out, and in the grass
> Ridges of sand, and driftwood stripped of bark.

The heart of this dialogue poem is a discussion of a brook, situated (apparently) at the top of the mountain whose shadow darkens the small village at its base. A visitor, after interrupting a laboring farmer by asking him, " 'What town is this?' " is soon treated to a loving digression (the farmer seemed almost to be waiting for the opportunity):

> "There's a brook
> That starts up on it somewhere—I've heard say
> Right on the top, tip-top—a curious thing.
> But what would interest you about the brook,
> It's always cold in summer, warm in winter.
> One of the great sights going is to see
> It steam in winter like an ox's breath,
> Until the bushes all along its banks
> Are inch-deep with the frosty spines and bristles—
> You know the kind. Then let the sun shine on it!"

But the visitor is not very interested in the brook and comments that there ought to be a fine view of the area from the top. The farmer replies,

> "As to that I can't say. But there's the spring,
> Right on the summit, almost like a fountain.
> That ought to be worth seeing."

It soon dawns upon the visitor that the farmer has never seen the brook because he has never been to the top—nor, it turns out, has the farmer ever known anybody who has seen the brook.

The farmer "can't say" about the view from the top but he can "say" about the brook. The implicit distinction that he has made, casually, unobtrusively, and unconsciously, is the one between the experientially verifiable and the nonexperiential—the wholly imagined reality: the view from the top of the mountain the farmer is willing to relegate to the experiential; the brook and its special character he allows to live in his imagination alone. But the visitor's empirical curiosity is aroused, once the farmer admits that he has never really been to the top, and he probes further for the "truth":

> "Warm in December, cold in June, you say?"

> "I don't suppose the water's changed at all.
> You and I know enough to know it's warm
> Compared with cold, and cold compared with warm.
> But all the fun's in how you say a thing."

Now thoroughly disappointed, the visitor changes the subject:

> "You've lived here all your life?"
>   "Ever since Hor [the mountain]

Was no bigger than a —" What, I did not hear.
He drew the oxen toward him with light touches
Of his slim goad on nose and offside flank,
Gave them their marching orders and was moving.

And that is the way the poem ends. It seems as much about the playfully free and creative spirit, here manifesting itself in the indigenous
speech of a country man, as it is a poem about a brook. Or perhaps it is
more accurate to say that the brook provides the proper setting for the release of imaginative energy. Unlike the dangerous river, the brook does
not change nature and seems not to make much of a difference in the
farmer's everyday world. Though a natural force, it is of the gentlest sort;
it does not assert against us an ominous autonomous power; it lends itself
to the manipulations of imaginative consciousness.

For the farmer the contemplation of the brook signals the beginning
of a creative holiday, a spot of playful freedom embedded within a context of labor. When he contemplates the brook he must account no longer
for rivers and for oxen—things that make a difference at the observable
level of his experience. He becomes accountable only to himself and his
need to redeem experience—drab, routine, workaday experience—in and
through language. The creation of a mysterious reality in language defies
the facts, but the facts be damned because "all the fun's in how you say a
thing." The contemplation of the brook leads him to the fictionalizing
moment of figurative linkage: "One of the great sights going is to
see / It steam in winter like an ox's breath." One would need to be versed
in aesthetic things to see this sight which is to be distinguished from the
kind of view that our visitor desires from the top of the mountain. And
when asked the name of the mountain Frost's farmer reveals with wit an
agile poetic sensibility which allows him to project the fiction of aesthetic
consciousness as well as to stand outside the fiction—to view it for what
it is. He knows that his "saying" is the making of his world; that it is the
symbolizing power of human consciousness which gives the world its
peculiarly human identity as it transforms the inhuman thing-in-itself:
"We call it Hor: I don't know if that's right."

But our poet-farmer's precious freedom to do with the world what he wills in the anarchic moment of imagination is carefully circumscribed. The figurative moment is approached again in the poem's conclusion— " 'Ever since Hor / Was no bigger than a —' " but not quite realized. The poem's circular movement is completed: the aesthetic process is broken off because the farmer understands that his visitor does not share his fun of figurative play and has refused to enter with him into the imaginative experience; the laboring process must begin again. Though representative of the anti-aesthetic, labor is not representative of disvalue in this poem, because only within certain carefully prescribed limits, defined by labor, is the self released into the aesthetic state where it may experience the healing powers of an imaginative freedom that lifts us briefly out of what Wallace Stevens aptly called the "malady of the quotidian," the dull, ritualized rhythms of our every day lives.

2

In "The Generations of Men,"[3] a long dialogue poem from *North of Boston*, the brook not only encourages the flow of a redeeming imaginative vision but is implicated, as well, with the themes of history, change, and love. The characters are two, a young man and woman, far distant cousins who have returned to the town of Bow, New Hampshire, for a gathering of all those named Stark; the original ancestors are traced back to Bow, and, specifically, to an "old cellar hole in a by-road / The origin of all the family there." Generally it is difficult, sometimes impossible, to probe the objects in Frost's landscape in isolation. In "The Generations of Men" the figure of the brook is entangled with the figure of this cellar hole—the house that is no more a house—which we met earlier in "Ghost House." Like the cellar hole in "Ghost House," this one becomes a dwelling place for the mind, the occasion for a wide-ranging meditation.

With a soft rain falling, and with most of the Stark clan settled in for the day, the young man and woman wander separately to the old homestead; there they meet and make each other's acquaintance. As they sit upon the cellar wall, with their legs dangling among the raspberry vines, and with a brook hidden among trees, rushing away on down the hill, they begin to question each other about why they have returned to Bow; why they are drawn to the cellar hole "Like wild geese on a lake before a storm?" The question, asked by the young man, spurs a series of imaginative journeys. First the girl:

"The Indians had a myth of Chicamoztoc,
Which means The-Seven-Caves-that-We-Came-Out-of.
This is the pit from which we Starks were digged."

"You must be learned. That's what you see in it?"

"And what do you see?"

"Yes, what *do* I see?
First let me look. I see raspberry vines—"

But she will have none of his humorous skepticism and bids him to join her in a synesthetic experience—an imaginative kind of seeing: " 'Oh, if you're going to use your eyes, just hear / What *I* see. It's a little, little boy. . . .' " Her spirit is infectious and he pretends to join her with his own visions of Grandsir and Granny Stark. But it is soon clear to her that he will not suspend disbelief; that he won't journey into imagination's country without taking along his ironical defenses. So she makes to leave and that stops him. The prospect of not seeing her again presses him on to visions that are free from the drag of irony. He tells her, in so many words, we have been using the eye of imagination—" 'We have seen visions' "—but if we wish to go to the depths we must "consult the voices," we must use the ear of imagination:

"Yes, you must go; we can't stay here forever.
But wait until I give you a hand up.
A head of silver water more or less,
Strung on your hair, won't hurt your summer looks.
I wanted to try something with the noise
That the brook raises in the empty valley.
We have seen visions—now consult the voices.

. . . .
I've never listened in among the sounds
That a brook makes in such a wild descent
It ought to give a purer oracle."

The hitherto skeptical young man begins to reveal to his companion what looks to be a religious consciousness. The incomplete comparative "a purer oracle" distinguishes the voice of the brook from the flow of personal vision by suggesting that personal visions are merely imposed structures—they are nostalgic memories of the past that have no basis in objective necessity. But the sound of the brook is the pure voice of history itself, flowing forward into the present, delivering its lessons to a younger generation. The girl is at least as hardheaded as he is. She does not believe in communications from sacred objects. The brook is not the true voice of history: it is rather an encouragement to the imagination buried in the self, it beckons, draws it out, becomes the occasion for self-conscious visionary experiences:

> "It's as you throw a picture on a screen:
> The meaning of it all is out of you;
> The voices give you what you wish to hear."

The source of imaginative vision is argued briefly—" 'Strangely, it's anything they wish to give.' " / " 'Then I don't know. It must be strange enough. / I wonder if it's not your make-believe.' " He continues to insist: " 'I'll tell you what the voices really say.' " But he has been playing elaborately all along. When the voice of the past speaking through the brook is translated by him it is quite clear that the message is his "make-believe" and that he has been creating out of desire, not translating the language of history. She knows it and accepts it with warm and gentle humor:

> "The voices seem to say:
> Call her Nausicaä, the unafraid
> Of an acquaintance made adventurously."

> "I let you say that—on consideration."

> . . . .
> "Call her Nausicaä, and take a timber
> That you shall find lies in the cellar, charred
> Among the raspberries, and hew and shape it
> For a doorsill or other corner piece
> In a new cottage on the ancient spot.
> The life is not yet all gone out of it.
> And come and make your summer dwelling here,
> And perhaps she will come, still unafraid,
> And sit before you in the open door
> With flowers in her lap until they fade, . . . "

> "I wonder where your oracle is tending."

The brook cannot deliver to the present the voice of the past. In a sense it does something more important: it becomes an inducement for imaginative play—it encourages the creative energy within the self to throw up against change and decay what Frost called, in his definition of poetic value, a "momentary stay." The boy and girl respond to the brook with the harmonies of their love-to-be. These lovers, like poets, make a world opposed to the one of their immediate experience and by so doing redeem the past by asserting in the face of its crumbling remains the will to renewal. It is not Granny Stark who says " 'You take the timber— / It's as sound as the day when it was cut— / And begin over—'." The pun in the poem's title becomes the ultimate clue to its meaning: it is a poem about how the love spurred by the "generations" of a young man can finally link "generations," making that continuity, the marriage of present with past—not a gift of time, but an achievement of the will that must be periodically rewon with acts of the mind and heart.

The conjunction of the image of the brook with the theme of love occurs again in "Hyla Brook."[4] "Going For Water," "The Tuft of Flowers," and "The Generations of Men" are poems in which an experience of a brook initiates imaginative journeys, and imaginative journeys either lead to or are accompanied by a sense of intimacy between self and world, self and time, self and self. (In "Hyla Brook" the tone of an embracing intimacy is established quickly in the first line: it is "our brook.") The closeness in human relations dramatized in "Going For Water" and "The Generations of Men" stands in sharp contrast to the failure of contact that is evoked in "The Mountain"; even as the willingness of the selves projected in "Going For Water" and "The Generations of Men" to experience the brook in an imaginative way stands in opposition to the unwillingness of the visitor in "The Mountain" to take anything but the deadening empirical view of the brook as object.

For Frost, the very basis of human love is an act of the imagination. In "Hyla Brook" he insists that to love the thing itself, to make a cherishing, sympathetic identification with an object of nature sometimes requires that the thing be remade in poetic figuration; that it be taken into the interior of self:

> By June our brook's run out of song and speed.
> Sought for much after that, it will be found
> Either to have gone groping underground
> (And taken with it all the Hyla breed
> That shouted in the mist a month ago,
> Like ghost of sleigh bells in a ghost of snow)—

Or flourished and come up in jewelweed,
Weak foliage that is blown upon and bent,
Even against the way its waters went.
Its bed is left a faded paper sheet
Of dead leaves stuck together by the heat—
A brook to none but who remember long.
This as it will be seen is other far
Than with brooks taken otherwhere in song.
We love the things we love for what they are.

The poem roots Frost's musings over the relations of imagination and love in the image of the vanished brook and, as it comments obliquely on a well-known poem for children by Tennyson, speaks about changing modes of poetry as well. Frost will not be sentimental about his brook; it simply isn't true that it will "go on forever," as Tennyson says. Frost's brook has vanished and Reuben Brower's remark that the last line is ironic, not didactic,[5] is exactly to the point: "We love the things we love for what they are." This line, Brower says, refers us to a brook which is *not*. But I would add, which *is* in a kind of remembering that poets are especially capable of experiencing. Poets know how to "remember long"; it is the poet's memory, metaphorically charged, that can recall, via personification, "our brook" in June, humanized, "groping underground"; that can bring back the brook's croaking frogs of a month past as "ghost of sleigh bells"—or that can "see" the brook in weak "jewelweed" that bends even against the direction that its waters used to flow. Once again, it is poetic memory that marries present and past.

If the ability to love requires the cherishing of someone for what she is, then the ability to love a brook sometimes requires the power of seeing it where it is not. For the fact is that a brook doesn't stand much of a chance in nature; almost any dry spell will kill it, a heavy rain may make it more than it is, and little boys at play divert and dissipate its gentle flow at will. It needs to be paid homage to by a memorializing act of imagination. And in that memorializing act both vanished brook and self are drawn together, integrated in a remembered world where Frost's brook comes to life as the spark of vitality is forced across the gap between self and nature by the animism projected in the poet's language. Like the brook in "The Generations of Men" this one's sacredness lies in its receptiveness to being taken on an imaginative excursion. The brook spurs the visionary spirit in its search for integration, even though it remains, in empirical reality, a "faded paper sheet / Of dead leaves stuck together."

3

"A Brook in the City"[6] is a brooding and troubled meditation which darkens the meaning of an obsessive image. As it figures and celebrates the innocence and free impulse of the country scene now smothered by a creeping and monolithic urbanization, the image of the brook illuminates Frost's vision which we may describe with Leo Marx as "complex pastoral-ism,"[7] the destructive penetration of the city within the pastoral garden of unpremeditated pleasure. The quiet personifications of brook and farm-house throughout (as humanized nature and naturalized self) point us to the romantic core of Frost's psychological parable: the self, once free, integrated with its natural environment, and child-like, becomes in the urban setting repressed, civilized (read "unnatural"), and self-conscious:

> The farmhouse lingers, though averse to square
> With the new city street it has to wear
> A number in. But what about the brook
> That held the house as in an elbow-crook?
> I ask as one who knew the brook, its strength
> And impulse, having dipped a finger length
> And made it leap my knuckle. . . .

The farmhouse, pinned and fixed in the stasis of artificiality, ("it has to wear / A number") has become a house in the city. The farmhouse as farmhouse now "lingers," at the point of death. Once, though, the brook, "that was the water of the house," in the words of "Directive," was a kind of mother and the farmhouse nestled in the protective enclosure of her "elbow-crook." But the brook as brook has been stilled (it flows now as a sewer stream)—the farmhouse has lost its function, and adult life must go on unprotected. The perspective in the poem is that of an adult's divided consciousness, severely differentiated from the life around it. The use of simile ("as in an elbow-crook") is probably deliberate. For Frost it is the perfect way of suggesting his complex pastoralism because the simile generates, at once, a vision of integration and beneficent pastoral en-closure, even as it negates that vision by insisting on the radical difference between the brook and the human arm. Still, though the farmhouse and brook cannot stand emblematically for a fully integrated self and natural world that are no more, and though the poet refuses to indulge a sentimentalized vision of the vanishing pastoral way of life, he is yet held in essential awe by the brook, by "immortal force,"

> thrown
> Deep in a sewer dungeon under stone
> In fetid darkness still to live and run—
> And all for nothing it had ever done,
> Except forget to go in fear . . .

Lastly, the brook is psychologically emblematic of the way the natural self, though pushed underground, and repressed in the adult self, refuses to succumb to the discontents of a civilized world which fears the self's impulsive and anarchic energies. Our "brook" self runs on deep within us, haunting our mature lives:

> But I wonder
> If from its being kept forever under,
> The thoughts may not have risen that so keep
> This new-built city from both work and sleep.

With this last nuance of meaning, as figure of the irrepressible, underground self, we prepare to approach the symbolic sense of the brook that seems intended in the title poem of Frost's fifth volume of poetry, *West-Running Brook*. A philosophical dialogue carried on by a young married couple, "West-Running Brook"[8] is Frost's most extended and self-conscious treatment of the brook as fixed object in his landscape. The poem builds on the initial observation of the wife that this brook runs west while "all other country brooks flow east / To reach the ocean." Fascinated by this oddity, she proceeds to connect, casually, the contrariness of the brook with their relationship:

> "It must be the brook
> Can trust itself to go by contraries
> The way I can with you—and you with me—"

Becoming more fascinated by the connection she has made, she offers her husband a romantic vision of marriage as metaphor for the interdependent relations of self and nature:

> "We've said we two. Let's change that to we three.
> As you and I are married to each other,
> We'll both be married to the brook. We'll build
> Our bridge across it, and the bridge shall be
> Our arm thrown over it asleep beside it.
> Look, look, it's waving to us with a wave
> To let us know it hears me."

Her husband, Fred, is not the type to entertain such lovely romantic visions and he begins to undercut her with his own observation: " 'Why, my dear, / That wave's been standing off this jut of shore—' " but before he can complete his thought he interrupts himself with this complicated digression:

> (The black stream, catching on a sunken rock,
> Flung backward on itself in one white wave,
> And the white water rode the black forever,
> Not gaining but not losing, like a bird
> White feathers from the struggle of whose breast
> Flecked the dark stream and flecked the darker pool. . . .)
> "Ever since rivers, I was going to say,
> Were made in heaven. It wasn't waved to us."

In the very process of denying the viability of his wife's romantic vision with hard fact, Fred makes a metaphoric leap of his own to the poem's thematic center. The image of the "bird / White feathers from the struggle . . ." becomes emblematic of the action of the human will. Neither seems aware, for the moment, of his metaphor-making, and they argue briefly over whether or not the wave means what she says it means: " 'If not to you, / It was to me—in an annunciation.' " He replies, in exasperation: " 'Oh, if you take it off to lady-land, / As't were the country of the Amazons . . . it is your brook! I have no more to say.' " She is shrewder than he will credit her for, though, and understanding that her husband has already begun to suggest a great deal, urges him to extend his metaphoric digression: " 'Yes, you have, too. Go on. You thought of something.' "

He seemed to be waiting for the encouragement and promptly returns to his concentrated metaphor:

> "Speaking of contraries, see how the brook
> In that white wave runs counter to itself.

> It is from that in water we were from
> Long, long before we were from any creature."

It is not that he sees in water a primary form of being. Frost is not making Fred play Thales in modern dress. It is that the brook's double movement of flow and counterflow supplies his explanation of human existence. Existence, like the ever-changing, ever-moving brook is " 'The stream of everything that runs away,' " the Bergsonian flux:

> "It seriously, sadly, runs away
> To fill the abyss's void with emptiness.
> It flows beside us in this water brook,
> But it flows over us. It flows between us
> To separate us for a panic moment.
> It flows between us, over us, and *with* us.
> And it is time, strength, tone, light, life, and love—
> And even substance lapsing unsubstantial;
> The universal cataract of death
> That spends to nothingness—. . . ."

The philosophic darkness of this passage, buttressed by once popular theories of entropy, has no equal in Frost (and few equals in twentieth-century poetry). It is relieved only in the way that Frost typically relieves "the horror"—in a maneuver of wit; here, in "West-Running Brook," in the shrewd latinate play on "unsubstantial." Existence does not simply flow over the edge of fullness into the abyss of emptiness—that would be bad enough. The flux of existence is itself generative of nothingness. It is life itself that spills emptiness into the abyss—nothingness feeds the void —and as the water flows by the two standing at the brook's edge, the man senses that it is more than just the irrepeatable flow of time that saddens: it is the emptiness within the core of substance, the emptiness within the love that binds them, and the emptiness that separates and drowns them as it flows over and between them.

But if the dominant flow of the brook—its westward flow to death— figures the flux of existence that "spends to nothingness—and unresisted," then its minor counterflow, the water "flung backward on itself in one white wave" like a struggling white bird "whose breast / Flecked the dark stream," suggests the resistance of the human will itself, engulfed and caught in the flux, but pressing back against it, keeping its integrity by asserting its contrariness to nature (though "Not gaining," "not losing" either).

"Not just a swerving, but a throwing back,
As if regret were in it and were sacred. . . .
It is this backward motion toward the source,
Against the stream, that most we see ourselves in,
The tribute of the current to the source.
It is from this in nature we are from,
It is most us."

These lines not only speak about the contrariness of will but render as well a desperation of tone that is appropriate to the speaker's theme. It takes an act of humanizing imagination—a seeing of ourselves *in*, a forcing of humanness into the nonhuman—to make the little counterwave (it *must* be us) the metaphor of the resistent force which defines our humanness. And the repetition of the key line—" 'that most we see ourselves in' "—" 'It is most us' "—suggests the terrible minimal consolation of that little counterwave. But despite the uncertainties, and despite the terrors of a world in decay, for Fred and his wife the brook has been the basis of understanding, of a coming together not unlike the union suggested in "The Pasture." The poem's last line speaks only of resolution: "Today will be the day of what we both said."

4

As representative of an objective feature of Frost's given New England world, and as inhabitant of an interiorized landscape, the brook shuttles in and out, joining self and the landscape across which self moves. This dual status of the brook is reflected in "The Mountain," where the brook is both brute fact and the motivating object of playful fantasy; in "The Generations of Men," where it encourages visions of continuity even as it represents change; in "Hyla Brook" where it is both a vanished empirical object and present as vision; in "A Brook in the City," where it is both a sewer stream and a figure of an innocent, repressed self; and, finally, in an image from "West-Running Brook" that could not be more precise, an image of flow and counterflow, the brook is emblematic of death and of the life-force of resistive will. The brook can embrace such contraries because Frost has constructed, in the cumulative interrelations of all his brook poems, a symbol of the polar movements of his consciousness; its movement toward redemption of self and nature within an aesthetic universe, and its movement toward an ironic awareness of the way things are.

Though the function of Frost's brook is similar to the function of other major recurrent features of his landscape, it would be misleading to assume that these objects in the landscape all coalesce one complex of experience. The brook stands uniquely in Frost's world as the motive of redemptive vision. It rarely fails to elicit from the lonely figure who meets it, as he moves across the forlorn landscape, a sense of wonder from being cut loose from the entanglements of his life; a sense of freedom and of psychic integration, and, if not an experience of wonder and inner wholeness, then a powerful desire for such experiences. So, though the brook never loses completely its ironic drag—it continues to speak, in "A Brook in the City," to a self psychically divided against itself, and severed irreparably from nature—it alone among Frost's symbols encourages a thrust of the mind powerful enough to free self from the fallen state of self-consciousness. Encountering the brook, the self in the poem finds himself released into an enveloping serenity, trust, and innocence which flow from a recovery of unself-consciousness in the imaginative moment, and which tell him that the split within, the split between self and nature, and the split between self and others, has been miraculously healed. Better things do not happen to the selves dramatized in Frost's poems.

Yet there is no "miracle." Frost's redemptions occur only within the imaginative and not within the religious experience; only within private and minor moments of secular consciousness in the ordinary life, not within spectacular moments of cosmic significance. The value of an imaginative experience, as Frost focuses it in his brook poems, is that it briefly lifts the self above subtle psychological forces of erosion that eventually break us. Though he generally eschews metaphysical and eschatological pretension, Frost continues to insist that the experience of the imaginative moment is of immense value, is necessary on a day-by-day basis because it supplies those moments of contact and resolution that can brace us, and makes the irresolvable longer haul bearable. He never believed, as Wallace Stevens sometimes did, that the imagination could take the place of God and that a poetic canon could replace the Bible. Neither does the farmer in "The Mountain" listen with T. S. Eliot for the distant sounds of thunder which will bring the waste land to life again. He has wrung a little joy out of today but tomorrow is entirely another problem.

3. The House

One need not be a Chamber—to be Haunted—
One need not be a house—
The Brain has Corridors—surpassing
Material Place—

Far safer, of a Midnight Meeting
External Ghost
Than its interior Confronting—
That Cooler Host.

Far safer, through an Abbey gallop,
The Stones a'chase—
Than Unarmed, one's a'self encounter—
In lonesome Place—

Ourself behind ourself, concealed—
Should startle most—
Assassin hid in our Apartment
Be Horror's least.

The Body—Borrows a Revolver—
He bolts the Door—
O'erlooking a superior spectre—
Or More—

(Emily Dickinson, #670)

. . . the images I want to examine are the quite simple images of
felicitous space. In this orientation, these investigations would deserve
to be called topophilia. They seek to determine the human value of
the sorts of space that may be grasped, that may be defended against
adverse forces, the space we love. For diverse reasons, and with the
differences entailed by poetic shadings, this is eulogized space. At-

tached to its protective value, which can be a positive one, are also imagined values, which soon become dominant. (Gaston Bachelard, *The Poetics of Space*)

The image of enclosure, especially when it refers to the house, is one of the more psychologically compelling images in Frost's poetry and essays. I comment in chapter 7 on the significance of enclosure for Frost's poetics as a metaphor for the poem itself, and we have already seen, in chapter 1, its crucial recurrence within his first volume in such poems as "Ghost House," "Storm Fear," and "Rose Pogonias." Enclosures, be they natural or human constructions, tend in Frost to correlate with structures which are entirely mental, often becoming figures for the interior space of self. But be they natural, artificial, or mental, such structures of enclosure serve mainly as havens; as places which the self in the poem, governed by his harboring instinct, seeks out in an effort to protect himself, to fend off destructive experience in the terror of free space.

One of the severest lessons of Frost's poetry is that although the mind may close out a world dangerous to psychic balance, it may as well, when divided against itself, enclose experiences that are potentially fatal to mental serenity. In Frost's pastoral world, where overt violence from without is a minimal consideration, the self may turn inward in its freedom from externally generated tensions, often to discover and confront threats from interior demons far more difficult to control than those of our public experience. As objects in his poetic landscape, the house and the woods differ importantly from the brook in that they often expose the most disturbing dimensions of Frost's vision. Both objects reveal the way the imaginatively redeemed world of desire, which is experienced in the brook poems, can become oppressive when the imagination is uncontrolled—a place more destructive to self than our world of shared experience. The house (be it actual or a figure for the mind) can be sanctuary, but it can be inescapable hell as well.

1

In "A Brook in the City" what Frost saw reflected in the water was not simply the wreckage of the pastoral ideal but also, as I understand the meaning of his personification, a reflection of the open and unself-conscious self (which "forgot to go in fear") now repressed and buried; driven underground by the closed, adult self which was figured in the house and which never forgets to go in fear. To look ahead to "Directive," in the brook of "A Brook in the City" we perceive what keeps us awake in the dark night of this "now" that is "too much for us"; it is what, repressed in us, motivates the quest of "Directive" for the children's playhouse; it is what presses us to recover the source of our psychic wholeness. The prophetic tone of the last lines of "A Brook in the City" seems to promise the apocalyse of this renewal of self.

A critical awareness of Frost's brook poems should help to prepare the entrance for a dramatically (and diametrically) different self that I find revealed in the house poems; it should help as well to alter the portrait of Frost that emerges in a very influential study, Roy Harvey Pearce's *The Continuity of American Poetry*. For Pearce the whole Frost is revealed in the house poems: the self that has, in Pearce's words, renounced "faith in the ultimate equivalence of the 'I' and 'we,'" and by so doing has established a "community of one," a "sense of the concrete, particular, bounded 'I.'"[1] Pearce's interpretation of Frost is not politically based in any narrow sense, but his final evaluation is in curious agreement with the self-conscious political interpretations of Frost's liberal, social critics. Inordinately irritated by the poet's explicit and caustic anti-Rooseveltian conservatism, these critics find him a basically ungenerous human being. What Pearce and the liberal critics tend not to see is that the lonely people haunting Frost's landscapes are agonized to the core. In his poems of enclosure Frost has written psycho-dramas of the private self. I find little in those poems to suggest that Frost is pleased with the alienation which he dramatizes, which he often felt in his own life, and which, on occasion, he seems even to have sought out.

Though based on a close reading of all of Frost, Pearce's conclusions reflect but one thrust of self—the self radiated by the house poems, where self finds itself surrounded by hostile and malevolent forces, unable to trust in anything but itself. Redemptions are sometimes achieved in the house poems, but they work for one man only, at the cost of severing all human relations, and at the cost of disvaluing all objects beyond the self. (House poems are never, like "Going For Water," or "Two Look at Two," poems of "we.") Houses are ultimately revelations in Frost of a crisis-focused self-consciousness, of an alienated self that can turn nowhere but to its made, private, and enclosed world for salvation, because neither nature nor other humans are to be trusted. There is a strong tendency in Frost to see the world as a place of darkness. For such a vision the only antidote is a secure, well-lighted room, but a well-lighted room is often hard to find.

2

A number of the isolated and disturbed characters in Frost's longer dialogue-narratives are extreme forms of the selves projected in his lyrics. These are people who are sick unto death, either physically, as in "The Death of the Hired Man," or mentally, as in "Home Burial," "A Servant to Servants," and "The Witch of Coös." Their loneliness is surpassed only by their inability to defend themselves. They do not know the warm, soothing feeling of enclosure, all danger safely shut out, the world fully there inside, and the self master of it all. A full analysis of these characters within their literary contexts is, regrettably, somewhat beyond the scope of my essay, but I think they make the perfect dialectical introduction to the symbol of the house as a place of sanctuary.

The pathetic figure of Silas, an unreliable hired hand who has come back to Mary and Warren, his old employers, very ill, broken in body and in spirit, is an example of what I have in mind. The entire discussion in "The Death of the Hired Man"[2] turns on Warren's reluctance "to be kind," as his wife puts it. The disreputable old wanderer is the black sheep of his family and hence is forced to turn, in his extremity, to Mary and Warren, expecting (with no good reason) that they will provide him his last "harbor":

> "Warren," she said, "he has come home to die:
> You needn't be afraid he'll leave you this time."
>
> "Home," he mocked gently.

Warren defines home cynically as "the place where, when you have to go there, / They have to take you in." His wife counters with "I should have called it / Something you somehow haven't to deserve." The matrix of pain in so many of Frost's poems is exactly this circumstance of needing enclosure very badly but not getting it. Too often the dramatically rendered character in the longer narrative, or the lyric self of the shorter poem finds himself, as Silas did, facing things alone and with no chance of sanctuary. The terrible vulnerability of such a figure is evoked metonymically toward the end of "The Death of the Hired Man" when Mary says,

> "he hurt my heart the way he lay
> And rolled his old head on that sharp-edged chair-back. . . .
>   he's broken."

In comparison to other of Frost's characters Silas is fortunate because his death is an escape from the razor edges of experience. More unfortunate than he are those broken in mind, those whose bodies are sound enough but who must endure the living death of an intermittent mental sickness. I refer to Frost's memorable women, particularly the wife in "Home Burial," the servant in "A Servant to Servants," and the witch in "The Witch of Coös." These women suffer for different reasons—one has lost a child, another appears to have inherited madness which manifests itself in sexual suggestion, and the third has buckled under a deserved burden of guilt—but all of them share in a naked vulnerability, a torturous state brought about by obsessive recollections which penetrate every defense. For these women there is no possibility of sanctuary. Frost's intention seems to be to focus the climax of his poems precisely in images of abject helplessness. Thus the wife in "Home Burial"[3] must brood daily on the family graveyard where her child is buried—it is framed perfectly by an upstairs window. Out of that window it is not only the graveyard that she sees, but an externalization of something that she carries within herself: "She was starting down, / Looking back over her shoulder at some fear." Her room with a view touches off morbidly detailed recollections of the day that her husband dug the grave:

> "I saw you from that very window there,
> Making the gravel leap and leap in air,
> Leap up, like that, like that, and land so lightly
> And roll back down the mound beside the hole. . . .
> You could sit there with the stains on your shoes
> Of the fresh earth from your own baby's grave
> And talk about your everyday concerns."

It is exactly his ability to talk about everyday rituals (*"You*—oh, you think the talk is all") and to retreat into language that save him from the constant reexperiencing of his child's death. It is her inability to erect barriers between the present and her destructive memories that places her at the mercy of the image of those awful stains on her husband's shoes:

"I can repeat the very words you were saying:
'Three foggy mornings and one rainy day
Will rot the best birch fence a man can build.'
Think of it, talk like that at such a time!
What had how long it takes a birch to rot
To do with what was in the darkened parlor?
You *couldn't* care!"

Women are frequently distinguished from men in Frost's poems by their serious lack of drive to preserve self. They are much too open to shock, seem not to have the strength—the wife in "Home Burial" would say "callousness"—to throw up against psychological chaos a momentary stay like the old saw "Three foggy mornings and one rainy day / Will rot the best birch fence a man can build" which, contrary to what she says, has everything to do with what was in the "darkened parlor." Unlike his wife, the husband in "Home Burial" has been able to establish his security within the haven of everyday banality while she must flounder about, continually reconfronting the crisis of her baby's death—"miserable," "frightening," and "jumbled." Perhaps the last clue to the wife's problem in "Home Burial" is in the macabre play of the title itself which suggests a triple home burial. This is a poem not only about the burial of a first-born, but also about the burial of a relationship; it is a poem about the way a woman buries herself a little bit every day in the domestic setting—as if smothered she says, "I must get air."

It is questionable whether she truly wants to come out of her painful isolation, or whether she would prefer to sink even deeper into her aloneness, in masochistic compensation for her child's death. She needs to see her husband as unfeeling and unresponsive because she needs, in her masochism, to destroy their marriage as a context of mutuality. Having convinced herself that mutual responsiveness is not possible, she may drive inward with self-annihilating logic to final isolation. When, casually, her husband sentimentally describes the small family graveyard as "Not so much larger than a bedroom," Amy's distorted version of him is authenticated: she takes him to be alluding very obliquely and very maliciously to the act of sexual love that brought their child to the world and, by painful extension, to death. In her resentment of her husband's ability to survive, she has cruelly confused his sanity with callousness, his surface calm with interior indifference. She says, in effect, if you were really as affected as I was you, too, would crack. When she speaks bitterly in generalities to her husband of "friends" and the way they react to the "dying," she means to speak of *him*, his despised toughness, and her spiritual death:

> The nearest friends can go
> With anyone to death, comes so far short
> They might as well not try to go at all.
> No, from the time when one is sick to death,
> One is alone, and he dies more alone.

In the poem's conclusion she threatens to leave the house and her husband. But escape is not possible because there is no cure for self, as E. A. Robinson once put it; no leave-taking of those imprisoning fixations on the death of her child which keep her in deep isolation and throw into poignant relief her husband's futile plea for contact: "Let me into your grief."

The woman in "A Servant to Servants"[4] is probably the most miserable of all Frost's *miserables* because she half understands that she is "all gone wrong" and that despite what her husband says no kind of medicine will cure her ailment:

> "He thinks I'll be all right
> With doctoring. But it's not medicine—
> Lowe is the only doctor's dared to say so—"

Four crude boarders rob her of her privacy, sometimes insult her sensibility, and whet fears of being raped within the very place where she should expect to be safe:

> "We have four here to board . . .
> Sprawling about the kitchen with their talk
> While I fry their bacon. Much they care!
> No more put out in what they do or say
> Than if I wasn't in the room at all. . . .
> I don't learn what their names are, let alone
> Their characters, or whether they are safe
> To have inside the house with doors unlocked."

She moves from this last thought of sexual violence to the area of her worst fears, a core of obsessive images relating to her uncle's madness—his shouted obscenities in the night, her feeling that her home is no asylum at all and that the true asylum is "The State Asylum" where she had once been. Folks, she says, think it more humane to keep their mad relatives at home. "But it's not so: the place is the asylum."

Like most of his wounded females, Frost's bound-up, housed servant carries on dialogue with others, but mainly she speaks to some voice hidden within, some coherent and controlled identity that might have been. Such inner dialogue tends to be paralytic and abates only when, for brief moments, the self is opened up to the landscape so that there is an energizing symbolic flow from the outside, from nature into the self:

> There's nothing but a voice-like left inside
> That seems to tell me how I ought to feel,
> And would feel if I wasn't all gone wrong.
> You take the lake. . . .
> It took my mind off doughnuts and soda biscuit
> To step outdoors and take the water dazzle
> A sunny morning, or take the rising wind
> About my face and body and through my wrapper,
> When a storm threatened from the Dragon's Den,
> And a cold chill shivered across the lake.
> I see it's a fair, pretty sheet of water,
> Our Willoughby! . . .

The many telling pauses and sentence fragments ("I guess you'd find. . . ." "But it's not medicine—") are expressive of the servant's confusion and disunified consciousness. Frost's style defines his psychological substance: the servant's monologue moves roughly and haltingly, leaping sometimes forward, sometimes backward, without those little transitional words and phrases that suggest an inner wholeness and connectedness of thought; she might begin dissociating, though it does not quite happen in the poem. The servant's psychological disorders have frozen her ability to express her feelings and even, in some part, have frozen her physical self ("It seems to me / I can't express my feelings any more / Than I can raise my voice or want to lift / My hand . . ."). But in one unguarded and therapeutic moment she breaks out of her frozen self and tells all to a total stranger. She has her "fancies," as she puts it, and in a remarkable passage evokes the nightmare vision which periodically haunts her, robs her of the possibility of normalcy:

> "My father's brother, he went mad quite young.
> Some thought he had been bitten by a dog,

Because his violence took on the form
Of carrying his pillow in his teeth;
But it's more likely he was crossed in love,
Or so the story goes. It was some girl.
Anyway all he talked about was love.
They soon saw he would do someone a mischief
If he wa'n't kept strict watch of, and it ended
In father's building him a sort of cage,
Or room within a room, of hickory poles,
Like stanchions in the barn, from floor to ceiling—
A narrow passage all the way around.
Anything they put in for furniture
He'd tear to pieces, even a bed to lie on.
So they made the place comfortable with straw,
Like a beast's stall, to ease their consciences.
Of course they had to feed him without dishes.
They tried to keep him clothed, but he paraded
With his clothes on his arm—all of his clothes.
Cruel—it sounds. I s'pose they did the best
They knew. And just when he was at the height,
Father and mother married, and mother came,
A bride, to help take care of such a creature,
And accommodate her young life to his.
That was what marrying father meant to her.
She had to lie and hear love things made dreadful
By his shouts in the night."

The servant reveals that until very recently she and her husband lived in her father's house and that her uncle's pen was still there in the attic. By the poem's end the form of her madness becomes somewhat clarified. Certain details appear to fit a pattern: the rough, profane speech of the boarders; the fear of what they might do to her with free access to the house; the lingering on her uncle's nakedness ("he paraded / With his clothes on his arm—all his clothes"); the identification with her mother as bride, making love in the night to the accompaniment of her uncle's dreadful screams; the last chilling identification with the uncle himself, whom she never saw, forced upon her by his "room within a room," a constant reminder of her mother's experience and an emblem of her own destiny (only "half-fooling," she says, "It's time I took my turn upstairs in jail"). Like the wife in "Home Burial," like the witch in "The Witch of Coös," the memory of the servant in "A Servant to Servants" encloses a set of images which are potentially fatal to mental balance if not expelled or suppressed.

But these women have no means of suppression: their imaginations function in such ways as to deepen and extend their nightmares, not relieve them. Like the figures in "Stars" and "Storm Fear" they create their own "desert places" because they are locked into the projections from their own deranged minds. The mad uncle's "room within a room" becomes a horrifying metaphor for the enemy lurking within the sanctuary of self—not really lurking, but more horrible, having a place there of its own—and an objective correlative of the way the mind's peaceful place can be invaded. Once that room is constructed in the mind it becomes an indestructible, inescapable prison whose ever-expanding boundaries eventually claim the total house of self (not just a room) and convert it from sanctuary to the residence of pandemonium.

From the point of view of neo-Freudian studies (especially those of Eric Erikson), the servant defines herself destructively—subverts her mental balance from within, as it were, since she locates her identity in her father's house, and her father's house encloses within it a place of caged madness. The servant's sense of who she is and what she desires is painfully unsure: a characteristic habit of her speech is "but I don't know!" With blunt honesty she says, "It's got so I don't even know for sure / Whether I *am* glad, sorry, or anything." Her identity hovers dangerously between what she recalls and what she imagines of her sick uncle and of her traumatized mother. The servant learns, as the wife in "Home Burial" does not, that she cannot escape a fictive room by moving out of a real house.

3

Taken in the context of the poems just discussed, the psychological orientation of Frost's definition of a poem as a "figure of the will braving alien entanglements" becomes very clear. Frost's portraits of the exposed self are figures of the will not braving, but succumbing to alien entanglements; not composing itself by making soothing circles of enclosed form, but destroying itself by projecting and enclosing itself in forms of horror. Viewed in this perspective, these are portraits of the aesthetically impoverished; of minds unequipped with the poet's ironic consciousness and his ability to constitute his reality in such ways as to retain control over various destructive elements in his experience that originate in the empirically objective and in the darker recesses of his subjectivity.

The mad, adulterous witch of Coös,[5] who helped her husband bury her paramour in their cellar after he murdered him, is almost a parable of the problem of deranged imagination and its relationship to the symbol of the house. She, like the pitiful servant, has her visions, but the witch has gone over the edge. She is convinced that her murdered lover's bones on one cold winter evening walked up the cellar stairs and into the bedroom. That no one else has ever seen the bones seems not to give her pause; she believes it was only her own native shrewdness (she tricked them into the attic where they are now locked) that saved her from whatever it was the bones wanted to do to her. The metaphors associated with the long-dead lover—a "rattling of a shutter," a "chandelier," a "pile of dishes"— attest to the close and choking intimacy of the visionary bones: for the crazy witch and her simpleton son, they are a "familiar" domestic reality. Just as the servant's "room within a room" robs her of the possibility of sanctuary, so the attic where the bones are locked becomes the witch's "room within a room" which violates her mind's sanctuary by paralyzing the rationalizing reflex that would absolve her of complicity in the murder. The journey of the bones from cellar to attic is figurative for the emergence of the witch's sexual guilt from out of the depths of her unconscious. To extend the metaphor: when memory raids the things in the mind's cellar and helps them to take over the attic of conscious awareness, then do the "dark" forces of the irrational overwhelm "well-lighted" places of rationality. The Freudian parallel here is exact. Freud often implicitly compares the mind to a house; his special interest tends to be in the cellar—for him a metaphor for the submerged unconscious and its unpleasant contents. It is possible to argue that the witch has overcome her problem because she can speak so easily (and amusingly) about it. I would argue just the opposite, however: the shocking ease with which she accepts the business of the bones is a clue that she is long beyond help; that she has merged her mad dream world with mundane reality. Such poems as "The Death of the Hired Man," "Home Burial," "A Servant to Servants" and "The Witch of Coös" lead us to direct consideration of the symbol of the house (as *actual* as well as psychological structure) in "The Hill Wife."[6] "The Hill Wife" blends thematically with these poems but structurally it is unusual for Frost and unusually elusive.

Not narrative but mosaic (and dreamlike) in form, its discontinuous (though probably organic) fragments hint at complex troubles too deeply buried in the psyche to be examined. Again the central figure is a disturbed woman, this one young and recently married. (The poem's direction is somewhat diverted, unfortunately, because of Frost's refusal to allow a controlling point of view; at the end of the poem he swings away from his young woman to her husband, and this shift in point of view truncates the emerging psychological revelation.) The first of the poem's five sections is presented from the first person point of view and is a reflection on loneliness in quasi-philosophical dimension that seems a cover for more immediate and psychic troubles. In ways that anticipate a later poem, "The Need of Being Versed in Country Things," the wife remarks on the cleavage of the human world from the natural world. Then, with the natural world as a reflector of what ought to be, she suggests implicitly another, more disturbing cleavage within her relationship with her husband:

> One ought not to have to care
>   So much as you and I
> Care when the birds come round the house
>   To seem to say good-by;
>
> Or care so much when they come back
>   With whatever it is they sing;
> The truth being we are as much
>   Too glad for the one thing
>
> As we are too sad for the other here—
>   With birds that fill their breasts
> But with each other and themselves
>   And their built or driven nests.

It is more likely the absence of deep, empathetic perception from her husband's end of the relationship, rather than alienation from nature, that is at the root of her trouble and that raises for her a landscape radiating loneliness and fear from the facts of the real landscape: a vulnerable farmhouse far from everywhere. A latent paranoia, aggravated and exposed perhaps by the sexual shock of marriage, shows itself in the hill wife's dreams in which her protected intimacy, the private space of the house of self, is penetrated by an alien force. Like the unfaithful wife of "The Fear," the young hill wife projects her interior insecurities onto the house itself:

Always—I tell you this they learned—
Always at night when they returned
To the lonely house from far away,
To lamps unlighted and fire gone gray,
They learned to rattle the lock and key
To give whatever might chance to be,
Warning and time to be off in flight. . . .

A passing stranger becomes the cause of paranoic speculation in the third
section ("I wonder how far down the road he's got. / He's watching from
the woods as like as not"), and in part four the presentation of a recur-
ring nightmare evokes the paranoic vision projected onto nature itself,
imaged here as an actively malicious agent that tries tirelessly to invade
and assault those within the house.

Frost's imagery is once more open to Freudian interpretation: the
"dark pine" is decidedly phallic and the house is a representation of the
female genitals, suggesting what in particular about marriage troubles this
young woman, and what in particular in her experience is the basis of her
paranoia. (In an earlier version of the poem references to the "tree" were
rendered with the third person singular masculine pronoun.) From a
psycho-sexual perspective we can understand why only one of the two
feared the "tree":

She had no saying dark enough
    For the dark pine that kept
Forever trying the windowlatch
    Of the room where they slept. . . .

It never had been inside the room,
    And only one of the two
Was afraid in an oft-repeated dream
    Of what the tree might do.

In part five, "The Impulse," Frost records the sudden departure of the
wife and hints at something that reminds us strongly of "Home Burial":
the ability of the male to survive psychological assault even as his mate
appears to be succumbing. In "Home Burial" the husband's grip on
normality is suggested by the way he can reimmerse himself in common
everyday realities after the death of his child, while his wife's inability to
return to routine, and her morbid brooding over certain images—the way
those images seem to have utterly entranced and magnetized her attention
—all of these things suggest her precarious mental condition. The last

section of "The Hill Wife" seems to me intimately related to "Home Burial," an illumination of the motives of two women:

> It was too lonely for her there,
>   And too wild,
> And since there were but two of them
>   And no child,
>
> And work was little in the house,
>   She was free,
> And followed where he furrowed field,
>   Or felled tree.

And, then, one fine day out walking while her husband works she just keeps on walking and never returns. The context of her departure suggests that there is something dangerous about unanchored freedom when it is mixed in with loneliness, her special kind of house fears, the recurrent nightmares. When cut loose from the quotidian, the free mind may wander toward the perilous point where common sense's force of gravity can no longer be felt; the point where the mind, free from the comforts of dull fact and the pleasurable constrictions of daily work, can entertain without check grotesque visions which, once fully experienced, destroy the possibility of a return to normality.

The dominant character in "The Fear" is another guilt-ridden woman— a close psychological relative of the witch in "The Witch of Coös"—who has deserted one lover and is keeping house with another far from town. In "The Fear" the real landscape—a barn, a single farmhouse, and a road enveloped in night—begins to feed a frightened mind:

> "You speak as if this were a traveled road.
> You forget where we are. What is beyond
> That he'd be going to or coming from
> At such an hour of the night, and on foot too?"

The farmhouse is miles from everywhere, and somewhere out there stands a threatening figure who has perhaps been within the house itself. Once enclosed in the frightened woman's awareness, the real landscape becomes transmuted and emerges as an interiorized landscape of paranoia, haunted by a dangerous demonic figure who has the power of being everywhere at once. Safe nowhere, because her one sanctuary has been penetrated at will (or so she believes), she is pressed to the edge of hysteria:

"And now's the time to have it out with him
While we know definitely where he is,
Let him get off and he'll be everywhere
Around us, looking out of trees and bushes
Till I shan't dare to set a foot outdoors.
And I can't stand it.

The poem climaxes when she moves out, lantern in hand, beyond the comforting barn, to confront the figure in the dark. He emerges: but it is only a stranger and a little boy out for a long walk. For them the night-time landscape holds no hidden, fearful surprises: it is a pleasant thing. (The entrance of the man and boy into the poem is dramatically strategic: their mundane normality sharply circumscribes and highlights the constricted and guilty woman's consciousness.) The poem moves rapidly downhill, with tension apparently resolved, then suddenly reverses and ends on a note of terror. The lantern accidentally hits the ground and goes out. The woman is left alone with the darkness, frozen with objectless fear:

"—Joel—you realize—
You won't think anything. You understand?
You understand that we have to be careful.
This is a very, very lonely place.—
Joel!" She spoke as if she couldn't turn.
The swinging lantern lengthened to the ground,
It touched, it struck, it clattered and went out.

The cumulative effect of "Home Burial," "A Servant to Servants," "The Witch of Coös," "The Hill Wife," and "The Fear" points us toward a sense of what constitutes psychological balance from the perspective of the poet's aesthetic values. The poet's mind becomes, as I. A. Richards noted some time ago, a touchstone of psychological fitness; what the poet needs to create is emblematic of what is needed by the rest of us in our transactions with our everyday world. It is "everybody's sanity . . . to live by form," as Frost put it in his "Letter to *The Amherst Student*." A poetic act of imagination is typically seen in Frost as a building of formal structures of enclosures—he takes his metaphor seriously—the erecting of a "room" for the mind to withdraw to.[7]

Yet Frost insists in his poetics that aesthetic enclosures be not too well shielded from the light of ordinary reality; that however much we may need to be rescued from ourselves and our world, we had better stay in contact, via an ironic consciousness, lest we slip away never to return. The "better world" of the sanctuary will transform into the nightmare world of a mind out of control when the delicate balances of ironic consciousness are upset; when the boundary separating the mind's personal inner world from the push and urgency of the common realities outside is obliterated. The crazed, the half-crazed, and the about-to-be crazed women that Frost writes about are projections of a self that he fears might have been, a self forced to live, as the wife in "Home Burial," as his deranged sister Jeannie lived, in a room with only one view—that of the graveyard.[8]

4

The continuity between the psychological dialogues which expose the naked vulnerability of the self and some of the meditative lyrics has rarely been noticed, but Frost has forged such continuity by rooting a number of the lyrics in the symbol of the house. Frost seems to have wanted many of the shorter poems to bear the full weight of the symbol, and to have constructed them in such ways that all of the desperation that clings to the symbol as psychological enclosure hovers about the edges of these shorter poems in which the dramatized self meditates directly upon actual, physical enclosures. In the lyrics, however—and this tends to distinguish them sharply from the dialogue poems just examined—the house is not a metaphor for a crippled self on the verge of a crack-up, imprisoned in its own obsessions, but, rather, a metaphor for a serene, protected, and ordered existence.

The voice heard in "Good Hours,"[9] for example, or again in "Acquainted With the Night," or in such an apparently light piece as "The Runaway" is quiet in tone, measured, even casual in its gestures. The effort is to project quite deliberately a tone of matter-of-factness in order to suppress the terror (not so far below the surface) in contemplating a life without therapeutic structures of enclosure. In "Good Hours" we meet the familiar Frost figure of the solitary man out walking in the night. He wanders out "for my winter evening walk," notes the few cottages on the way gleaming with light, a sounding violin here, some "youthful forms and youthful faces" there. He walks out beyond the village line, turns around and walks back. But now it is late, everyone has gone to bed, and the night walker sheepishly and whimsically says,

Over the snow my creaking feet
Disturbed the slumbering village street
Like profanation, by your leave,
At ten o'clock of a winter eve.

The playfulness of the direct address to the reader in the closing lines is a kind of whistling in the dark which the speaker must subconsciously hope will obliterate his glimpse of stark aloneness given in the poem's penultimate stanza:

I had such company outward bound.
I went till there were no cottages found.
I turned and repented, but coming back
I saw no window but that was black.

We are quite close to the speaker in "The Vantage Point" whose art of living demanded an exquisite balancing of the requirements of community and the need for the freedom of isolation. The speaker in "Good Hours" has gone out too far and, sensing more than anything else the burden of isolation, he returns. For a moment he experiences the feeling of being perhaps too late—of being cut off forever—but it is only an evening walk, he can return home.

The significance of the frightened little Morgan colt in "The Runaway"[10] is certainly deepened if the objective description in the poem is seen as enveloped by the speaker's inner world of muted fears. The image of the colt bolting about in a mountain pasture, his mother nowhere in sight, with night and the year's first snow falling fast, may or may not be disturbing in itself; but the image is intended to correlate with the speaker who is envisioning himself as the colt—

"Whoever it is that leaves him out so late,
When other creatures have gone to stall and bin,
Ought to be told to come and take him in."

and can imagine himself without a place to go, with no one to take him in. Both "Good Hours" and "The Runaway" are slight poems and I do not want to make too much of them. My point is only that their real power is communicated when they are seen to be circling about one of the major objects in Frost's landscape which radiates the complex fate of the solitary encounter of consciousness with its world.

There is no danger of distorting value with "Acquainted With the

Night,"[11] Frost's quintessential dramatic lyric of homelessness. Unlike the anguish experienced by the psychotic women in the dialogue poems, the terror of loneliness experienced by the self projected in "Acquainted With the Night" is not a terror that flows from a landscape bathed in a deranged consciousness. Lionel Trilling once remarked that reading Frost won't help one to sleep at night. "Acquainted With the Night" is one of those poems that will keep the most hard-headed among us awake for its terror flows from a fully aware and mature consciousness:

> I have been one acquainted with the night.
> I have walked out in rain—and back in rain.
> I have outwalked the furthest city light.
>
> I have looked down the saddest city lane.
> I have passed by the watchman on his beat
> And dropped my eyes, unwilling to explain.
>
> I have stood still and stopped the sound of feet
> When far away an interrupted cry
> Came over houses from another street,
>
> But not to call me back or say good-by;
> And further still at an unearthly height
> One luminary clock against the sky
>
> Proclaimed the time was neither wrong nor right.
> I have been one acquainted with the night.

Now "Good Hours" seems more a preliminary study for "Acquainted With the Night." One coincidence of detail in particular deserves special noting: the night walker in "Good Hours" like the night walker in "Acquainted With the Night" goes beyond city lights by intention. The line from "Good Hours," "I turned and repented" foreshadows the line from the later poem, "I have passed by the city watchman on his beat / And dropped my eyes, unwilling to explain." A deeply etched pattern of movement of the solitary man in Frost is being extended in these poems: we reach back to its origins in his first volume of poetry, in "Into My Own" and in "Ghost House," where the willful flight of self from human engagement is explicit and where the pleasures of darkness and of isolation are actively sought. The journey outward in "Ghost House" is balanced by the journey back. Frost's pattern is often a dialectical one, the horror of darkness drives the imagination to building anew upon the crumbling foundations of the house that is no more. One senses in the repentance of the figure in "Good Hours" and in the unwillingness to explain of the figure in "Acquainted With the Night" a submerged desire to seek the darkness of the places far beyond the city lights, to sever all relations with community (the meaning of "acquaintance" in this poem is a not unfriendly relationship) and, accompanying that desire, a guilt in entertaining it.

The sense of homelessness in "Acquainted With the Night" becomes acute when the speaker is granted his wish and the full burden of loneliness descends upon him. When the interrupted cry breaks over the roofs from another street, he stops his feet, but it is a cry that concerns him not at all—no one calls him home. And when his glimpse at the clock tower (or perhaps it is the moon) suggests to him the indifference of time—it neither guides nor judges his journey, it just flows on inexorably—his homelessness begins to reveal its cosmological dimension. The cruel irony of his "acquaintance" with the night surfaces when the poem circles back to repeat its opening line which now begins to implicate the real state of the human condition with the state of darkness itself—they are reciprocally complementary—and the state of darkness begins to figure living without enclosure, with man on the outside and all the windows of the universe darkened.

"Acquainted With the Night" speaks to the confrontation with nothingness, to what Wallace Stevens called the "experience of annihilation." It was God who died, Stevens wrote, and we share in that death because we are left feeling "dispossessed and alone in a solitude, like children without parents, in a home that seemed deserted, in which the amical rooms and halls had taken on a look of hardness and emptiness."[12] The furthest range of Frost's poem merges with Stevens's meditation on the feeling of metaphysical homelessness. With all chances gone for a harmonized relation of self and nature, the only enclosure possible is the one which the self can make and impose on an inhospitable universe. The image of self that we are left with in "Acquainted With the Night" is an image of frozen will, of feet stopped, with darkness all around and no constructive act forthcoming.

5

"Acquainted With the Night" is an especially passive moment for the self consistently dramatized in Frost's poetry. The pressing back of imagination against such desolation is the usual cure for homelessness in Frost.

One's humanness is defined by vigorous creative acts of mind, the manipulation of things by consciousness, both Frost and William James believed, and many of the poems dramatize the exercising of creative consciousness within an inhuman environment. One of the most eloquent statements on the relationship of the *topus* of enclosure and the modern mind is Santayana's:

> The universe, apart from us, is a chaos, but it may be made a cosmos by our efforts and in our own minds. The laws of events, apart from us, are inhuman and irrational, but in the sphere of human activity they may be dominated. . . . We are a part of the blind energy behind Nature, but by virtue of that energy we impose our purposes on the part of Nature which we constitute or control. We can turn from the stupefying contemplation of an alien universe to the building of our own house. . . .[13]

Frost's most explicit meditation on the symbol of the house occurs in a lyrical passage from "The Black Cottage,"[14] another fine dialogue poem from *North of Boston,* in which the central figure is a minister made melancholy and brooding by his continual contemplation of a deserted cottage which always seemed to him forsaken, even when it was lived in. And now that "The warping boards pull out their own old nails / With none to tread and put them in their place" the deserted house comes to represent to him the inevitable decay and destruction of all things made; the fleetingness and impermanence of the human moment itself; the instability of stays and enclosures against an overpowering flux. Proceeding analogically—a habit of the clerical mind—he discovers that even more discouraging is the way that truths seem to move in the flux of change just as artifacts of the human will do, suggesting to him the Nietzschean observation that perhaps truth is just another human construction. The forsaken and deserted cottage, hard evidence for what time does, becomes in the poem's conclusion the motivation for an imaginative contemplation of permanence; for a construction of a house in the mind, immune to the flux of time, which protects the self and where being is *well-being.*

> As I sit here, and oftentimes, I wish
> I could be monarch of a desert land
> I could devote and dedicate forever
> To the truths we keep coming back and back to.
> So desert it would have to be, so walled
> By mountain ranges half in summer snow,

No one would covet it or think it worth
The pains of conquering to force change on.
Scattered oases where men dwelt, but mostly
Sand dunes held loosely in tamarisk
Blown over and over themselves in idleness.
Sand grains should sugar in the natal dew
The babe born to the desert, the sand storm
Retard mid-waste my cowering caravans—
"There are bees in this wall." He struck the clapboards,
Fierce heads looked out; small bodies pivoted.
We rose to go. Sunset blazed on the windows.

The world of desire projected in the minister's mind is as far beyond change as any natural place can be. As a desert it barely knows the change of seasons and its enclosing mountain ranges make it physically isolated, a kind of world apart. Its hostility to vegetative life is topped only by its hostility to human beings, those makers of truths various and shifting. And, best of all, if his wish were granted, the minister could lord it over this fortress-home of permanent truths.

But such an imaginative vision of a world free from human and natural contamination is self-destructive. By brooding over the *facts* of desolation the minister has spurred himself to an even more inhuman *vision* of desolation. It is difficult to praise too much Frost's shrewd manipulation of the minister's vision as he makes it flow into a self-denying rhetorical pattern. For it is when the minister begins to imagine the birth of a child —"a babe born to the desert"—that he unconsciously takes his vision to its *reductio ad absurdum*: the image of a baby sucking sweetness out of sand grains coupled with the image of his "cowering caravans"—his people retarded "mid-waste" (amidst the waste land which a desert is and perhaps also in the sense of stopped "mid-waist," paralyzed in a sand storm)—these images bring his revery to the tellingly abrupt halt of self-realization as he discovers in the very language of vision the mocking nuances of the ironist. The last three lines stand in masterful juxtaposition to the preceding passage of vision: in them Frost brings back the reality of the setting, not as emblems of destructive flux, but as emblems of a fierce natural vitality—sheer facts which seem a healthy corrective to the sterility of purely imagined worlds, of enclosures too well shielded from the glare of reality's light.

The census-taker, in the poem of the same name, seems more justified than the minister in turning to the life of the mind. The minister is confronted with only one desolate cottage while the census-taker must face a landscape that seems devastated by some terrible holocaust. His journey in blackened, burnt-out wastes to count people where there are none would seem to earn him his imaginative excursions. Both "The Black Cottage" and "The Census-Taker"[15] are controlled by the symbol of enclosure. The deserted house in both poems stimulates the creation of a house in the mind that will supply what the real thing can no longer supply: the sense of having locked out the dangerous world outside, the sense of being free from the cycles of process.

As far as I know no one has cared to identify Frost with the self-conscious centers of existentialism, and with good reason. But "The Census-Taker," which outdoes Eliot as it exposes the waste land and the self trapped in it with no hope for redemption in the far off sound of thunder, is as explicit a confrontation with nothingness as anything in modern American poetry. Frost's quester

> . . . came as census-taker to the waste
> To count the people in it and found none,
> None in the hundred miles, none in the house,
> Where I came last with some hope, but not much,
> After hours' overlooking from the cliffs
> An emptiness flayed to the very stone.

Nature is so desolated that it seems unnatural:

> The time was autumn, but [no one]
> Could tell the time of year when every tree
> That could have dropped a leaf was down itself
> And nothing but the stump of it was left
> Now bringing out its rings in sugar of pitch. . . .

Unlike some self-styled existentialists who take pleasure in this landscape of death, Frost's census-taker is motivated almost immediately (and, I think, unconsciously) to an act of humanistic transmutation of what he experiences. The landscape of death begins to come back to life when he says "I found no people that dared show themselves, / None not in hiding from the outward eye." It is the irrepressible inward eye of imagination that generates rebirth as it begins to entertain the humorous vision of folks hiding from the intruding census-taker. As his search proceeds, the imaginative element shows itself openly; he becomes preoccupied with the projections of his mind as his sense of futility deepens:

Perhaps the wind the more without the help
Of breathing trees said something of the time
Of year or day the way it swung a door
Forever off the latch, as if rude men
Passed in and slammed it shut each one behind him
For the next one to open for himself.
I counted nine I had no right to count
(But this was dreamy unofficial counting)
Before I made the tenth across the threshold.
Where was my supper? Where was anyone's?

In a series of negative assertions, he proceeds with his dreamy unofficial counting by projecting familiar and comforting domestic images:

They were not on the table with their elbows.
They were not sleeping in the shelves of bunks.
I saw no men there and no bones of men there.

Preferring to be scared by a skeleton or ghost, rather than by nothingness,

I armed myself against such bones as might be
With the pitch-blackened stub of an ax-handle
I picked up off the straw-dust-covered floor.

But he is denied the pleasure of having that kind of human fear for very long. He must acknowledge, it was "Not bones, but the ill-fitted window rattled." The census-taker says he must think about "What to do that could be done— / About the house—about the people not there." In a sense he has already done what could be done. It may not (from some points of view) be much, since it happens only in illusion and is good only for one man. But Frost's men are generally men alone who need first to save themselves. His poems are not antihumanistic, as some liberal, social critics have thought. They are elementary visions of men in a difficult, presocietal state.

6

We have become accustomed in the past few decades to reading poetry written since the romantic period as a poetry essentially concerned with the question of the limits and powers of poetic imagination. For all of the large historical claims made for the continuity of romantic and modern (i.e., symbolist and postsymbolist) imagination, it is becoming increasingly clear that a number of our central moderns are making much more guarded and modest claims for imagination than their romantic forebears did and certainly more modest claims than some of their enthusiastic interpreters claim in their names. I am claiming Frost as a central modern —as central as Wallace Stevens, though few would be ready to grant that much—and "The Need of Being Versed in Country Things"[16] as a centrally modern poem; one of his subtlest treatments of the problem of personal salvation through the redemptive act of imagination.

The poem opens with the evocation of a familiar symbol and with an attempt by the speaker to suppress a pervasive funereal attitude toward his circumstance:

> The house had gone to bring again
> To the midnight sky a sunset glow.
> Now the chimney was all of the house that stood,
> Like a pistil after the petals go.
>
> The barn opposed across the way,
> That would have joined the house in flame
> Had it been the will of the wind, was left
> To bear forsaken the place's name.

The effort to blend the emotions that attend the witnessing of a house's destruction with what one is likely to feel while watching a lovely sunset cannot be expected to succeed when the one attempting such a union of disparates is a figure in a poem by Robert Frost.

In the middle two stanzas the self in the poem indulges his memory of things past—specifically of the "teams that came by the stony road / To drum on the floor with scurrying hoofs." His feelings appear to become excessive, for the moment, particularly in the lines about the barn that remains and the birds that live in it:

> The birds that came to it through the air
> At broken windows flew out and in,
> Their murmur more like a sigh we sigh
> From too much dwelling on what has been.

The speaker saves himself from sentimentalism by taking back his incipient romantic predication of interdependence of the human and natural realms.

For them there was really nothing sad.
But though they rejoiced in the nest they kept,
One had to be versed in country things
Not to believe the phoebes wept.

But if skeptical and self-ironic treatment of romantic attitudes is what makes Frost's poem centrally modern, then perhaps we need not read far beyond certain well-enough known Victorian and *fin-de-siècle* expressions of similar attitudes toward man's relationship to nature.

There truly is a solid individual talent at work in "The Need of Being Versed in Country Things," but the whole performance is brought off with such deceptive ease that we tend to miss the display of virtuosity. Frost's tack in this poem is to manipulate (rather quietly) perspectives on nature and time. His major differentiation is between kinds of memory: it is only the human mind, he suggests, that is capable of the enormous leap backwards in time. The curse of human memory is that it alone is capable of recalling a past that can never return, that has been destroyed utterly and irrevocably by the fire. "Bird-memory" has little grasp of a human past. Human beings flash across the scene of bird-awareness but (blessedly) the grooves of impression are rarely made: only the larger features of a scene and the broad patterns of seasonal change are retained. The phoebes belong to a separate order of reality and "for them the lilac renewed its leaf."

Returning again to the poem's opening stanza, the lines "The house had gone to bring again / To the midnight sky a sunset glow" evoke the image of the dramatic persona as one who is consciously assuming something other than his human perspective, for it is from the perspective of the bird's awareness that the sudden redness in the night sky can be correlated to a sunset glow. Contrarily, in the penultimate stanza, the line "The dry pump flung up an awkward arm," though given from the perspective of the phoebe is actually the speaker's. In the first instance the speaker's attempt is to mitigate the facts of destruction by viewing them as a natural happening; while in the second instance he attempts to blend human and bird perspectives on nature by attributing to the bird humanizing powers. Both are acts of sympathetic imagination which may be modestly valued as acts which lead the self into the fictive world where no ontological discoveries are made, but where the precious state of serenity is restored, where enclosure is regained and the burden of the human awareness of temporality is lifted:

> Now the chimney was all of the house that stood,
> Like a pistil after the petals go.

The self in the poem attempts to link human artifice and nature in a poetic figure. His comparison of the chimney with the pistil of a flower "after the petals go" raises the image of the rebirth of the artificial human enclosure: the house will come back even as the flowers shall bloom again. But such expectations cannot be satisfied, and one versed in country things knows that very well. The simile compels ironic consciousness: an awareness of the image of the destroyed house as transmuted in the figure and a simultaneous awareness of the impossible-to-traverse gulf between human artifice and nature's flowers. Destroyed houses regenerate themselves only in the illusions projected in the poet's language, not in reality; the value (and disvalue, as we saw earlier) of enclosures is guaranteed by an act of the mind or not at all, and this constitutes knowledge of poetic things.

7

The treatment of the house as a distinctive feature of Frost's landscape could be extended much further: it controls such poems as "An Old Man's Winter Night,"[17] "The Exposed Nest"[18] (a fine, complex, but rarely noticed poem), "The Thatch,"[19] and "In the Home Stretch."[20] The house makes brief but controlling appearances in "Snow,"[21] "The Investment,"[22] "The Woodpile,"[23] and "Willful Homing."[24] Most intriguingly it appears in "Directive," where its coordination with the brook and the woods makes this poem Frost's *summa*. I now close this chapter with a brief discussion of enclosure in its "natural" phase, in "The Last Mowing," "Iris By Night," and "The Quest of the Purple-Fringed."

The indispensable key to Frost's poems of natural enclosure is a poem that I have already looked at in chapter 1, "Rose Pogonias." The great fascination of poems like "The Last Mowing,"[25] "Iris By Night,"[26] or "The Quest of the Purple-Fringed"[27] is that in them the wandering solitary figure seems to discover—really there in nature—an enclosure that will grant immunity from the ravages of experience; for a brief moment all redemption is given, artificial enclosures seem superfluous, and the world as it is seems paradise enough. But true to expectations earlier generated in "Rose Pogonias," the precious value of the moment within enclosure lies in the precariousness of the enclosure itself. Like his symbols of artificial enclosure, this one of natural enclosure is vulnerable to attack and destruction. The self seeking solace within "Faraway Meadow," where "We never shall mow in again," does not hope to luxuriate unendingly in a pleasure garden because

> trees, seeing the opening,
> March into a shadowy claim.
> The trees are all I'm afraid of,
> The flowers can't bloom in the shade of. . . .

The realization that the trees will advance in time to reclaim the meadow is a reminder to him that a human act has had something to do with the existence of meadows, after all, and that like all efforts of the human will to wrest a place from nature, this one must eventually fail. "The place," he says, "is ours," but only "for the moment."

In "Iris By Night" an unusual night walk is recollected, unusual because it was not taken alone but with a good friend. Here is one of the few night poems in Frost that is not saturated in the sense of terror. The mood is all of a harmony too good to be true. The poem ends with a fairytale-like denouement that seems unreal for this poet:

> Bow and rainbow as it bent,
> Instead of moving with us as we went
> (To keep the pots of gold from being found),
> It lifted from its dewy pediment
> Its two mote-swimming many-colored ends
> And gathered them together in a ring.
> And we stood in it softly circled round
> From all division time or foe can bring
> In a relation of elected friends.

The fact, however, is that only one has survived—an echo from *Moby Dick*, "And I alone of us have lived to tell" suggests a violent death for one of the friends, which does not say much for the protective powers of the lovely circle of form, the fortress against "time and foe."

Lastly, in "The Quest of the Purple-Fringed," the flower-gatherer, hoping to get there before the scythe which will spare him no loveliness, seems to be led mystically by nature itself—

> Till I saw the path where the slender fox had come
> And gone panting by.
>
> Then at last and following him I found—. . . .

The discovery of the obscure place of the purple-fringed leads to the purest celebratory moment in Frost's poetry:

> There stood the purple spires with no breath of air
> Nor headlong bee
> To disturb their perfect poise the livelong day
> 'Neath the alder tree.
>
> I only knelt and putting the boughs aside
> Looked, or at most
> Counted them all to the buds in the copse's depth. . . .

There, in the copse, he experiences a beautiful moment of integration and absolution. For the lonely man who haunts Frost's poems, it almost makes everything else seem bearable.

In "The Quest of the Purple-Fringed" all of the hard postromantic lessons do not apply; the "mind lays by its trouble," as Stevens put it in "Credences of Summer," and the fact of consciousness is not coincident with the fact of alienation, of self-consciousness. In the pure moment, enclosure and all need for enclosure is broken down, and self feels harmoniously located within nature, as it abandons itself to the pure object, refusing to fix the object within the symbolic net:

> The place for the moment is ours
> For you, O tumultuous flowers,
> To go to waste and go wild in,
> All shapes and colors of flowers,
> I needn't call you by name.

4. The Woods

We do not have to be long in the woods to experience the always rather anxious impression of "going deeper and deeper" into a limitless world. Soon, if we do not know where we are going, we no longer know where we are. It would be easy to furnish literary documents that would be so many variations on the theme of this limitless world, which is a primary attribute of the forest. But the following passage, marked with rare psychological depth, from Marcault and Thérèse Brosse's excellent work, [L'education de demain] will help us to determine the main theme: "Forests, especially, with the mystery of their space prolonged indefinitely beyond the veil of tree-trunks and leaves, space that is veiled for our eyes, but transparent to action, are veritable psychological transcendents." I myself should have hesitated to use the term psychological transcendents. But at least it is a good indicator for directing phenomenological research towards the transcendencies of present-day psychology. It would be difficult to express better that here functions of description—psychological as well as objective—are ineffective. One feels that there is something else to be expressed besides what is offered for objective expression. (Gaston Bachelard, The Poetics of Space)

Because of the snug relationships of Frost's major images it is difficult not to anticipate his experience of the woods, particularly in the previous chapter, where an understanding of the psychological values suggested by the house often depended upon our awareness of Frost's attitude toward the exterior world. In the image of the woods Frost finds his synecdoche for nature and external reality. The experience of the woods becomes definitive, for a dangerous moment, of the whole world of Robert Frost. Though like two other significant objects in his landscape—the woods has a subjective as well as an objective phase—it is more thoroughly bathed in the darker recesses of his inner life than any other object in his poems. Despite exceptions that I have already noted in "Rose Pogonias," "Going For Water," "The Last Mowing," and "The Quest of the Purple-Fringed," the woods radiates in Frost's landscape the destructive urges of self. It is a metaphor of the irrational. We may remember with nostalgia Emerson's high romantic faith that in the woods we recover the vital spiritual center of self in an organic reciprocity of subject and object. Frost will never indulge us on this matter. In his dark wood the self is damned, not redeemed, because what may be unveiled and unloosed there is everything in us which must be kept under tightest control.

To enter the dark wood in Frost is to plunge to the underside of consciousness, to retreat from all human contact, and to wander in the limitless immensities of our internal worlds. There, though released from the troublesome and often dangerous external pressures of community, the self finds itself confronting its own dangerous impulses. The "Demon" is discovered "far in the sameness of the wood," as Frost put it in a little-known poem from his first volume called "The Demiurge's Laugh." As we read on through the poetic canon, it becomes clear that he means to locate that "Demon" in the interior. Once again, "outer" and "inner" landscapes merge in a single, reverberating image.

1

From the very beginning, in "Into My Own," to the very end in "The Draft Horse" (*In the Clearing*, 1963), the image of the woods captures our attention with its load of psychological significance. The self in the poem is immediately and often inexplicably fascinated by the woods; the poet behind the poem is a good deal closer than usual to his dramatized selves; he seems as entranced, so entranced that the power of the natural object extinguishes the power of the self-conscious, manipulating craftsman and appears to free itself from control—for the moment, it stands alone, magnetizing the consciousness of the poet like a totemic object.

The image of the woods is often expressive of paradoxical experience (rendered in oxymoronic language) which suggests that nature is the ground of hostile, more than natural forces. Whether these forces are actually grounded in nature, or whether they are unconscious (and destructive) projections from the self dramatized in the poem is the core interest out of which flows the central conflict in much of Frost's work. What had seemed so safely objectified in those female characters who veered to the edge of sanity now comes very close to home in the dark wood lyrics. In the first poem in *A Boy's Will*, "Into My Own," "those dark trees" represent for the self seeking permanent exit from community a "vastness" which swallows up the self and thereby swallows up as well the pain of our separateness and self-consciousness. But the desire to move beyond the human world presses the self into the recesses of a private realm—the "vastness" is located in the interior of the speaker. The trees, "so old and firm," are not really the patch of woods situated some yards beyond the farmhouse. Their quality of "not showing the breeze," or scarcely so, is a vague gesture toward the idea that these trees are not hedged by the facts of the empirical world, but expand infinitely in the mind's infinite universe. The dark wood is situated in a psychological no-man's-land.

A lifetime of preoccupation with the symbol of the trees comes to completion appropriately and inevitably in the first two stanzas of "The Draft Horse":[1]

> With a lantern that wouldn't burn
> In too frail a buggy we drove
> Behind too heavy a horse
> Through a pitch-dark limitless grove.
>
> And a man came out of the trees
> And took our horse by the head
> And reaching back to his ribs
> Deliberately stabbed him dead.

The malicious act, inexplicable at the level of common sense, does makes sense in a nightmare vision of a universe under demonic control. Linked (horrifyingly) with the darkness and the trees—no more appropriate relation of setting and act could be imagined, not even by Kafka—the treacherous stabbing is raised above the level of an ordinary event in the ordinary world by the blatant and strange oxymoron, "limitless grove," a phrase that may finally give us entry to a mind which, as it relives in dream the experience of the dark wood, slips into a private and crazy world swamped in unmotivated violence. Frost's pleonastic judgment ("Deliberately stabbed") is a key to the speaker's shock. His precise descriptive detail evokes the mad logic of dream and the sense of hopeless inevitability that often marks the irrational mind; we can see it all coming, for is not the buggy "too frail," the horse "too heavy"? (And why have these country folks, who ought to know better, hitched a draft horse to a buggy?)

There is more—the poet is not quite his persona. In the middle stanza of the poem we find this:

> The ponderous beast went down
> With a crack of a broken shaft.
> And the night drew through the trees
> In one long invidious draft.

In his daring play on "draft" Frost has made an invidious comparison. We may think of the breed of horse that he is writing about, but that would not take us very far; better, we may think of the wind whistling through the woods, and that gets us closer to his joke. This story is a "lot of wind," dear reader, don't take me too seriously. Frost has punned himself free from the nightmare of demonism, has distanced himself from his persona. The last stanza of the poem is offered by the poem's speaker as an explanation, but the gap between event and explanation is so astonishingly wide that we can only take the last lines as a sort of defensive black humor. The final effect of the poem is one of irresolution. Frost's intentions seem ultimately hidden.

> We assumed that the man himself
> Or someone he had to obey
> Wanted us to get down
> And walk the rest of the way.

A remark by one of the characters in "Snow," written in Frost's early career, bristles with new significance when read within this psychological context. And we begin to understand a bit better what houses are for:

> "You make a little foursquare block of air,
> Quiet and light and warm, in spite of all
> The illimitable dark and cold and storm.". . .²

2

Three poems from the volume *West-Running Brook*, "Spring Pools,"³ "Once By the Pacific,"⁴ and "Sand Dunes"⁵ are rooted in visions of violence. "Spring Pools" is focused on the image of the dark wood and the other two extend the symbolism of "Spring Pools" by exchanging the symbol of the dark wood for the symbol of a raging ocean:

> These pools that, though in forests, still reflect
> The total sky almost without defect,
> And like the flowers beside them, chill and shiver,
> Will like the flowers beside them soon be gone,
> And yet not out by any brook or river,
> But up by roots to bring dark foliage on.
>
> The trees that have it in their pent-up buds
> To darken nature and be summer woods—
> Let them think twice before they use their powers
> To blot out and drink up and sweep away
> These flowery waters and these watery flowers
> From snow that melted only yesterday.

The tiny forest pools and the flowers of spring growing beside them, both magnetizing the poet's loving attention, enjoy only a precarious existence. The poem is at once a lament for the transience of precarious things, and an evocation of the dominant destructive element in nature—seasonal process—which obliterates nature's own momentary shows of beauty and peace.

Frost suggests the complex theme of his poem by contrasting the images of pools and dark woods. Pools in spring are associated by the poet with a sense of openness, with a sense of nature in light: the barren trees of spring allow the figure by the pool a free expanse of vision. Under the fully leaved trees of summer very little can be seen, vision is severely truncated, and the self in the poem feels suffocating entrapment. "Spring Pools" is surely as much about shifting subjective states which are touched off by changes in the objective world as it is about nature itself. The self's peaceful moment of rest, figured in the stillness of the pool's surface, is swept away in the flux; not, however, in ways that the eye can trace ("not out by any brook or river") but via the mysterious transmutation worked by sucking roots of trees that change water to dark foliage. It is in the last thematic configuration (of stasis versus flux) that we can see the dramatized self in the poem driven to the animism of psychological response. In the phrase "Let them think twice" the lament for the passing of spring beauty shifts suddenly into the stridency of tone of a disturbed man personifying his fears like the besieged figure in "Storm Fear," or the troubled women in "The Fear" and "The Hill Wife." In "Spring Pools" there is about to be perpetrated an unnameable psychological violence to which the only proper response seems to be the scream: for what is lost in the passing of spring flowers and spring pools is an inner state of resolution as well as an outer loveliness.

The self rendered in "Once By the Pacific" is subjected to a more explicitly violent scene as he watches from the palisades high above the water sea waves crash against the shore. The imagination of the terror-ridden self demonizes the world and thereby upsets all possibility for that serenity of vision and detachment from immediate conflict that is the stuff of mental balance. The figure in "Once By the Pacific" is on the verge of losing his control, as he is reduced to a frightened little boy crying out against a diabolical "night of dark intent." He sees great waves "looking over each other," thinking of "doing something to the shore / That water never did to land before." He gazes above and sees in the clouds a maddened face, "low and hairy in the skies." The shrill nervousness of tone in "Let them think twice" from "Spring Pools" is caught once again in the line "Someone had better be prepared for rage."

"Sand Dunes" fits the pattern of intention borne by "Spring Pools" and "Once By the Pacific" with one important exception: the perspective in the latter two poems is that of the dramatized self, the figure of a man alone reacting to a particular scene and setting; while the perspective in "Sand Dunes" is that of the poet himself who is situated somewhere above the scene. But the two perspectives from within mesh with the perspective from above, suggesting again that the distance between Frost and his projected personae is not really very great, and that the human figures in his poems are variations on a single, central self who envelops all of the poems in his presence. The psychological identity of the speaker is continuous from "Spring Pools" through "Once By the Pacific" and "Sand Dunes." The chief difference between "Sand Dunes," on the one hand, and "Spring Pools" and "Once By the Pacific," on the other, is that in "Sand Dunes" the voice is controlled, measured, and confident of the ordering powers of mind, while in the other two the voice is desperate and fearful because the self seems on the verge of being diminished and overwhelmed by natural forces beyond human control.

> Sea waves are green and wet,
> But up from where they die
> Rise others vaster yet,
> And those are brown and dry.

They are the sea made land
To come at the fisher town
And bury in solid sand
The men she could not drown.

She may know cove and cape,
But she does not know mankind
If by any change of shape
She hopes to cut off mind.

Men left her a ship to sink:
They can leave her a hut as well;
And be but more free to think
For the one more cast-off shell.

The ocean, like the dark wood, figures a force of terrifying violence which (more terrifying yet) is not mere physical energy but the arm of a cunning and malicious mind whose single purpose is to destroy man. Despite the assured tones of "Sand Dunes" it is not difficult to hear the potential for fear and inner crisis which is actualized in "Once By the Pacific" and "Spring Pools"; the voice of the fear-struck self of "Storm Fear" who watches, alone, the raging blizzard in the night. Shockingly, the hostile and calculating force within the sea waves has the ability (like an evil, ubiquitous god) to transmute itself, to come at man as sand dunes.

Salvation lies in neither ship nor hut. When the last physical enclosures are beat down there is still "form to go on," as Frost put it in the "Letter to *The Amherst Student*"; there is that act of imagination—nature cannot hope "to cut off mind"—which can erect the necessary barriers, build the proper kind of enclosure, a place for the mind to hide. The only safe and integrated worlds are those created by the mind, when mind itself is not out of control, but even those not for long. In poems like "The Aim Was Song,"[6] or "Never Again Would Birds' Song Be the Same"[7] or, of more interest at this point, in a poem called "Canis Major,"[8] which faces "Sand Dunes" in *Complete Poems* and seems to be its proper companion, the act of imaginative consciousness is dramatized. One of Frost's prime lessons is that this redeeming act of mind need not be embedded in a grim context of cosmic significance. These acts of redemption can be minor, personal, and evocative of lightly comic moods. William James's suggestion[9] that we begin to defeat the coldness of the universe in the very fact of consciousness, by projecting human interest onto it—as when we isolate groups of stars and give them a name—is probably the background of

But tonight I will bark
With the great Overdog
That romps through the dark.

and evidence enough that epistemological problems need not always be the stuff of which lectures are made.

Such saving acts of mind, whether gay or solemn, are not, unfortunately, always forthcoming. The dangerously magnetic woods often stays free of the manipulations of will. As a brute unshapeable given, the dark wood tends to drive the self to dangerous inner places. More than any other group of related poems, those focused in the image of the woods evoke the will on the verge of being overwhelmed. The line from "Spring Pools"—"Let them think twice"—and the line from "Once By the Pacific"—"Someone had better be prepared for rage"—suggest fears in excess of the facts as given, and by so doing indicate that what motivates the tone of urgency in these poems comes as much from some unnameable thing within as from some specifically frightening thing outside. The moment of encounter, when the self faces the dark wood or the raging ocean, is the moment of fear's dominion. Whether fear is motivated in the interior or in the exterior (and very often in Frost we are unable to make that determination with any confidence), the immediate problem remains one of psychological survival. We have explicit examples of this moment of crisis; the opening lines from "The Onset"[10] dramatize the submerging of self in a setting bathed with fear:

Always the same, when on a fated night
At last the gathered snow lets down as white
As may be in dark woods, and with a song
It shall not make again all winter long
Of hissing on the yet uncovered ground,
I almost stumble looking up and round,
As one who overtaken by the end
Gives up his errand, and lets death descend
Upon him where he is. . . .

In the second half of "The Onset" the self suppresses the subversive, animistic projection of its own mind, and transcends fear and the fearful implications of the morbidly tempting dark woods of winter. It is precisely the possibility of imagining a redeemed future by envisioning a renewed spring scene which ensures the speaker's poise. Frost transforms the snake of winter into benevolent April water:

Yet all the precedent is on my side:
I know that winter death has never tried
The earth but it has failed: the snow may heap
In long storms an undrifted four feet deep
As measured against maple, birch, and oak,
It cannot check the peeper's silver croak;
And I shall see the snow all go downhill
In water of a slender April rill. . . .

In "Bereft,"[11] however, psychological balance seems fatally endangered as the self is wholly overcome, strangled by the malevolent fictions of a sick mind that projects the world as an actively hostile force. "Bereft" is Frost's perfect coordination of the house, as metaphor of a painfully vulnerable and isolated human identity, with the woods, the metaphor of all out there that is destructive to the self:

Summer was past and day was past.
Somber clouds in the west were massed.
Out in the porch's sagging floor
Leaves got up in a coil and hissed,
Blindly struck at my knee and missed.
Something sinister in the tone
Told me my secret must be known:
Word I was in the house alone
Somehow must have gotten abroad,
Word I was in my life alone,
Word I had no one left but God.

3

We approach three closely interrelated poems which need the full context of Frost's symbolism of the dark wood, "Stopping By Woods on a Snowy Evening,"[12] "Desert Places,"[13] and "Come In."[14] Repeated readings begin to convince one that the creation of "Stopping By Woods" was more or less spontaneous, an unself-conscious flow from the poet's deepest experiences of certain constant features in the natural landscape, or (what may be more likely), a carefully calculated effort to give that very impression. The shrewd high art of Frost's dark wood poems lies in the "artless" realism of their psychological immediacy. What makes this poem particularly elusive is the way it reaches into mutually exclusive areas of experience. Many readers emphasize the loveliness of the woods filling up with snow—that is why the speaker stops his horse to watch—but that particular image in "Desert Places" and in "The Onset" evokes from the dramatic personae quite different emotions from the apparent serenity of the speaker in "Stopping By Woods." And, in "Stopping By Woods" itself, one notes that, after all, the speaker does not stop for long, perhaps because, in his fascination with the woods, he senses in their darkness, in their inhuman otherness, suggestions of his personal end.

And yet the morbid aspect of the symbolism of "Stopping By Woods" has probably been overplayed. It is a "quiet little poem," as Frost once said at a public reading, and the poised, classic regularity of sound and rhythm suggests that the poem's speaker can maintain his poise, as he rests in a moment of contemplative detachment and reasoned serenity which is sharply contrasting to the agitated and agonized voices of "Bereft" and "Desert Places." Frost's poise is that of aesthetic man who can resist all instinctual urgings toward the death of natural submersion ("these woods are me"), and all utilitarian demands to say "these woods are mine." His aesthetic moment is defined as a moment of stillness that is engendered by pure contemplative appreciation: these woods are lovely. But the moment of stillness and freedom is tightly circumscribed: he must get moving on; our aesthetic man must yield to quotidian man. How, after all, could he do otherwise?

Certain resonances of "Stopping By Woods" will not be dismissed. It is the "darkest evening of the year," the woods themselves are not just "lovely" but "dark and deep." If with many of Frost's readers we take the woods to represent some sort of death-wish—and I think we have to, Frost's humorous public protestations to the contrary—then we may come to appreciate Frost's shrewd linguistic precision in his choice of the "but" of "But I have promises to keep." (The conjunction would be badly chosen, it would be syntactical overkill, if the woods represented only visual beauty, since "promises" do not in themselves condition visual beauty.) If the woods represents what most of us think it does, then "but" is the proper and healthy syntactical arrangement of life-urges against death-urges. What tantalizes is the way the symbol of the woods in this particular poem can evoke, without the support of immediate context, both the sense of full freedom, the delights of submersion in nature, as in "The Vantage Point," and the counter feeling of poems like "Ghost House," or "Into My Own," where the delights of ego-autonomy, of radical disengagement from community are seen for what they are: the prelude to extinction as a human kind of being. The real contexts of "Stopping By Woods" are not the linguistic configurations within the poem, but the quiet reverberations that sound through it when it is placed in the context of the Frost canon.

If we may say of "Stopping By Woods" that its poise of style reflects the poised voice of a secure man who is exerting final control over certain of his self-destructive tendencies, then we might say of "Desert Places" that some of its rhythmic, dictional, and tonal features reflect the poem's speaker in the act of taking a long look into the nothingness within the self and having to exert a special energy in order to keep hold and to maintain his humanness.

> Snow falling and night falling fast, oh, fast
> In a field I looked into going past,
> And the ground almost covered smooth in snow,
> But a few weeds and stubble showing last.
>
> The woods around it have it—it is theirs.
> All animals are smothered in their lairs.
> I am too absent-spirited to count;
> The loneliness includes me unawares.
>
> And lonely as it is, that loneliness
> Will be more lonely ere it will be less—
> A blanker whiteness of benighted snow
> With no expression, nothing to express.
>
> They cannot scare me with their empty spaces
> Between stars—on stars where no human race is.
> I have it in me so much nearer home
> To scare myself with my own desert places.

A sense of impending entrapment is established quickly in the first line with the ominous linkage of falling snow and metaphorically descending darkness. As usual, there is something sinister *out there* for Frost's solitary night walker. The speaker's cosmic fear (perhaps it is just to call it "cosmic paranoia") may be grasped tonally in the dirge of vowel sounds in line 1; it may be grasped in the deliberately awkward, halting rhythm of line 5, which encourages us to linger over the thrice repeated "it" and to consider the triple reference of "it." The force of the poem's grammatical logic would refer "it" to *snow* and *loneliness,* but the poem's "organic logic," the pressure of the total poem on the "it," ultimately refers "it," in all of its cool neutrality of gender, to nothing—to those "desert places," that palpable absence which the speaker "sees" all around him in the winter landscape. In the stunned quality of voice suggested by lines 11 and 12 we come to a sense of the speaker morbidly dwelling on nothingness in the fine Melvillean redundancy "blanker whiteness," and in "With no expression, nothing to express." (How nicely that caesura, halving the line, allows the repetition clearly to project the speaker's despair and shock. We suspect that only one expecting much more from nature would speak this way.) What we may come to understand in "Desert Places" is Frost's tragic sense of loss, for only a poet looking back longingly at the failed promises of high romantic faith could be so grieved at the cold, repelling natural world that he discovers.

But as shocking as the discovery of the void out there may be, there is the more shocking discovery of the void within. We grasp the psychological landscape emerging out of the actual landscape in the "smothered" animals, in the projection of loneliness into the woods, and in the speaker's awful perception that there may be no line between the human mode of being and the nonhuman—in his perception that, perhaps, humanness is dissolved in the confrontation with the dark winter woods. (Can we doubt for a moment who it is that is being "smothered"?) In the final line the ambiguous reference of the phrase "my own desert places" (the planet Earth's emptiness? interior emptiness?) radically shifts the tone of the poem as it raises a playful possibility: is the void merely my projection? That last nuance, reminding us of the wittily qualified last line of "Design," leads us to an awareness of a series of psychologically-saving linguistic plays in "absent-spirited," in "benighted snow," and in the comic rhyme "spaces / race is."

Probably no poem of Frost's so well accommodates the wide emotive swings of self which he probed from early on in his career. In "Desert Places" we watch the speaker go to the brink in his projection; then he comes back to normality, withdraws from dark vision, and rests in the stability of a balanced ironic consciousness. As well as any poem of dark vision that he wrote, "Desert Places" gives evidence of Frost's ability to achieve aesthetic detachment from certain sorts of destructive experience. A number of the dark woods poems are cast in the past tense—they are recollections in tranquility, consciously dramatized presentations of experience and, as such, both strong evidence that Frost's craft crucially supported his psychic serenity, and a firm reminder to Frost's critics that his poems are not to be taken as raw psychological data.

There is an affinity between the demented witch in "The Witch of Coös," the half-demented servant in "A Servant to Servants," the wife of

"Home Burial," and the selves created in "Design," "Desert Places" and other dramatic lyrics. The figure in "Desert Places," unlike the three women, understands that he "scare[s himself] with [his] own desert places"—that the desert places belong peculiarly to him because they are projections of the self. Likewise, the "design of darkness" in "Design" is first, and perhaps last, a metaphorical projection of the brooding philosophical mind, not necessarily a reflection in poetry of ontological fact— and the poet understands this very well: "if design govern in a thing so small." Quite deliberately, in "Design," Frost counterpoints a mechanical, nursery-rhyme iambic rhythm against a scene of natural horror. The effect of such counterpointing is two-fold: first, it heightens the macabre quality of the scene imaged; second, it implies the presence of a self-conscious poetic craftsman who above all delights in manipulating the tools of his trade, in playing rhythm and image against each other. In both "Desert Places" and "Design" the poet's self-consciousness saves him; it allows the pressure of a difficult situation to be released. There is always an impregnable harbor for the self to retreat to, a room in the house of the mind that can never be penetrated, even if that room is sometimes only the self-directed ironic attitude.

The dark wood, which simultaneously attracts and repels, controls "Come In," a late lyric that is practically a paradigm of the problem that I have been sketching in this chapter:

> As I came to the edge of the woods,
> Thrush music—hark!
> Now if it was dusk outside,
> Inside it was dark.
>
> Too dark in the woods for a bird
> By sleight of wing
> To better its perch for the night,
> Though it still could sing.
>
> The last of the light of the sun
> That had died in the west
> Still lived for one song more
> In a thrush's breast.
>
> Far in the pillared dark
> Thrush music went—
> Almost like a call to come in
> To the dark and lament.

> But no, I was out for stars:
> I would not come in.
> I meant not even if asked,
> And I hadn't been.

Among the recurrent features that appear here (besides that of the dark wood) two are especially compelling: the lonely night walker and the habit (consciously played with in "The Need of Being Versed in Country Things") of first projecting and then immediately withdrawing the human imagination from an alien natural world.

The poem's dominant tones suggest a certain uneasiness, a nervous tenseness in the voice, that is projected in the abrupt, snapped-off rhythm of the last line ("And I hadn't been") and in the staccato, plodding rhythm of lines 3 and 4 ("Now if it was dusk outside / Inside it was dark"). These rhythms help to point up the puzzled unsureness, tinged with apprehension and anxiety, that lies behind the desperate syllogism of the "If-then" structure in lines 3 and 4. The mind may be on the verge of slipping off balance—an irrational energy once more is in control as the self confronts the dark wood. The figurative sense of the phrase "pillared dark" belongs peculiarly to the self of Frost's woods poems who, when he contemplates the woods at night, can see the trees as a kind of foundation for darkness which lies over the woods as if the clustered trees were, its proper place of rest.

Finally, the explicit withdrawal of human meaning from the bird's song must inevitably raise the question: why project such meaning? One answer is that the speaker is not concerned with the ontological problem of the continuity of self in the nonhuman world, but is consciously imagining himself within the wood, as the bird, lamenting in the dark. The landscape evoked in the poem is etched by the subjective turmoil of the speaker. The dark wood and the bird within, singing for the dying light, are reflections of self in the world, holding a precarious position ("Too dark . . . to better its perch") and enclosed by a deepening night of dark intent. But (again), Frost's playful wit ("sleight of wing"), inserted in this grim context, cautions against too much critical grimness—and reminds us (again) of his psychic toughness, his poise in the face of danger. The refusal to enter the woods is consciously willed—"But, no, I was out for stars"; the lure of self-centered and self-pitying images is fought off.

5. The Redemptive Imagination

*. . . there are no two things as important in life and art as being
threatened and being saved. What are ideals of form for if we aren't
going to be made to fear for them? All our ingenuity is lavished on
getting into danger legitimately so that we may be genuinely rescued.*
(R. F. in a letter, 7 June 1937)

*The relation of art to life is of the first importance especially in a
skeptical age since, in the absence of a belief in God, the mind turns
to its own creations and examines them, not alone from the aesthetic
point of view, but for what they reveal, for what they validate and
invalidate, for the support that they give.* (Wallace Stevens, Adagia)

In recent years a compelling and cogent argument for the skepticism of
the great English romantics has been made by Harold Bloom, Geoffrey
Hartman, David Perkins, David Ferry, and others. Directed with considerable polemical force (particularly by Bloom) at the antiromanticism
of the New Critics and their followers, this argument has convincingly
made Wordsworth and company charter members of the modern literary
community. It is not possible, now, not to see the romantics as fathers
of modernist poetry; not possible, now, to read them as noumenally naive
believers in the healing powers of imagination. But the case for skepticism
has been much overstated, as perhaps it had to be, and some ineradicable
(and crucial) discontinuities in literary history since Wordsworth have
been blurred. A stubborn and strange refusal by recent romantic critics to
acknowledge basic differences in the philosophical contexts of the early
romantics and certain twentieth-century writers has led to the postulation
of more continuity in the literary history of the past century and a half
than in fact exists. It is of course true that the malaise of self-conscious-

ness—a central point of comparison—has its origins in the romantic movement, and true that modern writers wrestle the problem. But it is also
true that our modern writers tend to have an even more minimal vision
of human community and the community of man and nature than do the
early romantics. A stricter accounting for the immense impact of naturalism (and for various other philosophical movements that contributed to
the "disappearance of God") might be sobering for the devotees of
romantic continuities.

Neither Robert Frost (nor Wallace Stevens, for example) feel a hatred
for the "limits of mortality"—to borrow the title of David Ferry's book on
Wordsworth—because neither Frost nor Stevens have in their cultural
contexts a paradigm and a *promise* (however difficult to realize) for the
ultimate romantic cure of alienation, the metaphysical continuity of subject and object which breaks down the prison of subjectivity. For Frost
the redemption of alienation is never an experience of metaphysical
transcendence, as it sometimes is in Wordsworth. For Frost the frequent
failure to redeem alienation is never accompanied (as it sometimes is in
Wordsworth) by the sense that human limitation has cruelly denied him
the experience of what he believes to be most profoundly true of human
beings and their relationship to the natural world. If we wish to seek
typological parallels for Frost and Wordsworth we would look to Nietzsche and Schelling respectively. And an awareness of the chasm that
separates these two philosophers may help us to keep separated the vari-
eties of romanticism.

The concept of a secularly generated "redemption," with its locus
within the moment of aesthetic imagining, is not an invention of Wallace
Stevens (despite rumors to the contrary), but a fundamental postulate
of romantic tradition. In the romantic formulation the concept is deeply
psychological, not theological. The model, though, is the Redeemer of the
Biblical story and His relationship to the creation. In the romantic and
postromantic transformation, the redemptive force gets transferred to
imaginative consciousness; it is a kind of creative perception, and the key
relationship becomes the epistemological one of subject (as redeemer)
and object (as that-to-be-redeemed). What most distinguishes Frost from
earlier apocalyptic romantics—who are often painfully aware of the dis-
junction of nature and consciousness—is his guarded awareness that redemptive consciousness is only human, all too human. The consolations
of imagination are at best modest and they tend to be limited to aesthetic
illusion. From the traditional perspective this is meager, perhaps even

meaningless stuff. But our best twentieth-century poets refuse to claim more.

Redemptive consciousness is reflected in Frost in the merging of self with another ("The Pasture," "Going For Water"); in the merging of lovers with history which is grasped, in their love, as a continuous whole ("The Generations of Men"); in the merging of self with nature ("Rose Pogonias," "The Quest of the Purple-Fringed"); in the merging of self with the workaday world (as that world is transformed by the self's play energies in a poem like "The Mountain"); in the serenity of self within an imagined world, an enclosure which fences out actuality ("The Black Cottage," "The Census Taker"); and, finally, because of any or all of these resolutions, redemptive consciousness is reflected in the resolution of inner tensions as the self comes into harmony with itself, feeling relief that passes all understanding.

Three qualifications need to be made. First, the moment of redemptive vision in Frost is only, usually, a moment. With few exceptions it tends to be hedged in by skeptical, ironic consciousness. (The last lines of "Two Look at Two" are a splendid example of this complexity.) And in an ironic consciousness separateness, finitude, and tensions plague the self once more. Second, the resolutions which occur in Frost occur wholly within imaginative awareness, and this emphasizes the purely phenomenological validity of those redemptive moments. Frost claims neither explicitly nor implicitly that his resolutions have a metaphysical correspondence in the nature of things, nor that they can work for anyone else. Though such redemptions and their ramifications are wholly psychological and personal, they are not any less valuable for Robert Frost. Third, redemptions need not result always in therapeutic experiences, because they are often projected out of counter-therapeutic acts of consciousness.

1

The mass of men lead lives of quiet desperation. . . . There is no play in them, for this comes after work. (Thoreau)

"Mending Wall"[1] is the opening poem of Frost's second volume, *North of Boston*. One of the dominating moods of this volume, forcefully established in such important poems as "The Death of the Hired Man," "Home Burial," "The Black Cottage," and "A Servant to Servants," and

carried through some of the minor pieces, flows from the tension of having to maintain balance at the precipitous edge of hysteria. With "The
Mountain" and with "A Hundred Collars," "Mending Wall" stands opposed to such visions of human existence; more precisely put, to existences
that are fashioned by the neurotic visions of central characters like the
wife in "Home Burial," the servant in "A Servant to Servants." "Mending
Wall" dramatizes the redemptive imagination in its playful phase, guided
surely and confidently by a man who has his world under full control, who
in his serenity is riding his realities, not being shocked by them into
traumatic response. The place of "Mending Wall" in the structure of
North of Boston suggests, in its sharp contrasts to the dark tones of some
of the major poems in the volume, the psychological necessities of sustaining supreme fictions.

The opening lines evoke the coy posture of the shrewd imaginative man
who understands the words of the farmer in "The Mountain": "All the
fun's in how you say a thing."

> Something there is that doesn't love a wall,
> That sends a frozen-ground-swell under it
> And spills the upper boulders in the sun,
> And makes gaps even two can pass abreast.

It does not take more than one reading of the poem to understand that
the speaker is not a country primitive who is easily spooked by the normal
processes of nature. He knows very well what it is "that doesn't love a
wall" (frost, of course). His fun lies in not naming it. And in not naming
the scientific truth he is able to manipulate intransigent fact into the
world of the mind where all things are pliable. The artful vagueness of
the phrase "Something there is" is enchanting and magical, suggesting
even the hushed tones of reverence before mystery in nature. And the
speaker (who is not at all reverent toward nature) consciously works at
deepening that sense of mystery:

> The work of hunters is another thing:
> I have come after them and made repair
> Where they would have left not one stone on a stone,
> But they would have the rabbit out of hiding,
> To please the yelping dogs. The gaps I mean,
> No one has seen them made or heard them made,
> But at spring mending-time we find them there.

The play of the mature, imaginative man is grounded in ironic awareness —and must be. Even as he excludes verifiable realities from his fictive world the unmistakable tone of scorn for the hunters comes seeping through. He may step into a fictive world but not before glancing back briefly at the brutality that attends upon the play of others. Having paid for his imaginaive excursions by establishing his complex awareness, he is free to close the magic circle cast out by his playful energies, and close out the world reported by the senses ("No one has seen them made or heard them made"). In knowing how to say a thing in and through adroit linguistic manipulation, the fiction of the "something" that doesn't love a wall is created; the imagined reality stands formed before him, ready to be entered.

Like the selves dramatized in "Going For Water" and "The Tuft of Flowers," this persona would prefer not to be alone in his imaginative journey:

> I let my neighbor know beyond the hill;
> And on a day we meet to walk the line
> And set the wall between us once again.
> We keep the wall between us as we go.
> To each the boulders that have fallen to each.
> And some are loaves and some so nearly balls
> We have to use a spell to make them balance:
> "Stay where you are until our backs are turned!"
> We wear our fingers rough with handling them.
> Oh, just another kind of outdoor game,
> One on a side. It comes to little more:
> There where it is we do not need the wall:
> He is all pine and I am apple orchard.
> My apple trees will never get across
> And eat the cones under his pines, I tell him.
> He only says, "Good fences make good neighbors."

If the fact of a broken wall is excuse enough to make a fiction about why it got that way, then that same fact may be the occasion for two together to take a journey in the mind. For those still tempted to read "Mending Wall" as political allegory (the narrator standing for a broad-minded liberal internationalism, the thick-headed second speaker representing a selfish super-patriot) they must first face the line "I let my neighbor know beyond the hill." "Mending Wall" has nothing to do with one-world political ideals, with good or bad neighbor policies: on this point the title of the poem is helpful. It is a poem that celebrates a process, not the thing itself. It is a poem, furthermore, that distinguishes between two kinds of people: one who seizes the particular occasion of mending as fuel for the imagination and as a release from the dull ritual of work each spring and one who is trapped by work and by the New England past as it comes down to him in the form of his father's cliché. Tied as he is to his father's words that "Good fences make good neighbors," the neighbor beyond the hill is committed to an end, the fence's completion. His participation in the process of rebuilding is sheer work—he never plays the outdoor game. The narrator, however, is not committed to ends, but to the process itself which he sees as having nonutilitarian value: "There where it is we do not need the wall." The process itself is the matrix of the play that redeems work by transforming it into the pleasure of an outdoor game in which you need to cast spells to make rocks balance. Overt magic-making is acceptable in the world of this poem because we are governed by the narrator's perspective; we are in the fictive world where all things are possible, where walls go tumbling for mysterious reasons. Kant's theory that work and the aesthetic activity are antagonistic, polar activities of man is, in effect, disproven, as the narrator makes work take on the aesthetic dimension. The real differences between the two people in the poem is that one moves in a world of freedom; aware of the resources of the mind, he nurtures the latent imaginative power within himself and makes it a factor in everyday living; while the other, unaware of the value of imagination, must live his unliberated life without it. And this difference makes a difference in the quality of the life lived.

The narrator of "Mending Wall" does not give up easily: he tries again to tempt his neighbor to enter into the fictive world with him and to share his experience of play:

> Spring is the mischief in me, and I wonder
> If I could put a notion in his head:
> "*Why* do they make good neighbors? Isn't it
> Where there are cows? But here there are no cows.
> Before I built a wall I'd ask to know
> What I was walling in or walling out,
> And to whom I was like to give offense.
> Something there is that doesn't love a wall,
> That wants it down." I could say "Elves" to him,

But it's not elves exactly, and I'd rather
He said it for himself.

All to no avail: the outrageously appropriate pun on "offense"—a linguistic emblem of the poem's spirit of play and freedom—falls on deaf ears. The neighbor won't say "elves," those little folk who don't love a wall; he will not enter the play world of imagination. He moves in "darkness," our narrator concludes, "like an old-stone savage armed." The characterization is philosophically precise in the logic of post-Kantian aesthetics; the recalcitrant and plodding neighbor is a slave to the rituals of the quotidian, a primitive whose spirit has not been freed by the artistic consciousness that lies dormant within. It is the play spirit of imagination, as Schiller suggests, which distinguishes the civilized man from his cave-dwelling ancestor—that "old-stone savage" who moved in "darkness."

2

In "Birches"[2] (*Mountain Interval*, 1916) Frost begins to probe the power of his redemptive imagination as it moves from its playful phase toward the brink of dangerous transcendence. The movement into transcendence is a movement into a realm of radical imaginative freedom where (because redemption has succeeded too well) all possibilities of engagement with the common realities of experience are dissolved. In its moderation, a redemptive consciousness motivates union between selves as we have seen in "The Generations of Men," or in any number of Frost's love poems. But in its extreme forms, redemptive consciousness can become self-defeating as it presses the imaginative man into deepest isolation.

"Birches" begins by evoking its core image against the background of a darkly wooded landscape:

When I see birches bend to left and right
Across the lines of straighter darker trees,
I like to think some boy's been swinging them.
But swinging doesn't bend them down to stay
As ice storms do.

The pliable, malleable quality of the birch tree captures the poet's attention and kicks off his meditation. Perhaps young boys don't bend birches down to stay, but swing them they do and thus bend them momentarily. Those "straighter, darker trees," like the trees of "Into My Own" that "scarcely show the breeze," stand ominously free from human manipulation, menacing in their irresponsiveness to acts of the will. The malleability of the birches is not total, however, and the poet is forced to admit this fact into the presence of his desire, like it or not. The ultimate shape of mature birch trees is the work of objective natural force, not human activity. Yet after conceding the boundaries of imagination's subjective world, the poet seems not to have constricted himself but to have been released.

> Often you must have seen them
> Loaded with ice a sunny winter morning
> After a rain. They click upon themselves
> As the breeze rises, and turn many-colored
> As the stir cracks and crazes their enamel.
> Soon the sun's warmth makes them shed crystal shells
> Shattering and avalanching on the snow crust—
> Such heaps of broken glass to sweep away
> You'd think the inner dome of heaven had fallen.

Fascinated as he is by the show of loveliness before him, and admiring as he is of nature as it performs the potter's art, cracking and crazing the enamel of ice coating on the birch trees, it is not finally the thing itself (the ice-coated trees) that interests the poet but the strange association he is tempted to make: "You'd think the inner dome of heaven had fallen." Certainly there is no question of belief involved here. The linkage of the scientifically discredited medieval sphere with the heaps of cracked ice suggests rather the poet's need to break beyond the rigid standard of empirical truth, that he himself has already allowed into the poem, and faintly suggests as well the kind of apocalyptic destruction that the imagination seeks when unleashed (the idea that the inner dome has been smashed clearly pleases the speaker). Eventually Frost in "Birches" comes round to exploring in much more sophisticated ways the complex problem broached by this statement from a later poem, "On Looking Up By Chance At the Constellations":[3]

> The sun and moon get crossed, but they never touch,
> Nor strike out fire from each other, nor crash out loud.
> The planets seem to interfere in their curves,

But nothing ever happens, no harm is done.
We may as well go patiently on with our life,
And look elsewhere than to stars and moon and sun
For the shocks and changes we need to keep us sane.

In "Birches" Frost looks not to natural catastrophe for those "shocks and changes" that "keep us sane" but to his resources as a poet:

You may see their trunks arching in the woods
Years afterwards, trailing their leaves on the ground
Like girls on hands and knees that throw their hair
Before them over their heads to dry in the sun.

Manipulating the simile, the overt figure of comparison, is a dangerous ploy for the poet, implying often that he does not have the courage of his vision and does not believe that his mode of language can generate a distinctive perspective on experience. For Frost, however, and for any poet who is rooted in what I call the aesthetics of the fiction, the simile is the perfect figure of comparison, subtler even than metaphor. Its overtness becomes its virtue: in its insistence on the disparateness of the things compared (as well as their likeness) it can sustain a divided vision; can at once transmute the birches—for a brief moment nature stands humanized and the poet has transcended the scientific universe—and, at the same time, can allow the fictive world to be penetrated by the impurities of experience that resist the transmutative process of imagination. It is at such moments as this in Frost's work that the strategies and motives of a poetry of play are revealed. There is never any intention of competing with science, and, therefore, there is no problem at all (as we generally sense with many modern poets and critics) of claiming a special cognitive value for poetry. In his playful and redemptive mode, Frost's motive for poetry is not cognitive but psychological in the sense that he is willfully seeking to bathe his consciousness and, if the reader consents, his reader's as well, in a free-floating, epistemologically unsanctioned vision of the world which, even as it is undermined by the very language in which it is anchored, brings a satisfaction of relief when contemplated. It may be argued that the satisfaction is greatest when it is autonomous: the more firmly the poet insists upon the severance of his vision from the order of things as they are and the more clearly that he makes no claim for knowledge, the emotive power of the poem may emerge uncontaminated by the morass of philosophical problems that are bound to dog him should he make claims for knowledge. Both poet and reader may submerge themselves without regret (because without epistemological pretension) in aesthetic illusion.

> But I was going to say when Truth broke in
> With all her matter of fact about the ice storm,
> I should prefer to have some boy bend them
> As he went out and in to fetch the cows—
> Some boy too far from town to learn baseball,
> Whose only play was what he found himself,
> Summer or winter, and could play alone.

The shrewdness in Frost's strategy now surfaces. While claiming to have paid homage to the rigid standards of empirical truth in his digression on the ice-loaded branches, what he has actually done is to digress into the language of fictions. When he turns to the desired vision of the young boy swinging birches, he is not, as he says, turning from truth to fiction, but from one kind of fiction to another kind of fiction: from the fiction of cosmic change and humanized nature to the fiction of the human will riding roughshod over a pliable external world. And the motives for all of this fooling? I think there are two: one is that Frost intends to fox his naturalistically persuaded readers; a second is that this is what his poem is all about—the thrusting of little fictions within alien, antifictive contexts.* As he evokes the image of the boy, playing in isolation, too far from the community to engage in a team kind of sport, he evokes, as well, his cherished theme of the imaginative man who, essentially alone in the world, either makes it or doesn't on the strength of his creative resources. And now he indulges to the full the desired vision that he could not allow himself in the poem's opening lines:

> One by one he subdued his father's trees
> By riding them down over and over again
> Until he took the stiffness out of them,
> And not one but hung limp, not one was left

---

* The swings in consciousness between fictive and objective worlds are reflected in a series of perfectly placed linguistic pivots. Consider: the conjunctive "but," lines 5, 21; or the conjunctive "and," lines 42, 49, 55; or the subtle semantic ambiguity of "shed" (line 10) and "trailing" (line 18) which points us simultaneously outward (in objective reference) to the inhuman world of nature—of birches as birches—and inward (expressive reference) to the warm, ambient world of Frost's consciousness, of bent birches as girls throwing their hair before them, drying in the sun.

> For him to conquer. He learned all there was
> To learn about not launching out too soon
> And so not carrying the tree away
> Clear to the ground. He always kept his poise
> To the top branches, climbing carefully
> With the same pains you use to fill a cup
> Up to the brim, and even above the brim.
> Then he flung outward, feet first, with a swish,
> Kicking his way down through the air to the ground.

One figure seems to imply another—the image of the farm youth swinging up, out, and down to earth again recalls the boyhood of the poet:

> So was I once myself a swinger of birches.
> And so I dream of going back to be.
> It's when I'm weary of considerations,
> And life is too much like a pathless wood
> Where your face burns and tickles with the cobwebs
> Broken across it, and one eye is weeping
> From a twig's having lashed across it open.

For anyone but Frost the "pathless wood" is trite. But for him it carries a complex of meaning fashioned elsewhere. The upward swinging of the boy becomes an emblem for imagination's swing away from the tangled, dark wood; a swing away from the "straighter, darker trees"; a swing into the absolute freedom of isolation, the severing of all "considerations." This is the transcendental phase of redemptive consciousness, a game that one plays alone. The downward movement of redemptive imagination to earth, contrarily, is a movement into community, engagement, love—the games that two play together:

> I'd like to get away from earth awhile
> And then come back to it and begin over.
> May no fate willfully misunderstand me
> And half grant what I wish and snatch me away
> Not to return. Earth's the right place for love:
> I don't know where it's likely to go better.
> I'd like to go by climbing a birch tree,
> And climb black branches up a snow-white trunk
> *Toward* heaven, till the tree could bear no more,

But dipped its top and set me down again.
That would be good both going and coming back.
One could do worse than be a swinger of birches.

One really has no choice but to be a swinger of birches. In the moment when, catapulting upward, the poet is half-granted his wish, when transcendence is about to be complete and the self, in its disdain for earth, has lofted itself into absolute autonomy, nothing having any claim upon it, and no return possible, then, at that moment, the blessed pull of the earth is felt again, and the apocalypse desired by a transcending imagination, which seemed so imminent, is repressed. At the end of "Birches" a precious balance has been restored between the claims of a redeeming imagination in its extreme, transcendent form, and the claims of common sense reality. To put it in another way, the psychic needs of change—supplied best by redemptive imagination—are balanced by the equally deep psychic need—supplied by skeptical ironic awareness—for the therapy of dull realities and everyday considerations.

3

In its difficult and dense linguistic configurations within which a complex network of meanings is embedded, in its rapid and radical shifts of tone and attitude that evoke a wide range of responses, and in its masterful blank verse rhythms that sustain his ultimate in lyrical expression, we are pointed to one idea: that "Directive"[4] is Frost's *summa*, his most compelling and encompassing meditation on the possibilities of redemption through the imagination, the one poem that a critic of Frost must sooner or later confront if he hopes to grasp the poet's commitment to his art as a way of saving himself, and to understand the astonishing unity of his life's work at last fully revealed here in this major poem of his later career. The interlocking motifs and symbols from the earlier poems are there: the lonely man out on an even lonelier journey, seeking to withdraw; the image of the house now only a crumbling foundation overgrown with wild flowers; the deliberate, self-conscious projecting of illusions; the image of the woods; the overt references to play; the image of a vanishing human world; lastly, the crucial reference to the brook. But "Directive" is no collection of old stories: it does not represent the artist in his last phase as the great pretender, reduced in his aesthetic poverty to imitating himself. The landscape established in many other poems emerges in "Directive," but it is fashioned anew, the context is fresh.

In the poem's opening lines the narrator issues the first of several "directives" to his reader:

> Back out of all this now too much for us,
> Back in a time made simple by the loss
> Of detail, burned, dissolved, and broken off
> Like graveyard marble sculpture in the weather,
> There is a house that is no more a house
> Upon a farm that is no more a farm
> And in a town that is no more a town.

Possibly only the poet can risk issuing such directives which, because of their ambiguous and even contradictory implications, lead not to action— as the rhetorician's language is calculated to so prompt us—but to troubled and bewildered contemplation. We must immediately acclimatize ourselves to a context within which linguistic playfulness and the grimmest of issues are the most compatible friends. The imperative tone in the opening lines is lost if we do not recognize the play over the phrases "Back out of," "Back in" which idiomatically refer us to time past—and in part that is what the poet intends—but which literally command us to a certain kind of movement. We are being asked to "back off," really, to withdraw from overwhelming confusion. The image projected in these lines is of a man overcome, warily withdrawing from the present with both eyes fixed on the "now" that is "too much," as if it were a cunning enemy that you could not for a moment turn your back on. It is painful but true that the value of withdrawal rests on the continuing presence (at least in the mind) of that which one no longer wants present: the rushing, unmanageable present itself and a number of facts about the human condition that Frost will not let us conceal from ourselves. His first directive is curious, finally, not only because it is cast in the language of double talk but also because unlike most directives it is issued not from above, from one who is situated outside of the chaos that he orders us out of. "Now" is "too much for us"—the poet's directive has self-reflexive force.

However strong the desire for withdrawal may be, we might finally find ourselves frozen in our backward movement: what we are withdrawing *to* seems hardly more promising than what we are withdrawing *from*. It is difficult to feel nostalgic about the trip back through time when it gives all the appearances of being a trip through decay and destruction, through nature's morgue. Our journey through time promises to take us by monuments of time's conflagration: things "burned," things "dissolved," things "broken off." And when we finally make it to the desired simplicity of the promised land, we will be rewarded with three images of desertion and death: the house, the farm, and the town that are no more. At this point the journey doesn't seem worth our trouble. I would venture the guess, though, that the poet's intention is to make it as difficult as possible, and to warn us that it will be hard from the very outset. As he put it in "Mowing," he does not offer "easy gold at the hand of fay or elf." The "wrong ones," as he suggests in the concluding lines of "Directive," echoing St. Mark, will be discouraged long before he can lead them to the treasures of a special kind of redemption—they won't "get saved." He insists that those who do get saved have an encompassing kind of consciousness that can entertain and retain clashing values and visions. Frost's ideal man of imagination has to be a tough and resilient type who can stay whole though he is pulled in opposite directions by powerful forces, hung between a present that is confusing and unliveable and a past that is littered with death's remains. He has, apparently, nowhere to go, even as he withdraws.

The narrator continues, with qualification, in gentle tones not at all typical of those who issue directives:

> The road there, if you'll let a guide direct you
> Who has at heart your getting lost,
> May seem as if it should have been a quarry—
> Great monolithic knees the former town
> Long since gave up pretence of keeping covered.

The guide is the poet-narrator and the journey that he is asking us to take with him—if we should consent—is more than a long walk on one of Frost's long-closed New England roads that lead back, even today, to towns where nobody lives. We are taking with him a journey in the imagination, backing up the stream of time, and the lostness that he hopes we shall come to feel will be something different from a sense of spatial dislocation, with our compasses all out of order. We are, or so we hope, going to lose one kind of existence in order to gain a more valuable one.

The progress (and direction) of our steady withdrawal can be measured by the changes wrought by the forces of nature. Just below the busted road laid down by the men of the town long ago sits the imperturbable, eternal raw rock. Its cold and hard face again dominates the

scene and the "pretence" of human control has been shattered, sub-
verted from beneath, as it were. This image makes it clear that no salvation awaits us in the barren rock-ribbed hills; this is a setting that will not
caress the bruised psyche. The narrator is inviting us, with ever so much
tact, quietly destroying any last harbored romantic illusions about our
relations to history and the external universe, but simultaneously intro-
ducing more modest illusions of his own, hoping now not to command us
but to beguile, hoping to slip inside our defenses against the enchant-
ments of a difficult trip.

> And there's a story in a book about it:
> Besides the wear of iron wagon wheels
> The ledges show lines ruled southeast-northwest,
> The chisel work of an enormous Glacier
> That braced his feet against the Arctic Pole.
> You must not mind a certain coolness from him
> Still said to haunt this side of Panther Mountain.
> Nor need you mind the serial ordeal
> Of being watched from forty cellar holes
> As if by eye pairs out of forty firkins.

Implicitly we are being invited to assume the magic of the poet's perspective in order to ease the burdens of a lonely journey. Geological history—and specifically that part of it belonging to the Ice Age—is casually
mythologized. Historical record when seen as "a story in a book" takes on
the quality of an imagined—a constructed—reality and its forbidding
posture as intransigent fact is dissolved away in whimsical personification.
A humanized nature, projected in this myth, however cool, is preferable
to the thing really there beneath the myth. The lightness of Frost's touch
in this passage, markedly contrasting to the tone of the poem's beginning,
is meant to get us over a difficult place in the journey, to take us deeper
with the least amount of pain. The comparison, purposely left submerged,
is between the kind of force that it took to chisel a lasting mark on the
stony face of nature—a force massive and beyond comprehension—and the
embarrassingly puny and futile human effort, the pretence to keep those
forbidding knees covered. Frost generally builds in an escape hatch: in
this passage, if we should grasp the unstated comparison between nature
and man, if we should then become disillusioned at the image of the
human will given, why then there are the lines, alongside those made by
the Glacier, worn in rock by our wagon wheels, years and years of wagon

wheels, attesting to our tenacious stamina. We are not all that ephemeral, after all, unless, that is, we insist on scrutinizing Frost's compliment a little too carefully. Then we shall be reminded that human history is but a drop in the sea of geological history. And that is what scares—that is the true serial ordeal concealed beneath the false ordeal of being watched by the eyes from the crumbling ruins of old houses. The eyes are not really there; the *as if* is meant to underscore that fact. But the man who journeys with Frost (if he be a true knight) must see all around the poet's figures, must glimpse into the harshness beneath. He has to prove himself capable of first grasping and then maintaining the multiple visions built into the poet's context; must prove, as well, that he can shoulder the burden of the knowledge of human time, comprehended, as Frost insists, within the frame of geological time.

Then, as if to intensify the ordeal of such encompassing vision:

> As for the woods' excitement over you
> That sends light rustle rushes to their leaves,
> Charge that to upstart inexperience.
> Where were they all not twenty years ago?
> They think too much of having shaded out
> A few old pecker-fretted apple trees.

The animated woods might make us feel at home, for a brief moment, but the pleasure of such a welcoming is taken away as soon as it is given. The question "Where were they all not twenty years ago?" is enough to put them in their place, far below the abiding rock, implying that whatever has the spark of organic life, trees or humans, is, from the perspective of geological time, doomed to quick extinction. The rock remains, impervious to the gouging chisels of Glacier and wagon wheels, but the apple trees are vulnerable to the damage that woodpeckers can do—they are "pecker-fretted." The troubled apple trees stand alone as the last sentient objects in the insentient landscape projected in the poem, and as a hint of the landscape of human suffering that we soon discover in our trip up history's stream.

And now, approaching our destination, the poet directs us to engage our imagination:

> Make yourself up a cheering song of how
> Someone's road home from work this once was,
> Who may be just ahead of you on foot
> Or creaking with a buggy load of grain.

The height of the adventure is the height
Of country where two village cultures faded
Into each other. Both of them are lost.
And if you're lost enough to find yourself
By now, pull in your ladder road behind you
And put up a sign CLOSED to all but me.

In the face of all the barrenness, the imagination begins to infuse its life-giving powers into a long-dead human scene. The isolated and wandering knight of "Directive" needs something more than the promise of a special grail waiting for him, one of the right ones, at the end of his long journey. Bereft of community he begins to make his own in song (like whistling in the dark?); the precise and homely detail of "creaking with a buggy load of grain" is not a sentimental gesture but a projection from a mind made desperate by its needs of the comforts of common human realities. The height of adventure is not the finding of imagination's desired realities, but the finding of the vestiges of human culture. The height of adventure, to put it another way, is not the verification of imagination's humanizing illusions, but the pressing of imagination to its furthest reaches by the discovery of the final evidence of the abject sadness of the human condition in a human-repelling universe. Our climb up into the higher country is a metaphor for the journey of imagination (echoing the swinging metaphor from "Birches") and Frost is quick to seize upon the conceit buried in the idea of the old "ladder road" to emphasize that the final stage of a journey in the mind has been reached and that it is a journey that can be completed only by solitary men. The imagination pours forth its greatest energies only after it has realized its anarchic potential, severing itself from all connections: "CLOSED to all but me."

We have traveled far, passing through geological, cultural, and organic time in our search for the serenity that the present could not give. Now firmly situated in country hospitable only to the imagination, we must take stock of what we have been given:

Then make yourself at home. The only field
Now left's no bigger than a harness gall.
First there's the children's house of make-believe,
Some shattered dishes underneath a pine,
The playthings in the playhouse of the children.
Weep for what little things could make them glad.
Then for the house that is no more a house.

> But only a belilaced cellar hole,
> Now slowly closing like a dent in dough.
> This was no playhouse but a house in earnest.

It hardly seems credible that history's graveyard could be imagination's proper place. All around are the signs of death and pain: the phrase "no bigger than a harness gall," like the phrase "pecker-fretted apple trees," thrusts an image of suffering onto the natural landscape; better there than someplace else. Actually, the galled and the fretted are those who threw up against a hostile environment the "house in earnest," now a "belilaced cellar hole" being sucked slowly into the earth—a fitting finale to the constant minor irritants, the little open sores which, like a harness gall, rarely claim a life, just supply the daily portion of misery. The failed "house in earnest"—an all too vulnerable enclosure—is opposed by the house that never was in reality and therefore still is in "make believe"—an enclosure beyond assault. What fascinates the poet most about this entire scene is not the image of failure and futility, but those shattered, useless dishes that are the playthings in the children's dreamy play world.

> Your destination and your destiny's
> A brook that was the water of the house,
> Cold as a spring as yet so near its source,
> Too lofty and original to rage.
> (We know the valley streams that when aroused
> Will leave their tatters hung on barb and thorn.)
> I have kept hidden in the instep arch
> Of an old cedar at the waterside
> A broken drinking goblet like the Grail
> Under a spell so the wrong ones can't find it,
> So can't get saved, as Saint Mark says they mustn't.
> (I stole the goblet from the children's playhouse.)
> Here are your waters and your watering place.
> Drink and be whole again beyond confusion.

The brook is our destination *and* destiny: both the end of the physical journey and the inevitable fated object of our imagination's teleological process. Unlike the valley stream which when swollen with spring rains can wreak destruction, the brook does not rage, does not disturb the life around it. It alone among natural forces harmonizes with human existence. Once the lifeblood of the house that is no more, now we are drawn to the waters of the brook as to the sacred waters of baptism. We have not, finally, traveled back through public history, but through private, inner time. What we recover, if we brave the various assaults that the poet has subjected us to, is the pristine moment of our childhood imagination—a moment that stands outside time—the embryo moment of our maturer imaginative faculty. Unfettered by ironic habits of vision, the mind of the child can build up out of the broken objects of the adult life the purer fantasies that occupy his days.

And now we return to that sacred source to renew ourselves, to make ourselves whole again, and to overcome the confusion we have left and to which we shall and must return. But if we would drink out of the goblet that is "like the Grail"—again the obtrusive simile drives home the ironic consciousness of the poet—then we must know that we drink from a broken goblet (hidden, appropriately, in the playhouse to which we must return to recover the root energies of adult imagination). Our transformation from confused adult to simple child is not complete and could not be complete. Yet this is what Frost's special kind of redemption has been all about, all along. The unself-conscious acts of child imagination foreshadow the deeply self-conscious imaginative visions of adult life. The child gives the example to the adult, for even as the children in play can transmute the shattered dishes into the fixtures of their magic world, so the adult, with examples of failure and suffering all around him, must somehow transform what he sees into a better world: we really have no choice—either we recreate the world better than it is, or we live an un bearable existence. We shall drink as much as a broken goblet will allow, even as we shall build up (but only within imagination's proper residence: the playhouse) a universe as humanized as the inhuman universe will permit. Perhaps the last lesson of a man of redemptive consciousness, of a self seeking to be "whole again beyond confusion," is that imagination's journey is ended only when the projection of imagination's shapes of hope and desire is accompanied by a sober self-consciousness that will keep us in touch with ourselves and the limits of our redemption, and keep us from projecting fantasy worlds that will spurn the law of gravity and spur us into anarchic solipsism.

Part Two: Landscapes of Modern Poetics

6. Organicism and Subjectivity

The creative process . . . involves a search for language that adequately captures in and through itself the object that, somehow, until it is successfully captured by language, lies tantalizingly just beyond the reach of consciousness. (Eliseo Vivas, *Creation and Discovery*)

Is it not in the last analysis cruel to face a human being with merely an object as such, a being which is less than a person? As soon as contemplation enters beyond a certain state of awareness, is not the human being going to be unsatisfied if he cannot find another, a person, a you, in whatever it is he is concerned with? (Walter J. Ong, *The Barbarian Within*)

The critical metaphor most frequently associated with New Critics, that of the poem as "object," distills the important modern aesthetic doctrine, ultimately derived from Kant, that a poem is a discrete, self-bounded and self-sufficient entity, neither imitative of an external reality nor an expressive out-pouring of the poet himself, but rather a "world" of intrinsic meaning and value—an alternative nature, as Kant suggested, which operates autonomously according to its own laws. The poet who brings this aesthetic world into being with a creative act of his imagination stands like an aloof God, as James Joyce evoked him, coolly paring his nails, forever—and by choice—cut off from his creation. New Critical theory has preserved this hermetically sealed object from critical contamination by shrewd formulation of a series of fallacies: those of paraphrase and affect and, most crucially, the fallacy of intention which appears to bar the poet from his poem.

T. S. Eliot's chemical metaphor for the creative process is a perfect illustration of some of the aesthetic ideas of the leading New Critics. The act of the poet's consciousness is but a "catalyst," according to Eliot, and has no part in the finished "product" itself. Significant modern critics, by following Eliot's lead, make the poem into an inviolable "object," and take a giant and problematic step away from their romantic heritage. For the modern objectivist the romantic metaphor of the poem as "organism" is not nearly radical enough because organisms are not finally independent or self-sufficient; they die without a sustaining environment. A modern metaphor for the poem more central than MacLeish's "globed fruit" is Yeats's metallic bird, singing in eternity, beyond the processes and ravages of nature.

I believe that Robert Frost occupies a position somewhere between the neo-Kantian, object-oriented aesthetics of the New Critics and the proto-phenomenology and existentialism of William James which focuses almost exclusively on the uniqueness and privacy of person—what James somewhere called the "self of selves." With all his sympathy for postromantic theories of the poet's creative power I doubt that Frost would accept the cold, object metaphor of the New Criticism. The personalist and phenomenological perspective that I developed out of William James in the opening chapter encourages us to view all acts of the mind not as issuing from transpersonal epistemological categories, as neo-Kantians suggest, but as issuing from the unique affective life of a person, ineluctably saturated with the presence of person.

James's view may lead us, however, to despair—to be conscious is to be alienated. In his philosophy the unique person is available only in self-conscious introspection, a perception of the self which cannot be enjoyed by the "other": the breaches between personal minds, James concludes, are the most "absolute breaches in nature."[1] There is no possibility of contact because the self is forever enclosed behind what Pater called the "thick wall of personality"; we exist, as F. H. Bradley suggests, in the prison of self. The problem is more difficult than the existentialist devotees of Buber's "I-Thou" philosophy would allow, for it is not simply that we are made into objects by social stereotypes—that is only part of the problem; social stereotypes can be dealt with. But we have difficulty dealing with our own stereotypical self projections; we generalize and destroy our particularity as persons when we project ourselves through the generic forms of language.

Though alienation is one of Frost's fundamental themes, his is not ultimately a poetry of despair—he assumes and sometimes articulates a position taken by Walter J. Ong. Verbalization, Ong believes, can be an "amplification" of the hidden interior.[2] We need to add to Ong's theory only that there are good and bad amplifying systems. Since the conventions of language are recalcitrant, they tend to resist subjectification; most of us must lie tragically hidden behind the words we speak, as we "amplify" through language not our unique selves but conventionalized shapes of the self. Our self-consciousness is so heavily mediated by conventional language that the deepest levels of our own personal selfhood are inaccessible even to us. But the lyric poet of power, a supreme self-knower, can shape those very conventions to personal ends and make language constitutive of his subjectivity. His radically personal acts of consciousness—the sustaining environment of his poems—are not hidden in the cavern of an unformulated self because, when aesthetically successful, he creates his self in publicly accessible linguistic shapes. Frost's Jamesian reverence for subjectivity is matched by an organicist, New Critical reverence for the efficacy of language. The poem seen in these contrary perspectives is an "object" of sorts, since its language plays a creative role; but it is an "object" filled with a "subject." The finished poem becomes, as it were, a residence; it houses the poet's self, the quality of his awareness. The poetic analyses carried out above were essentially attempts to get at that housed subjectivity in the imaginative landscape; to find the poet in those exfoliations of self, the poems themselves.

It was John Dewey who brought some of James's basic psychological insights to aesthetic theory, and in so doing tied together in indissoluble unity the creative act of expression, the expressive object itself, and the revelation of selfhood. Among modern aestheticians of expression—including Croce, Collingwood, and Alexander—Dewey is most satisfying in his treatment of this problem because he fuses the typical concern of the romantic mind with self-expression and the modernist emphasis on the creative power of language:

> The act of expression that constitutes a work of art is a construction in time, not an instantaneous emission. And this statement signifies a great deal more than that it takes time for the painter to transfer his imaginative conception to canvas and for the sculptor to complete his chipping of marble. It means that the expression of the self in and through a medium, constituting the work of art, is *itself* a prolonged interaction of something issuing from the self with objective conditions, a process in which both of them acquire a form and order they did not at first possess.[3]

To ask how Frost's poems can capture, house, and constitute his "self of selves" is to ask a question that his mentor in philosophy did not pose. Believing with Descartes in the inaccessibility of the self, James could not have sustained the New Critical faith in language. James, at any rate, wrote no poetics. Though Frost wrote no explicit poetics, on numerous occasions in letters, essays, and interviews he anticipated the linguistic concerns of the New Critics. Ironically, despite their familiar warnings about heresies and fallacies, the New Critics may have provided us with an important theoretical justification for entering the very realm of subjectivity which literary critics of the phenomenological school, in often acrimonious debate with New Critics, have claimed as their theoretically distinctive territory.

1

In their analysis of the function of language in poems, the New Critics often advanced, in their critical practice, beyond the initial claim for creativity which is rooted in the epistemological revolution of Kant, and which is applied to the act of the artistic imagination by Coleridge and, later, by Croce. By grounding his theory of imagination in German idealist philosophy Coleridge endowed poetic perception with a creative power not allowed by the major Western epistemological traditions of realism and empiricism. After Kant and Coleridge the mimetic view of the creative process began to drift out of the mainstream of philosophical aesthetics because the passive, mimetic view of mind in its act of knowing—archetypically imaged in Locke—was no longer considered an adequate explanation of the role of mind in cognitive activity. Rather than reflecting an independent, antecedent reality, the mind becomes in itself an originative source of the real.

Yet Coleridge—in Frost's American tradition, Emerson—and certainly Croce, curiously truncated their theoretical discussion of the creative process. As idealists they could assign the poet special power and value in his act of vision because their central epistemological assumption is that mind is in part creative of the world which it knows. (But this is a truly problematic claim of idealist aesthetics. Since poetic perception is subsumed under a general theory of knowing, it is difficult to understand how the poet can be assigned a uniquely creative mind because all minds are assigned creative or constitutive powers in idealist epistemology. The

distinction must be one of degree, not kind, as Wordsworth suggests.[4])
The strength of philosophical idealism is sometimes also its weakness—
Coleridge, Emerson, and Croce had difficulty in accepting into the creative
act, as a necessary formative factor, the "matter" of an artistic medium.
Coleridge's well known organicist commitments to the "word" are ultimately betrayed by his Schellingian commitments to an idealistic monism.
In Coleridge's theory of the imagination, as in the theory of most early
romantic poets, the act of creative vision is not coincidental with an act
of linguistic expression; the poem itself stands as "fading coal" to the
furnace of imaginative vision. This early romantic disdain for medium,
this exaltation of a vision which cannot be contained by the mere finite
reality of the medium of language, is no less evident in Croce who carefully distinguishes, as an idealist must, between the expressive act of
imagination and the mere externalization of that act: "We cannot will or
not will our aesthetic vision: we can however will or not will to externalize
it, or rather, to preserve and communicate to others, or not, the externalization produced."[5] The "real poem" for Croce is that unwilled and
apparently unconscious act of imagination—a poem complete and whole
prior to and independent of its "externalization" in language. Probably
Emerson put it most bluntly. Language cannot adequately sustain transcendental vision because words are "finite organs of the infinite mind.
They cannot cover the dimensions of what is in truth. They break, chop,
and impoverish it."[6]

What the New Critics urged in their modification of romantic imagination is the indispensable role of language in the creative process. By suggesting that the poet creatively discovers his poem in his linguistic medium, as he transforms ordinary language, the New Critic can make the
claim that the poem itself encloses within its boundaries indigenous meaning and value: the poet's world. Though he assumes the epistemology
of Kant and Coleridge, the New Critic switches the theoretical focus
from the constructive power of mind to the constructive power of the
poem itself. In the words of W. M. Urban, a modern idealist whose
extensions of Croce Cleanth Brooks found very attractive: "The artist
does not first intuit his object and then find the appropriate medium. It is
rather in and through his medium that he intuits the object. . . . The
poet . . . does well . . . to keep to his own symbolic form. For precisely
in that symbolic form an aspect of reality is given which cannot be adequately expressed otherwise."[7] Or in Brooks's own words: "The experience
which he [the poet] 'communicates' is itself created by the organization of

the symbols which he uses. The total poem is therefore the communication, and indistinguishable from it."[8] The idea that the poet's envisioned world is inseparable from the medium where it was creatively discovered is the basis of an object-oriented poetics that until very recently dominated the twentieth-century theoretical scene.

Frost felt little of the compulsion to apologize for poetry by defending it, as the New Critics did, against all enemies (especially against the monolithic cognitive claims of later nineteenth-century scientism and twentieth-century positivists), yet he proceeded along routes remarkably similar to those traveled by the New Critics. He sharply modified the earlier forms of romantic aesthetic and arrived at a view of the poem as a locus, a kind of residence for the poet's created world. The making of poems for the New Critic is a process of transforming a basically referential (and utilitarian) discourse, whose meaning seems to be given transparently *through* it, as through a window, into an aesthetic kind of discourse. Typically, poetic discourse is viewed by New Critics as an organic whole whose meaning is contingent upon the linguistic context itself.

Frost would agree with the broadly Symbolist implications of all of the above except for the characteristic New Critical claim that the distinction between poetic and nonpoetic discourse is the distinction between discourse which "means" organically and discourse which "means" referentially. Unlike the New Critics (or the contextualists as we have come to call them), he never accepted the dualistic theory of language, coming from I. A. Richards, which established an antagonism between aesthetic and referential functions of language, and seems not to have believed that there is any such thing as a sheerly referential function, either in scientific discourse or in ordinary, practical discourse. All modes of language, including the scientific mode, create a "world," because they are "metaphoric" as he delighted to point out. Frost's contemplations on the creative act are buttressed by the post-Kantian view of mind that he shared with James. In a casual way Frost appears to have anticipated Ernst Cassirer's epistemology of symbolic forms.

2

Before proceeding with the theoretical discussion of Frost's idea of the creative process, I want to turn back once more to his poems for the illumination and complication that they give to his poetics. Particularly problematic is his view of the role of consciousness in the formulation of the world. Frost often talked like a neo-Kantian philosopher of symbolic forms, implying, as we have just seen, that since metaphoric structures underlie all forms of discourse there is no such thing as referentiality in language. But the poems themselves seriously qualify and enrich his position. In such diverse poems as "All Revelation," "The Tuft of Flowers," "Mowing," "The Mountain," "The Black Cottage," and "Mending Wall," the symbolic and metaphor-making thrust of mind—the redemptive act of consciousness—is matched by an ironic, referential consciousness that recognizes the world of objects for what it is, for better and for worse. When Frost insists that metaphor is the foundation of all forms of language I do not believe that he wishes to deny that referentiality is a quality of language, or that there is a real world, but only that discourse is impure; that even as poetic discourse shapes the subjectively saturated, metaphoric world, it will acknowledge the brute given world, the unshapeable stuff of our common experience. It is more appropriate to speak of the tension in Frost's poems between the symbolic-redemptive and referential-ironic thrusts of mind and language as having a basis in the pragmatism of William James, rather than in the idealism of the neo-Kantians and the New Critics. It is peculiarly the strength of pragmatism to recognize a difficult real world that plays some determinative role in our lives, while also allowing for the possibility of the active consciousness to carve out, to a certain extent, the world of its desire. The very idea of redemption posits a real world out there, a something to be transformed, a something without which redemption would be meaningless. We have seen Frost shrewdly suggesting such a complex philosophical stance in his frequent employment of simile at the most crucial turns in his most crucial poems. Here it is in "Directive."

> I have kept in the instep arch
> Of an old cedar at the waterside
> A broken drinking goblet like the Grail . . .

Both in strategy and meaning "For Once, Then, Something" enacts the major coordinates of Frost's poetics. The poem raises the question of "frames." Is reality framed and structured by the self?

>   the water
> Gives me back in a shining surface picture
> Me myself in the summer heaven, godlike,
> Looking out of a wreath of fern and cloud puffs.

Frost comically deflates the serene, solipsistic world of his narcissistic self in ways that remind us of Wallace Stevens's treatment of Crispin, that Socrates of snails. For the framer is himself "framed"—and by the frame:

> Water came to rebuke the too clear water.
> One drop fell from a fern, and lo, a ripple
> Shook whatever it was lay there at bottom. . . .

There is free activity out there, in the world beyond self, and whatever that activity may disclose or disguise—be it transcendental truth of "whiteness," or the hard truth of naturalism, a "pebble of quartz"—the projective act of self into the world has been severely delimited. The water "rebukes" visionary revelation, not because there is Some*one* out there, toying with us for sport, but because natural fact (some*thing*) and natural energy—"lo, a ripple"—are ultimately autonomous, beyond control and containment by the mind's humanizing act. The self is framed, literally, by "Others"—the first word of the poem—and by "something," the last word of the poem.

And yet it is possible to overstate the force of natural fact and the extent to which the mind must take it into account. For what we are left with, in our uncertainty, is the mind's playing with possibility. The ironic reverberations of the last line, "Truth? A pebble of quartz?" do not so much cancel the alternatives, though in part that is the effect, as reestablish the power of the mind once more. The playful energies of mind are as irreducible as the natural energies of water. In play, in the hypothetical posing of alternatives, the way is opened once more for the reframing of reality in the terms of human needs.

3

I quote two passages from Frost's letters: the first, from a letter to Louis Untermeyer, was written in 1916; the second, from a letter to Sidney Cox, was written in 1932. The context of the first passage is a discussion of a book of poems recently published by Untermeyer; the context of the second passage is a discussion of a book on Frost that Cox was writing:

> . . . the poem wrote itself. That's what makes a poem. A poem is never a put up job so to speak. It begins as a lump in the throat, a sense of wrong, a homesickness, a lovesickness. It is never a thought

to begin with. It is at its best when it is a tantalizing vagueness. It finds its thought and succeeds, or doesn't find it and comes to nothing. It finds its thought or makes its thought. . . . Let's say again: a poem particularly must not begin thought first.[9]

A subject must be an object. . . . My objection to your larger book about me was that it came thrusting in where I did not want you. The idea is the thing with me. It would seem soft for instance to look in my life for the sentiments in the Death of the Hired Man. There's nothing to it believe me. I should fool you if you took me so. I'll tell you my notion of the contract you thought you had with me. The objective idea is all I ever cared about. Most of my ideas occur in verse.[10]

And here is a third and quite remarkable passage, written even earlier, in 1914:

You aren't influenced by that Beauty is Truth claptrap. In poetry and under emotion every word used is "moved" a little or much—moved from its old place, heightened, made, made new. See what Keats did to the word "alien" in the ode. But as he made it special in that place he made it his—and his only in that place. He could never have used it again with just that turn. It takes the little one horse poets to do that. I am probably the only Am[erican] poet who haven't used it after him. . . . I want the unmade words to work with, not the familiar made ones that everybody exclaims Poetry! at. . . . His [the poet's] pleasure must always be to make his own words as he goes and never to depend for effect on words already made even if they be his own.[11]

Frost's commitment to the ideas that he expressed in these letters was lifelong. From at least as early as 1914, to as late as 1959[12]—in letters to friends, in interviews for college newspapers, on a radio broadcast over the BBC and, in 1959, in an interview with Robert Penn Warren and Cleanth Brooks—he turned again and again to metaphors of quest to describe the poetic process: a poem is a "little voyage of discovery."[13] But the motif of discovery in language is just a bit misleading. To echo the title of a book which is deeply concerned with the nature of the creative process, it is not just discovery, but *creation* and discovery.[14] "Finding" in Frost is generally balanced by "making." The poem may not be understood, in terms of pre-Kantian literary theory, as a mirror reflection of a fully-structured, antecedent reality. As such it would be, Frost says, a "put up job"—not really a poem at all. Eliseo Vivas suggests the direction of Frost's mind when, in the spirit of Urban and Brooks, he writes:

> If all the artist does is represent or imitate, if he does not constitute, if he does not create in the act of discovery, all he can do with his language, at best, is to add an external adornment to the object of imitation. This is the doctrine of the Aristotelians. I believe it is easy to recognize that this view utterly fails to do justice to the way in which the language of poetry functions to say or mean what it does.[15]

If poetry's values are to earn their residence in the poem itself and not be tourists on vacation from the world of action, then we shall have to take quite seriously the remark by Frost that "the poem wrote itself. That's what makes a poem." I say take "seriously" because I think he meant his statement to be taken in that way, though I doubt that he would want it taken literally. (Among the contextualists, only I. A. Richards, as far as I know, has dared a similarly radical interpretation of the creative process. And he, curiously, seems to have meant it literally.[16] Implicitly, in their practical criticism, a number of New Critical epigones cut the poem away from the poet's delimited and organizing consciousness, and are thus led to assume the subjectivistic and irresponsible position that poems have an infinite multiplicity of meaning. Literary criticism, in this perspective, degenerates quickly into self-display.) The poet begins, Frost suggests, in his engagement with the linguistic medium, with a vague and "tantalizing" sense of something—a sense of something, but never a grasp of it. That something—the poem's object—is fully contextualized in the meandering process of composition. (In Frost that "something" tends to be a fixed object in his landscape, a perception of the brook, or of the house, or of the woods which has magnetized his consciousness.) As the vague and fascinating sense of the object tempts the poet, moves him, motivates his quest through language, the poet's mind and craftsmanship exert pressure on the medium in an attempt to shape that medium such that it will satisfy his tantalizing sense. But the medium presses back, as it were; the poem starts to "write itself" as the medium exerts its own pressures which are generated by the myriad conventions, structures, and technical resources of the language. When the resources of language become (in turn) shaped by the poet's creative act, they become more than constituents of technique: they become constitutive themselves of the poem's meaning and the poet's world. And then the object in the landscape that has magnetized the poet's shaping consciousness will have been transformed from its place in the real order to a new place in the reality of the poem where, as a fiction, it will both satisfy the poet's needs and radiate his shaping consciousness: "The artist must value himself as he snatches a thing from some previous order in time and space into a new order [the poem itself] with not so much as a ligature clinging to it of the old place where it was organic."[17] Thus understood, the poem becomes jointly revelatory of the world created in an act of Frost's consciousness, and of the creating consciousness itself which is the ambient and sustaining presence in that created world.

I would surmise that Frost intentionally exaggerates when he says the "poem wrote itself" in order to suggest (as the systematic romantic idealist cannot) the powerful formative role of an objective medium in the creative process. The poem lives there, in the medium, and not in the caverns of the poet's unformulated self: "The canvas is where the work of art is, where we make the conquest."[18] But if this discussion seems to exalt romantic irrationalism all over again by transposing it into the modern finite and agnostic critical key, if the stress here seems to make the artist the unconscious tool of some mysterious force—specifically, the tool of some magically alive medium—we might, then, recall Frost's suggestive vacillation between finding and making: "It finds its thought or makes its thought." The poet, he would argue more plausibly, not the poem, both finds and makes; he finds as he makes. As Frost paradoxically phrased it in his talk with Warren and Brooks: "You've got to be the happy discoverer of your ends."[19] With that remark he restores the balance between finding and making by restoring to the poet the shaping powers of his directed consciousness. The teleology of the creative act is a peculiar sort of purposiveness because although it posits a directed and dynamic artistic consciousness—a most unromantic, conscious, and willful sort of creativity —it cannot allow that consciousness the pleasure of fully knowing itself until it has discovered its "end" in language:

Brooks: That's a very fine way of phrasing it, "the happy discoverer of your end." Because otherwise it is contrived. You can see it coming a mile off.

Frost: A mile away. I've often said that another definition of poetry is dawn—that it's something dawning on you while you're writing it. It comes off if it really dawns when the light comes at the end. And the feeling of dawn—the freshness of dawn—that you didn't think this all out and write it in prose first and then translate it into verse. That's abhorrent![20]

(There may have been, at that point, a moment of private embarrassment for Brooks who, some twenty years earlier in *Modern Poetry and the Tradition,* could not quite bring himself to allow Frost into the tradition as he had newly defined it in his revisionary enthusiasm for the New Critical revolution.)

The last drops of passivity are squeezed out of Frost's conception of the creative process in his discussion of Keats. The metaphor of the poet as "discoverer" or "quester" does not quite do justice to Frost's vision of the poet as a dynamic agent who shapes as he seeks. The making of poetry is the making of the old word, the stuff of the medium, into a new mode of discourse whose uniqueness of meaning lies precisely in the uniqueness of its particular linguistic configurations: its context. In the "Ode to a Nightingale," Frost says, Keats rooted the word "alien" from its "old place"—its old context—and made it new (a clear echo of Ezra Pound) and he made it new by making a special place for it, a unique context. Keats created a nuance of meaning "but only in that place," Frost emphasized, only in *those* particular organic interrelations, only in that poem. "He could never have used it again with just that turn." Each and every poem, to make the logical extension, ought ideally to be a unique context of meaning, a new Mallarmean word, not in the sense of a palpably dense, opaque object,[21] a world of meaning utterly severed from the world we live in and act in, but in the sense of a unique form of discourse discontinuous not only with other forms of discourse but also with the discourse of all other poems. Those are large, extreme, and perhaps finally untenable and unwise claims for poetry. I believe, in fact, that Frost's own poetic practice rebuts this extreme of organicist theory (I discuss this paradox of theory and practice in my epilogue). Nevertheless, at a certain level they would seem to be Frost's claims because he conceives of the poet as a radically creative agent "who must always make his own words as he goes and never depend for effect on words already made even if they be his own." He will always transmute language in the alembic of the creative process; if, that is, he is not a "little one horse poet."

The one horse poet is passive, not dynamic; imitative, not creative. Pinned helplessly by the press of poetic convention and the received order and structure of language, the force of his own unique subjectivity is dissipated; he can only palely reflect the Keatsian mode. He is a prisoner of a pre-Kantian view of consciousness, so to speak; a prisoner of the world as it impacts on the quiescently receptive imagination; he is incapable of performing a creative act that must be grounded in an imposingly recalcitrant medium of language that resists all but the mind of the authentic artist. The authentic artist says with Robert Frost, "The canvas is where the work of art is, where we make the conquest."[22] According to the definition of the poet implicit in Frost and explicit in the aesthetics of Eliseo Vivas, the one horse poet is no poet at all (he offers us "put-up jobs") because the impulse to imitation is an antipoetic impulse. We may surmise that William James might have added that the impulse to imitation is an antihuman impulse because it is in the nature of consciousness to be excursive, to carry the person of the poet out into the objects of a public world.

4

The principle of the organic self-sufficiency of the poem is a difficult one to explain in language which is not finally tautological. Not surprisingly, those who believe in the idea have turned to metaphoric expression. The metaphor that has been used most successfully to explain organic structure in poetry is not the vegetative one, as one might expect; no metaphor drawn from nature, in fact, but one drawn from literature. I refer to the contention, familiar in the writings of New Critics, that dramatic structure is a metaphor for poetic structure in general. William Empson has used the concept to advantage in explicating a well-known line from *King Lear*; Allen Tate claims that certain famous lines in *Macbeth*, when seen in their proper dramatic context, are archetypal of the structure of meaning in poems, and Cleanth Brooks, in *The Well Wrought Urn*, seeks to make a theoretical principle out of the notion that he employed so convincingly in his analysis of the "Ode on a Grecian Urn."[23] Brooks's entire analysis turns on his desire to see the troublesome last lines of the poem not as propositional in intent, but as contextually controlled; not as thrusting toward a conceptual claim which might be said to stand freely independent of the context of the poem, but as a dramatic utterance whose meaning is properly understood only as it is fully integrated with the dramatic situation out of which it arose, even as the meaning of what a character says in a play is properly understood only when we are aware of its intimate connections with his character, the scene, the other characters, the whole "world" of the play.

In "The Heresy of Paraphrase" Brooks has explicit recourse to the dramatic metaphor. On the whole, Brooks writes, most of us are less inclined to force the concept of "statement" on drama than on a lyric poem; for the very nature of drama is that of something "acted out"—something which arrives at its conclusion through conflict—something which builds conflict into its very being. The dynamic nature of drama, in short, allows us to regard it as *an action* rather than as a formula for action or as a statement about action. For this reason, therefore, perhaps the most useful analogy by which to suggest the structure of poetry is that of the drama. . . .[24]

Brooks is now ready to make his all-crucial point about the contextual nature of poetic meaning:

any proposition asserted in a poem is not to be taken in abstraction but is justified, in terms of the poem, if it is justified at all, not by virtue of its scientific or historical or philosophical truth, but is justified in terms of a principle analogous to that of dramatic propriety. Thus, the proposition that "Beauty is truth, truth beauty" is given its precise meaning and significance by its relation to the total context of the poem.[25]

The purpose of Brooks and other New Critics, to make meaning in poems wholly contingent on context, is well illustrated by the principle of dramatic propriety. The problem, however, as R. S. Crane once pointed out in a critique of Brooks, is that the contextual theory of meaning applies to all forms of discourse, not just the poetic mode. Another problem, I would add, is that the New Critical specification of poetry's contextual self-sufficiency is finally not done with terms drawn from dramatic criticism, but rather with terms selected from the arsenal of rhetoric that would tend to force critics to read all poems as possessing the maximum amount of semantic complexity and density; hence, the stress on wit, irony, and paradox. Some great poems work that way, but other great ones clearly do not depend in any significant way on wit, irony, and paradox.

Frost, who is nothing like Donne and Eliot, has himself had recourse to the contextualist principle of dramatic propriety:

Everything written is as good as it is dramatic. It need not declare itself in form, but it is a drama or nothing. A least lyric alone may have a hard time, but it can make a beginning, and lyric will be piled on lyric till all are easily heard as sung or spoken by a person in a scene—in character, in a setting. By whom, where and when is the question.[26]

Frost's contextualism stresses not intellectual or even experiential complexity, the subtle reverberations of qualified meanings and motives, but (in keeping with his analogy) the dramatic preservation in language of self, voice, setting, and time; the preservation of *this* self, *this* place, *this* time. The distinctiveness of poetic discourse would lie not in its contextualism per se, since all modes of discourse may be seen in that way, nor in the dominance of any particular rhetorical strategy, such as irony, nor in the false (because too clean) division of the symbolic and the referential. It would lie in the superior ability of poetic language to capture the existential immediacy of a human act. In such a perspective, all ideas *as such* are not "in" the poem, strictly speaking, but abstractions of the critic from an experiential matrix. The basic human act in Frost, as I see it, is the movement of self across a particular landscape, the encounter of self with special objects in the landscape, and the constitution of self in language against those objects. The chapters in poetic analysis above were intended as an assay at the subjectivity of Frost, an attempt to capture the poet in his major recurrent dramatizations of self and place: as self and brook, self and enclosed space, self and woods. These particular intersections of self and place may be the keys to Robert Frost's identity.

The self and setting projected in Frost's poems are hypothetical, "fictive." A Frost poem is a "fiction" also in the sense (from the Latin: *fictio, fingere*) that it is the outcome of a freely constructive act of mind, and is itself a "construction," "shape," or "configuration," an artistic arrangement. Most poems are fictions in these two senses because most poems present arranged, hypothetical versions of reality. But Frost's poems are fictions in a special sense. As arrangements of reality they are creations of the world that he needs—a world that is, from the strictly realistic point of view, a "lie." Behind this third sense of fiction is an important, if somewhat neglected, tradition of modern poetics. It is the tradition elaborated by Kant, Schiller, Nietzsche, William James, Santayana, Vaihinger, and Kenneth Burke. It is my subject in the next chapter.

I close with three passages from the essay "The Figure a Poem Makes," written in 1939, and since then reprinted as the introduction to the various editions of Frost's collected poems. (When, in 1949, the essay "The Figure a Poem Makes" became the preface to *Complete Poems*, Frost made some minor revisions in it that made his contextualist bias even more apparent. The last sentence of the revised version reads: "Its most precious quality will remain its having run itself and carried away the poet with it. Read it a hundred times: it will forever keep its freshness as a metal keeps its fragrance. It can never lose its sense of a meaning that once unfolded by surprise as it went.") Ostensibly, the passages that I quote describe the poem itself: respectively, its inner logic, the unique relations of its elements, and its self-sustaining, organic structure. Fused to these descriptions of the poem is a description of the act which brings the poem into being:

> It has an outcome that though unforeseen was predestined from the first image of the original mood. . . .[27]
>
> It must be a revelation, or a series of revelations, as much for the poet as for the reader. For it to be that there must have been the greatest freedom of the materials to move about in it and to establish relations in it regardless of time and space, previous relation. . . .[28]
>
> The artist must value himself as he snatches a thing from some previous order in time and space into a new order [the poem itself] with not so much as a ligature clinging to it of the old place where it was organic.[29]

7. *The Scope and the Limits of Supreme Fictions*

I told them . . . I wished for impossible things, even for perpetual summer some times. But I wasn't going to commit suicide if things just went on being the way they always are—longer winters, higher taxes, older age, death at the end. (R. F. in an interview)

Life sways perilously at the confluence of opposing forces. Poetry in general plays perilously in the same wild place. In particular it plays perilously between truth and make-believe. It might be extravagant poetry to call it true make-believe—or making-believe what is so. (R. F. Selected Letters, p. 467)

Merely to give order . . . is to provide consolation, as De Quincey's opium did; and simple fictions are the opium of the people. But fictions too easy we call "escapist"; we want them not only to console but to make discoveries of the hard truth here and now, in the middest. We do not feel they are doing this if we cannot see the shadow of the gable, or hear the discoveries of dissonance, the word set against the word. The books which seal off the long perspectives, which sever us from our losses, which represent the world of potency as a world of act, these are the books which, when the drug wears off, go on to the dump with the other empty bottles. (Frank Kermode, The Sense of an Ending)

We have been a little insane about the truth. (Wallace Stevens)

Now, having isolated Frost's sense of the poem as self-sufficient, organic world—with special emphasis upon the *self* of "self-sufficient"—we face in Frost's aesthetics the problem that has plagued many theorists in the neo-

Kantian tradition: that of relating the apparently autonomous world of the poem to our bigger world of human experience.[1] When I refer to the "neo-Kantian tradition" I mean to evoke those traditions in poetics, mediated for English and American critics by Coleridge's *Biographia Literaria*, that originate from Kant's *Critique of Judgment* (the great source book of modern aesthetic and literary theory) and from his *Critique of Pure Reason* (the book he called his Copernican revolution in epistemology). In the *Critique of Judgment* Kant contended that art has unique, intrinsic values which distinguish it from other human activities. In his *Critique of Pure Reason* he elevated the respective places of the sensibility and the mind (in cognition) to the role of form-giving agents that construct the phenomenal world that we know and experience.

1

In his interpretation of Kant, Coleridge stressed the idea that through a shaping act of the mind the poet provides us with a special aesthetic way of knowing reality. What Coleridge did, in effect, was to endow creative imagination (which Kant had described in the *Critique of Judgment*) with a distinctive cognitive function that Kant himself had never allowed the imagination in its aesthetic phase.[2] If with many who follow in his footsteps we ignore the historical Coleridge's peculiar marriage of Kant with philosophers essentially alien to Kantian thought—various neo-Platonists, but especially the transcendentalist, F. W. J. Schelling—Coleridge's transformation of Kant's aesthetics becomes both a source and a model for the French Symbolists, the New Critics, and the philosophers of symbolic form who take off from Ernst Cassirer. By following the lead of Coleridge most neo-Kantians distort the meaning of Kant's third *Critique*. I believe that Frost and a significant modern tradition in aesthetic theory are oriented to the philosophical setting of the *Critique of Judgment*, where Kant, in opposition to what would become the obsessive epistemological interests of his neo-Kantian followers, stressed so heavily the affective value of the aesthetic experience. The epistemological defense of poetry in Kant's name is a keynote of modern literary theory, but as a defense it has been most often the way of the critics and the aestheticians, not the way of the poets themselves, not the way of Kant.

From the point of view of later aesthetic and literary theorists of organic autonomy and autotelicism, the most important passage in the *Critique of*

Judgment is where Kant compares the aesthetic object to a "nature" shaped out from the material that actual nature supplies to the artist. The germinal passage, to which I allude several times in the pages ahead, reads:

> . . . by an aesthetical idea I understand that representation of the imagination which occasions much thought, without however any definite thought, i.e. any *concept*, being capable of being adequate to it; it consequently cannot be completely compassed and made intelligible by language. We easily see that it is the counterpart (pendant) of a *rational idea*, which conversely is a concept to which no *intuition* (or representation of the imagination) can be adequate.
>
> The imagination (as a productive faculty of cognition) is very powerful in creating another nature, as it were, out of the material that actual nature gives it. We entertain ourselves with it when experience becomes too commonplace, and by it we remold experience, always indeed in accordance with analogical laws, but yet also in accordance with principles which occupy a higher place in reason (laws, too, which are just as natural to us as those by which understanding comprehends empirical nature). Thus we feel our freedom from the law of association (which attaches to the empirical employment of imagination), so that the material supplied to us by nature in accordance with this law can be worked up into something different which surpasses nature. (*Critique of Judgment*, p. 157)

Very schematically: the French Symbolists tend to translate Kant's "aesthetic nature" into an opaque, alternative nature,[3] forever independent of the world of action—"immaculate," as Mallarmé would have it. The New Critics, who derive almost all of their Kant from Coleridge, resist strongly the escapist and aestheticist tendencies of French Symbolist doctrine. The poem for them is not "pure"; never an entrance to a neo-Platonic / occultist realm of value. As self-contained organic unity the poem asks to be taken on its own aesthetic terms; so taken, it becomes a unique form of existential revelation, the vehicle of a special sort of aesthetic knowledge generally defined in rigid dialectical opposition to the language and knowledge of science.[4] Finally, there are those neo-Kantian philosophers of symbolic form who follow in the tradition of Ernst Cassirer, and who provide a broad cultural reinterpretation of Kant. The initial strategy of the philosophers of symbolic form is to generalize Kant's basic idealistic claim for the mind's constitutive action.[5] It is no longer the Kantian Understanding alone that possesses constitutive principles, the power to construct the phenomenal world, because all basic symbolizing acts of the mind are creative of the world. Each of man's major symbolic activities—the scientific, the aesthetic, the religious—allows us a vision of reality which is projected from the symbolizing form itself and is unique to the form. Thus, the creative act of artistic imagination, which shapes the symbolic forms of art, comes to have epistemological value.[6] In the neo-Kantian view, all of the symbolic activities are to be cherished because all are needed in a fully human culture.

For many humanists, the neo-Kantian philosophy is an ultimate response to an age of science and technology because it allows the arts to function in culture in a fashion equal to science. But art has no cognitive function in Kant's system. What it does have is an immense psychological role to play. Kant's "aesthetic nature" presents the "as if," regulative world—reality transmuted by our deepest needs. Though not cognitive in import, we need the aesthetic experience as desperately as we need the cognitive experience. Kant was a severe rationalist, but he recognized in the third *Critique* that we did not and could not live on reason alone.[7] For Robert Frost, as for Kant, the act of poetic imagining is the existentially urgent act of living humanly in the world by recreating the world in the terms of our purely human imperatives.

2

There is an underground tradition developing out of Kant, with complex nineteenth-century aesthetic and philosophical moorings, which is almost totally neglected by literary theorists and historians of criticism. Lost among the myriad entangled directions in nineteenth-century thought, the tradition flowers in the poetics of various twentieth-century writers. I choose to name it the tradition of the supreme fiction, after its most explicit adherent, Wallace Stevens.[8] An historically systematic account of the aesthetics of the supreme fiction would trace the linkage after Kant of a general theory of fictions with a more narrowly aesthetic theory. The account would begin with Kant, move through Nietzsche's pragmatic radicalization of the Kantian insights, then move through such diverse philosophers as George Santayana, William James, and Hans Vaihinger, whose *The Philosophy of 'As If'* is the single most important document for the general theory of fictions after Kant. The Jamesian character of Vaihinger's transformation of Kant is unmistakable, and unmistakably crucial to Frost's poetics: "It must be remembered that the object of the world of ideas as a whole is not the portrayal of reality . . . but rather to provide us with an *instrument for finding our way about more easily in this world*" (p. 15). The essential poetics of Robert Frost is an articulation of this tradition; oddly, a poetics simultaneously more modest and more complex (though less self-conscious) than we find in Stevens himself. The version of the aesthetics of the supreme fiction that I am proposing for Frost embraces both his dialogue and lyric poems; the aesthetics of the fiction is a philosophical and psychological characterization of the controlling vision of experience projected in Frost's work as a whole.

Stevens read about Kant in a handbook on philosophy[9] and Frost likely did not read even that little. I take it as a tribute to the depth of Kant's insights that Stevens and Frost, and others as well, come independently to similar conclusions: as "another nature," the poem is a "fictive" or "better" nature which achieves its value precisely because the Kantian imagination in its aesthetic phase does not perform an epistemological function, and does not pretend to yield what neo-Kantians under the influence of Cassirer call one of the constitutive forms of phenomenal reality. (Sidney's statement—and Scaliger's before him—that the poet "doth grow in effect another nature" is sometimes misleadingly cited by historians of literary theory as an anticipation of the thrust of post-Kantian aesthetics. Sidney had no intention of setting up the autonomy of poetry as we understand the concept of autonomy in post-Kantian thinking. His system of objective idealism, ultimately traceable to Plato, clearly subordinates poetry to the authority of moral philosophy.) As fictive nature the poem serves as psychic enclosure (a "room"[10] as Frost once described the poem), a place for the mind to hide. But as fictive nature the poem is not opaquely insulated from the world (as Mallarmean symbol tends to be) and is, in spite of itself, always engaging the world. As "other" than, or "better" than phenomenal reality, Kant's aesthetic nature subjects things as they are to a critique; demands that the "better nature" of art and the ordinary world of experience be apprehended dialectically by a consciousness which brings one against the other in ironic collision.

The essential claim of Kant's aesthetics is for a psychological value controlled directly and solely by the "better nature" of art which, because of its "purposiveness without purpose," induces a state of intransitive attention that locks the auditor into the art world in an ego-extinguishing transaction. In our experience of the supreme fiction, the aesthetic representation of reality, we discover the world of our supreme desire, a world which, in Kant's words, "surpasses nature"; a world the contemplation of which, Kant believed, brings about the interior harmony and free interplay of our mental faculties: the pleasurable feeling of psychological integration as our faculties are freed from all end-directed activity.[11] In the experience of the "better nature" we cease all end-directed seeking because all ends and "purposes" are *there*, satisfied in poetry's Edenic reconstruction of the world.

When we grasp Frost's landscape, the personal world shaped by the poet's consciousness in and through language, a world answering to the psychic needs of its shaper, we are not gaining a form of sharable knowledge of a common public reality. What we gain, initially, is a "better nature," a shaped vision of reality (a fiction) that the poet finds therapeutic. Insofar as we share in his human condition, it is a shaped vision which we, too, find therapeutic (hence, the fiction's affective value). This is not to deny that the object in the poet's landscape sits out there in a common public world, but only to affirm that the vision of the object, as shaped by the poet's medium, has its locus wholly within the unique consciousness of Robert Frost and tells us something special about the consciousness which has apprehended the object and nothing at all special about the object itself.

As expressions of self Frost's fictions do not transcend the privacy of his constituting consciousness. His particular shaping of reality could not have occurred within the consciousness of anyone else. And to affirm that is to affirm again the singularity of consciousness, and to affirm as well the common sense that tells us that Frost's poems have qualities shared by no other poems. Ultimately, though, as I shall argue in my epilogue, we do gain a kind of knowledge—a knowledge of interiority—when, thoroughly immersed in the poet's total canon, we come to have a sense of Frost's subjectivity (a "redeeming presence") which has invaded and surrounded the objects which his imagination has enveloped.

Historically viewed, the tradition of the supreme fiction surfaces in American poetics through George Santayana in the first two decades of our century. (In America, the Kantian aesthetics of the supreme fiction is routed through Santayana's *Interpretations of Poetry and Religion* [1900], a key text in the Harvard milieu of Frost and Stevens.) It follows immediately upon the flood tide of Symbolist and Aestheticist thought. This is one reason for its stress on the psychological values of poetry: the theorists of the fiction inherit a large dose of what Wilhelm Worringer called primitive space-shyness[12] and, as well, the fear of flux and time that is pervasive in the antinaturalistic poetry and poetics of the Symbolists and Aestheticists. But the fear of space and time, which informs the escapist poetics of Aestheticism, and which in part informs the aesthetics of the supreme fiction, is balanced in the theorists of the supreme fiction by an unwillingness to give up the world for the transcendent beauties of artifice; by a sense that apocalyptic transmutation is a more dreadful thing than the ugly pressures and messiness of the empirical world. As a theorist of the supreme fiction Frost believes that the poem as fictive nature preserves its value only insofar as it can meet, welcome, and enclose within its own boundaries the antifictive, which is revealed, as we have seen in so many of the poems, by moments of ironic consciousness.

3

In Frost's poetics the creative imagination comes alive only as it engages the linguistic medium: the locus or residence of the fictive nature is there, in the medium. From this organicist view of the creative process flow Frost's many statements on the poet's performance in language—the poet is a linguistic athlete for Frost—and particularly his many statements on the centrality of metaphor, its role as the master formative technique and strategy in the making of poems as fictive natures. But I would suggest that because the value of the poem as fictive nature is grasped only dialectically, Frost's sense of *actual* nature, his sense of reality's composition (more precisely, its frequent lack of composition) is what presses his redemptive impulse into action. The existential context of the poet as maker of fictive symbols is at once dangerously chaotic and threatening, and adventurously open and quiescent before the molding power of his imagination.

Through the philosophy of Nietzsche and his existential inheritors we have come to appreciate the frightening side of the "absurd"; we have come to understand very well the fact of "otherness" and flux and meaninglessness, and all of their dread-inducing implications. But we have not yet come to the proper appreciation of the absurd's loveliness, which is a beckoning formlessness that calls out for the shaping hand of the artist. It is not, I think, until William James, who came to feel—as Nietzsche rarely did—that the chaos of the given universe was not so frightening after all, who felt that a universe in part unshaped was the proper home for the shaping spirit of the mind, that we come to understand, for modern poets, the necessity of chaos. (It is perhaps clear that I am compromising the meaning of "chaos" with such hedged phrases as "frequent lack of composition" and "a universe in part unshaped." It would be a mistake, in Frost, to interpret "chaos" in an unqualified sense, though he himself has spoken of "utter chaos." He spoke more truly of his position when he spoke of that portion of experience not yet worked all the way up into form. I think that the meaning of "chaos" most applicable to Frost is that of "chasm" or "gulf." Whether reality is total disorder or not, it is "other"—there is a yawning separation between mind, its needs, and reality as it is: and it is that quality that moves the poet's imagination to project its fictions of an integrated self and world.) Frost felt often the impingement of a nightmare universe upon his inner serenity but he prized that nightmare as well as feared it because it was his aesthetic *raison d'être*, his motive for making metaphors:

> My object is true form—is and always will be. . . . I fight to be allowed to sit cross-legged on the old flint pile and flake a lump into an artifact.[13]

> You wish the world made better than it is, more poetical. You are that kind of poet. I would rate as the other kind. I wouldn't give a cent to see the world, the United States or even New York made better. I want them left just as they are for me to make poetical on paper. I don't ask anything done to them that I don't do to them myself. I'm a mere selfish artist most of the time. I have no quarrel with the material. The grief will be simply if I can't transmute it into poems. I don't want the world made safer for poetry or easier. To hell with it. That is its own lookout. Let it stew in its own materialism. No, not to Hell with it. Let it hold its own position while I do it in art. My whole anxiety is for myself as a performer. Am I any good?[14]

> I thank the Lord for crudity which is rawness, which is raw material, which is the part of life not yet worked up into form, or at least not worked all the way up. Meet with the fallacy of the foolish: having had a glimpse of finished art, they forever after pine for a life that shall be nothing but finished art. Why not a world safe for art as well as democracy. A real artist delights in roughness for what he can do to it. He's the brute who can knock the corners off the marble block. . . .[15]

One may detect in the above a tone of bravado, perhaps even a posture of callousness. Yet Frost is generally not so callous nor does he usually make a practice of whistling in the dark. As a poet he came to cherish chaos—it was his *materia poetica*, as Stevens put it—but his act of cherishing was fully earned because the man had already seen behind the surface crudeness and surface troubles, the politician's chaos, into the structure of misery which is the existential world. There is a difference between "griefs" and "grievances,"[16] Frost once said, and that is the difference between the "immedicable woes"—which are griefs—which "nothing can be done for" because they are built into the human condition, indeed define one's humanness as much as one's humanness is defined by the shaping or creative tendency of the mind. "Grievances," on the other hand, are things that can be medicated, even cured by the social do-gooders and liberal politicians who were the objects of Frost's scorn. Whatever pain *they* can ease, he suggested, is finally not real because not permanent. What the poet is possessed by—a vision of structural disturbances at the core of being—cannot be cured, is a "grief," the condition which constitutes the tragic vision and the condition which the poet must face and evoke in his poems. In a letter to Louis Untermeyer—who at the time was in his Marxist phase—Frost put this bitter pill to the liberal mind: "Leave the evils that can be remedied or even palliated. You are of age now to face essential Hell. Cease from the optimism as much that makes good as that sees good. Come with me into the place of tombs and outer darkness."[17] Fourteen years later Frost reminded Untermeyer again: "It was designed to be a sad world, how sad we won't keep on telling each other over and over. . . ."[18]

The setting of our lives, Frost wrote in his "Letter to *The Amherst Student*," is a setting of "hugeness and confusion," of "black and utter chaos"[19] and, his advice to Untermeyer to the contrary, he did keep telling himself that that was so. What Frost meant to say to Untermeyer, I believe, is that though this is so, it is in itself no reason to collapse, in a yielding mass of plaintiveness and fear, as William James put it,[20] and while giving in to the massiveness of all that confusion, give up as well the autonomy of our will and the creative force within us which may transmute painful confusion into poetry. I would not trace the origin of Frost's tragic vision to his terrible years at the Derry, New Hampshire farm—that, surely, is the kind of sociological pretension which makes "grievances" of "griefs"—but very early in his married life he composed a poem (a rather bad one) expressing a philosophical overview. (I mention the Derry years only to indicate that Frost came to his worldview early and maintained it unswervingly throughout his life, regardless of his personal and economic status: from the desperate early days in New Hampshire, when publishers only rarely looked upon his poems with favor; when his mental grip on things seemed always on the verge of slipping, and when his marriage seemed at the point of homicidal violence, to the late comfortable years of fame, the years of the fifties and early sixties, when he became the toast of nations and the friend of presidents and dictators.) The poem that I allude to, "The Trial by Existence,"[21] suggests with a tone of doctrinal assurance an image of the self trapped in a temporally enclosed world of endless bewilderment and pain-dealing circumstances. What is interesting about the poem is that it allows for the trapped self no hope whatsoever of freedom, no visionary glimpse into the resolution of the human condition. It is of the essence of the trial that the outcome be unknown and unknowable. For all we can know, here and now, and as long as we are bound up in flesh and bone, is overwhelming confusion. Our great triumph is our ability to survive, to maintain our serenity, and to hack out a personal order in the dangerous jungles of existence.

In a late poem called "The Delphic Oracle on Plotinus," W. B. Yeats evokes his questing hero swimming through the archetypal seas of experience, with salt caked into his burning but not quite blinded eyes. The quester moves steadily, with direction, toward the golden shore which is dim and very far away but finally apprehendable and finally reached in "News From the Delphic Oracle," a poem written in Yeats's last years. Yeats offers his "Delphic Oracle" poems at the end of a long career of search, not as fictions bearing only dramatic "truth," but as a bitterly won statement on the nature of things; the "Delphic Oracle" poems are meant to bear eschatological import. Frost's "The Trial by Existence," though inferior as poetic achievement, and tactlessly doctrinal as well, is thematically a far grimmer poem—it cuts the poet-quester off from any transcendental meaning—there is no golden shore—and leaves him only his salt-caked eyes to contemplate. In such circumstances the poetics of the supreme fiction flourishes.

The poet, then, has no choice but to confront as ultimate fact of human experience what Frost called the "larger excruciations"[22] and the poem itself becomes a "figure of the will braving alien entanglements."[23] The poet's addressing of pain and complexity marks the initiation of the creative process, engagement with the destructive element of real experience. There is, admittedly, a tone of dark psychological solemnity in this description of the creative process—perhaps too dark—and though it is in certain respects an accurate reflection of the situation of the artist

—an accurate reflection of the situation of every man, according to Frost —that tone is itself transmuted as the poet transmutes confusion, shapes the lump of crude experience into a structured artifact. The mood of dark solemnity gives way under the pressure of the creative act to a mood of delight. The poet delights in the roughness of the world because it is finally not an unbearable weight for him but the occasion of aesthetic muscle-flexing. In a striking passage Wallace Stevens said that the "violence without" is matched by an equal "violence from within"—the second kind of violence is imagination's.[24] The equivalent in Frost is the roughness outside which is met by the roughness from inside, the brute power of imagination which enables the poet-sculptor to smash the corners off the block of marble as he wills his creation of order.

4

All freedom from the excruciation of existence is purely aesthetic achievement. For the poet it has its locus in the process and completion of the act of creation. For the auditor the intransitive experience of the fiction freezes, for a moment, the relational thrust of his attention, encloses him in rapt contemplation of the wondrous transformations effected by the poem's metaphoric structure. The place of metaphor in poetry—"Poetry is simply made of metaphor,"[25] Frost said—and the place of metaphor in the affairs of consciousness is one of his favorite themes. Metaphoric vision is central not only to his poetics but to his general theory of knowing because, with Nietzsche and Vaihinger, he believes that metaphor is the basis of all thinking.

The pragmatic view of consciousness that we find in Frost and William James bears a family resemblance to the neo-Kantian epistemology of Ernst Cassirer, but there are crucial differences. Kant and the neo-Kantians trace the creative power of mind, its ability to project ordered, symbolic forms of the world, to the universally shared structure of our mental organization. Frost and James also see mind by its very nature as an active shaper of the world that it confronts. But they, unlike formal Kantian idealists, believe the acts of the mind to be impelled by our private needs and interests; the distinctive character of the individual consciousness, not the universal structure of mental organizations. Frost made numerous statements which suggest the indigenous creativity of mind and numerous others which suggest that all modes of thought—insofar as they project a coherently structured universe—are metaphoric in that they amalgamate into humanly meaningful wholes the disparate objects of nature's manifold.[26] The difference between Frost's position and Kantianism is a difference between an act of consciousness which functions within the poet's personal context of need, and one which functions epistemologically within the public context of a conceptual grasp of experience. Frost's metaphoric vision unifies his chaotic experience of lived reality:

> Greatest of all attempts to say one thing in terms of another is the philosophical attempt to say matter in terms of spirit, or spirit in terms of matter, to make final unity. That is the greatest attempt that ever failed. We stop just short there. But that is the height of all poetry, the height of all thinking, the height of all poetic thinking, the attempt to say matter in terms of spirit and spirit in terms of matter. It is wrong to call anybody a materialist simply because he tries to say spirit in terms of matter, as if that were a sin. Materialism is not the attempt to say all in terms of matter. The only materialist . . . is the man who gets lost in his material without a gathering metaphor to throw it into shape and order. He is the lost soul.[27]

Metaphor is the master figure for the poet like Frost[28] who would create the poem as fictive nature; in and through metaphor shape, order, and unity are engendered upon a disordered universe. Unity and order are not found "out there," discovered with the help of metaphor, because metaphoric vision is not a reflection of ontological structure (indeed, there is no ontological structure that can be known, in Frost's view): metaphor cannot be offered as having the cognitive value that a realist would claim for it. Neither, in Frost's thinking, is metaphor in poems constitutive in the precise idealistic sense that Kant said that the Understanding and its categories are constitutive of the phenomenal world, nor in the looser sense that Cassirer claimed for the different forms of consciousness and language.

In his broadening of Kant's idealistic theory of mind, Cassirer destroys the hegemony of scientific rationalism by allowing a variety of modes of consciousness to be constitutive of reality and to claim an area of knowledge each in their own distinctive way. Several of Cassirer's students, if not Cassirer himself, in a desire to save literature and the arts from extreme logical positivists like Rudolf Carnap and A. J. Ayer, argue in decidedly un-Kantian fashion that there is an aesthetic mode of constructing reality which yields a special kind of knowledge. The difficulty is that when Cassirer's students begin to define the world projected in art they do so wholly in terms of his categories of mythic consciousness—the mythic form of consciousness is not, however, peculiarly aesthetic. What Cassirer calls the "primeval mythico-religious" consciousness (especially attractive to students of Blake) is a quality of the primitive mind in general and its moments of monistic vision, when the spark of subjectivity jumps the gap between self and other, and a union between self and other is created. In the mythic consciousness of reality all phenomena become "positively identical with one another," exist as "one single plane of being."[29] Insofar as there are vestiges of the primitive mentality in modern men, mythic thinking becomes a universal mode of human experience. Cassirer insists as neo-Kantian that the mind of the poet is constitutive of the world in its act of creation, but he cannot ground the constitutive imagination in the personal subjectivity of the poet, the unique embodied self. For Cassirer it is not the poet's distinctive subjectivity which impells the constitutive imagination, but those categories of consciousness which the poet shares with all perceivers, and which originate in the transpersonal, mythic mind. Cassirer's is a theory that cannot account for original genius.

Though he may finally fail, Frost, unlike idealists, tries mightily to make metaphoric vision in poems distinctive to the poet's way of apprehending. He believes that the metaphoric habit is a basic, universal habit of mind, but he refuses to refer his unique vision to the neo-Kantian categories of poetic consciousness—that intersubjective poet in every man. He has too much respect for the demands of the linguistic medium, is too much aware of the powerful transformative effect of language on vision in the creative process to believe that there is anything but an unbridgeable chasm between aesthetic fictions and the fictions of everyday life, between the poet's act of the mind and all other acts of the mind.

We face perhaps the most radical implication in Frost's poetics. Since epistemology is the branch of philosophy which is concerned with the study of how and what we can all know, the aesthetics of the fiction stands outside the realm of epistemological implication because fictions, at least Frost's, are the aesthetic projections in language of what William James found to be an irreducibly unique and private consciousness. The study of Frost's aesthetic fictions moves us firmly into phenomenological psychology, into the study of the poet's individualized and varying acts of consciousness, as they are radiated in his poetic landscapes—from the fictions of redemption ("Going For Water"), to the fictions of self-damnation ("Bereft," "A Servant to Servants"). The fictions of poetry are for Frost, in contrast to neo-Kantians, epistemologically unsanctioned, free-floating structures. They are peculiar to the poet who projects them because they are embedded in a linguistic medium which preserves both the fictive world and the distinctive consciousness which has shaped it. Frost's imaginative landscapes are unveilings of the hidden self.

We can now measure more precisely the distance between Kant and the pragmatist Kantians of "as if," Hans Vaihinger and William James, by remembering that the constitutive acts of the mind in Kant's philosophy do not (as it is sometimes thought) give us "as if," fictive constructions of the world; they give us the necessary structure of the phenomenal world because our a priori categories of consciousness determine what we can experience. For Vaihinger, James, and other pragmatically oriented philosophers and poets of supreme fictions, the value of the "as if" act of mind lies exactly in our freely choosing to impose the fiction upon the phenomenal world, and then freely choosing to divest the phenomenal of the fictive, to see it for what it is in its brute facticity. Vaihinger, James, and Frost do not disagree seriously with Kant about the necessary structure of phenomenal experience—they are not solipsists; they begin where Kant leaves off. They are not concerned with universal (i.e., epistemological) questions, but with the freedom of the self to impose its personally needed structures upon a world which too often thwarts our deepest interests. Man is the symbol-making animal Cassirer says; man, because he is man, has really no choice about that. Kenneth Burke reminds us that man is also distinguished as the symbol-*using* animal, and that idea points us to the basis of an aesthetics of the supreme fiction.

The philosophy of the fictive, "as if" thrust of consciousness may be moored in the epistemology of Kant, as Vaihinger once demonstrated,[30] but it owes its modern aesthetic formulation much more to the psychology of William James, who allows the poet the freedom to become aware of his fictive projection *as* projection; the freedom to step outside of his fictions, so to speak, and watch them as they fall short—fail to reach beyond themselves to the thing itself. The poetics of the supreme fiction —which exalts the molding powers of the mind—is informed by a healthy Jamesian skepticism and humility, an ironic consciousness that creates in the poet a desire to extinguish the ever-mediating self and the carving, order-making needs of his mind and to acknowledge the given order, the things of this world in themselves, in their places. Frost rarely forgot the

stubborn things of this world that lay outside the fictive shapes of experience given in his poems. These things, in their chaos and in their
beauty, motivated him to write his poems. The things of the world, Frost
believed, finally resist the transformational magic of metaphor.

To extend the last point: the poetics of the supreme fiction blends the
modern phenomenological sense of realism with its idealism. (The later
James reminds us that even though the mind projects its pragmatically-
motivated constructions upon the world, there is something within experience itself, as the empiricists have defined that concept for us, that
makes irreducible demands upon our attention.) And this paradoxical
blend illuminates Frost's temperament. Though he believed in the dynamic shaping power of metaphoric integrations, I don't think that he
believed in the extreme idealism of the neo-Kantian tradition which often
celebrates human creativity at the expense of received experience (the poor
old "ordinary universe," as Denis Donoghue has called it). The mind is
creative, yes, but not because reality is utterly malleable before the poet's
shaping consciousness. Anyone familiar with Frost knows that an enormous hunk of "things as they are" (Stevens's *bête noire*) gets into his
poems. Frost once accused Stevens of writing about "bric-a-brac"; Stevens
retorted that Frost wrote about "subjects." The difference between "bric-a-
brac" and "subjects" underscores a profound difference in attitude toward
the given world. For Frost the creative mind goes to work on a world
which in large part resists imaginative change; a world with much fixed,
naturally-given symbolic meaning which insists on being there in the
poem; a world which the poet sometimes wants to be there because he
finds it not unreceptive to the needs of self. Frost's creative perceptions
never transmute experience beyond recognition: the experienced universe
is cherished even as the mind works its magic, quietly reshaping things to
fit his needs. Stevens's fictions are impelled by a more radical commitment to the idealistic position; the world of his poems is often cleanly
severed from the world of ordinary perception. Robert Frost's fictions are
modest: the fictive orders that his mind insinuates into experience are
sometimes difficult to see.

5

One of the distinctive marks of a poetic consciousness, Frost believed,
is its acute awareness of the self-enclosing nature of fictive unifications;

a self-conscious awareness of fiction as fiction which is built into poetic structure itself. The beauty of fictive metaphor—its primary value—is that it carries such divided consciousness; it breaks down, even as it projects the "better nature":

> . . . unless you are at home in the metaphor, unless you have had your proper poetical education in the metaphor, you are not safe anywhere. Because you are not at ease with figurative values: you don't know the metaphor in its strengths and in its weaknesses. You don't know how far you may expect to ride it and when it may break down with you.[31]

A critical difference between poetic vision and other kinds of metaphoric vision (that are not poetically educated) is that the poet's fictions (or metaphoric structures), unlike the metaphorical structures offered under the name of science and philosophy, do not pretend to broad operational value, or to grand, metaphysical validity. Poetic fictions are offered humbly, without arrogance. Poems are not, as Harry Berger, Jr. notes in an important critique of Frost, "vast systems but focused and practical acts addressed to individual occasions."[32] From this critical difference spring many consequences: among them, the poet's humane valuation of those mind-resisting objects of this world which dance free of his controlling vision, an act which occurs simultaneously with his act of creating the fictive shapes of reality in metaphor. This duality of vision demanded by Frost's theory of metaphor we have seen brilliantly poised several times in his employment of simile. It is just this duality—and the psychical tension engendered in the reader—that Hans Vaihinger saw as indigenous to what he called "comparative apperception"—the basic act of consciousness that gets reflected in the "as if" form of discourse; where in the "as" we transform utterly one thing by transferring to it the qualities of another, and in the "if" state the impossibility of the whole transaction.[33]

This limited, modest reach of fictive metaphor is, curiously, its greatest strength, a quality that enables it to perform a double function. Needing to brave "alien entanglements," not to succumb to them by allowing the mad flow of the world to engulf the mind, the poet finds in the harmonized worlds projected by his metaphor the required psychological caressing. Within the tight boundaries of the aesthetic enclosure the poet can project his fictive orders; can change the original block of unhewn marble by informing it, and, by informing it, redeem the old nature—the given, actual nature, into a "better nature." Frost never has illusions about the difference between the world that he contemplates in and through his fictions and the world that resists the fiction. Not only does he have no illusions about the limited grasp of poetic vision, but he insists that both worlds be there in the poem, that the demands of the antifictive be assented to. Though the beauty of untruth, a Nietzschean and Wildean theme, is clearly Frost's theme as well, Frost's poetics asks for something which his poems have shown us over and over again: the constant vigil of a delicate ironic consciousness. "Poetry," he said, is a "momentary stay against confusion."[34] It is of the essence of a "stay" that there be something for it to stay *against*. Somehow, that "hugeness and confusion," the antifictive element that lies outside the fictive orderings of metaphor, must be allowed its place in the poem.

In his aestheticism Frost follows not Oscar Wilde, who in his anti-naturalism would turn us away from existential reality, but Nietzsche, who in his meditation on the origins of Greek tragedy made a plea for the primacy of aesthetic values not because they allow us to transcend to fairy-land, but because they encourage us to bear and confront what is often unbearable and unconfrontable. From Nietzsche's perspective Frost's imagination is under the care of Apollo, the god of form, serenity, and illusion who helps us to face up to that dreadful wisdom of Silenus which forms the very substratum of the fictive world of art. Apollonian redemption must be earned, Nietzsche believed, must be threatened by Dionysian horror and chaos; just as the Kantian "better nature" of art must be apprehended dialectically against the less-than-desired phenomenal world, things as they are. Such tensions within poetic structure and in the experience of the poem are reflections of a more fundamental tension in the relationship of mind and reality. What Kantians describe as the inventive factor in consciousness becomes, after Darwin and the pragmatists, not merely the ground of a cognitively coherent phenomenal experience but a life-preserving response to a hostile, life-denying world. Hans Vaihinger's *The Philosophy of 'As If'* is the meeting point of the diverse traditions of Kant, Nietzsche, Darwin, and William James, and a clear anticipation of Frost's view of the function of poetic imagining:

The fictive activity of the mind is an expression of the fundamental psychical forces; *fictions* are *mental structures*. The psyche weaves this aid to thought out of itself; for the mind is inventive; under the compulsion of necessity, stimulated by the outer world, it discovers the store of contrivances that lie hidden within itself. The organism finds itself in a world full of contradictory sensations, it is exposed to the assaults of a hostile external world, and in order to preserve itself, it is forced to seek every possible means of assistance, external as well as internal. In necessity and pain mental evolution is begun, in contradiction and opposition consciousness awakes, and man owes his mental development more to his enemies than to his friends.[35]

The pressure from the antifictive—man's enemy in Vaihinger's terms—is guaranteed in Frost's poetics because the aesthetics of the supreme fiction subsumes the aesthetics of play as well. Together, the fictive and the playful thrusts of consciousness distinguish the poet's imagination and, together, they satisfy the expectations of Frost's organic view of the creative process by grounding imagination in a medium. The poet is a player in Frost, an athlete who performs freely in language, accomplishing magnificent feats therein.

Though the poet's act of the mind may resemble all acts of the mind insofar as all human perception is in some sense metaphoric, creative of the world, the poet's constructive vision is plagued by loneliness and the dissatisfaction of incompleteness until it finds a medium in which it can release its playful energies and in so doing reach beyond the purities of its own fictive shapings of reality. As he frees himself from the world by redeeming it in fictive order, Frost's playful, ironic consciousness ties the poem into the world as given, as unredeemed. The only mode of discourse, Frost implies, that can at once satisfy the fictive and the antifictive is poetic discourse. The distinctiveness of poetic discourse, of fictive metaphor, is that in the process of breaking down before reality it breaks itself down in its playfulness; it cleanly severs its fictive order, the better nature, from the real order, even as it recognizes the real order, welcomes it into the confines of the poem and gives the mind a reason to enclose itself. Poetic fictions can be "the opium of the people," in Frank Kermode's words, but not Frost's—his poems do not "sever us from our losses." They *do* allow us to make discoveries of the "hard truth here and now," "see the shadow of the gable," "hear the discoveries of dissonance."

At this juncture, an important qualification of Frost's aesthetics of the fiction is strongly urged by a series of poems which I have already discussed: among them, "Storm Fear," "Home Burial," "A Servant to Servants," "The Witch of Coös," "Bereft," and "Come In." Thus far, the underlying assumption in Frost's aesthetics has been the idea that the poetic fictions of redemptive imagination *always* surpass the given world, that the fictions transform actual nature into a "better nature," even as the skeptical consciousness of the poet will allow the difficult and alien world of nature to have its say. But poems such as "Bereft" and "A Servant to Servants" suggest that redemptive imagination, the dominant force in Frost's consciousness, has its black underside—actual nature can be transformed into a "lesser nature" when imagination is impelled by a disturbed consciousness. The telling sign of such self-destructive consciousness is its monolithic, absolutizing character: single vision reigns, the saving skepticism of ironic consciousness is extinguished. Enclosures then become houses of horror.

The contrary of an enclosure of horror is an enclosure of pure pleasure fantasy. But they, too, are the constructions of single vision; they, too, in their absolutizing tendency imprison the self in illusions through which the self and its world become constituted as an integrated, organic whole that can never be. Frost rarely sinks into the never-never land of heart's desire, though such poems as "Rose Pogonias" and "The Quest of the Purple-Fringed" come close. The ideal aesthetic enclosure contains contraries: the "better nature" of Frost's redemptive moments must accommodate the antifictive. Frost's best poems show us that redemptive consciousness must live side by side with ironic consciousness. No less important, the black fictions of his desperate moments of tragic vision must accommodate the common and innocent things of experience that do not threaten—the leaves in "Bereft" surely do not "hiss" and "strike." Such common things are themselves health-giving and redeeming *before* the poet's transforming consciousness goes to work on them. Some of Frost's better poems (I refer to "Going For Water" and "Two Look at Two" as examples) tell us that redemptive imagination may be encouraged to create fictions by nature's receptivity to self, by its loveliness, as well as by its nightmarish otherness and its terrors.

It may be helpful here to recall one historical fact of Frost's development as poet: he began to hit the stride of his poetic maturity in the era of Imagism. Although it is true that Frost's personal relations with Ezra Pound and Amy Lowell were never very warm, and his reactions to the doctrines of Imagism often harsh, the Imagist revolt did touch sympathetic chords in his poetic. The Imagist insistence that in poems the intellectual powers ought to be repressed in order that the objects of this world might emerge in all their preconceptual particularity generally recalls the earthy side of the Transcendentalist movement in America. Specifically it is an echo of some of the major attitudes that emerge in *Walden,* a book that Frost had intimate and loving knowledge of. The natural things of this world have a therapeutic effect on us, Thoreau believed, and we can see the consequences of that faith in the object in many of Frost's poems. Through the natural object, the anchor of inventive consciousness, Frost achieves his most powerful effects—certain evocative images emit a luminous after-glow that haunts us long, long after we have experienced the poem itself. It is thus that we remember the *bright green snake* of "Mowing"; those *bees in the wall* in "The Black Cottage"; the *broken drinking goblet* of "Directive"; the bed of *faded leaves stuck together* of "Hyla Brook"; the lumbering, *earth-bound oxen* of "The Mountain"; the *puzzled little horse* of "Stopping by Woods"; that *ripple of water* in "For Once, Then, Something."

6

I quote at some length, first from Frost's most suggestive summary statement of his poetics, the "Letter to *The Amherst Student,*" and second from a conversation with Sidney Cox which reenforces that statement:

> There is at least so much good in the world that it admits of form and the making of form. . . . When in doubt there is always form to go on with. Anyone who has achieved the least form to be sure of it, is lost to the larger excruciations. . . . The artist[,] the poet[,] might be expected to be the most aware of such assurance. But it is really everybody's sanity to feel it and live by it. Fortunately, too, no forms are more engrossing, gratifying, comforting, staying than those lesser ones we throw off like vortex rings of smoke . . . a basket, a letter, a garden, a room, an idea, a picture, a poem. . . . The background in hugeness and confusion shading away from where we stand into black and utter chaos; and against the background any small man-made figure of order and concentration. What pleasanter than this should be so? . . . we look out on it with an instrument or tackle it to reduce it. . . . We like it, we were born to it, born used to it and have practical reasons for wanting it there. To me any little form I assert upon it is velvet, as the saying is, and to be considered

for how much more it is than nothing. If I were a Platonist I should have to consider it, I suppose, for how much less it is than everything.[36]

Tragedy, yes, Robert said. There is always tragedy. That is what life is. But you must have heard me say a good many times that nothing is so composing to the spirit as composition. We make a little order where we are, and the big sweep of history on which we can have no effect doesn't overwhelm us. We do it with colors, or we do it with a garden, or we do it with the furnishings of a room, or we do it with sounds and words. We make a little form and we gain composure. One of the ways that goes far back into history, Robert said, is designing coins. Some of them are crude, of course, and have no form. But from the earliest times most of them have it, have design. They're always, or nearly always, circular. And within that little circle you make an animal or a face or some human figures, with proportion and appropriateness. . . . They are very lasting.[37]

A number of Frost's themes are here: the view of the poem as a form of psychic enclosure that shuts out the "larger excruciations" which must be there because they give the clean, well-lighted room of the poem a reason for being; the idea that the therapeutic values of the creative act are available to others besides the artist; the sense of the precariousness of the poem as psychological resting place, its smallness underscored by the "background in hugeness and confusion"; the status of the poem as subjective imposition which has no place in being. Aesthetic forms, unlike the Platonic Forms, Frost implies, have no objective value; they tell us nothing at all about the structure of reality, only about the needs of self in a universe which does not have Platonic kinds of explanation.

As a form of enclosure the aesthetic universe is responsive to the human will, encourages an expansiveness, the humanizing impulse of self. In actual nature, the self is a lost and ever-diminishing figure. Only in the aesthetic nature does the self, impelled by redemptive urges, become gardener of the world again: only in the aesthetic experience do we regain Eden. As form of enclosure the poem saves us from being what Frost called the world's only sinner, the man who cannot coerce experience into coherence. But the apocalypse of form is only partial in poems because the fictive universe does not consume the existential universe. The spirit of Northrop Frye hovers about this description of Frost's poetics. Perhaps we can understand Frost's position best if we compare his sense of the fiction created by metaphor with what Frye calls, variously, apocalyptic, archetypal, or radical metaphor—metaphor which, as it moves into what he calls its "anagogic" phase, projects a world of total identity.[38]

Frye and Frost both claim that the fictions of poetry have no epistemological or metaphysical values. Frye, a good neo-Kantian symbolist who sees the poem as a second nature, believes that the fictions of literature project the desires of man; that they are purely psychological in import, and appease, as Murray Krieger has suggested, the pleasure principle.[39] The crucial difference between Frye and Frost is that Frye's fiction-projecting metaphor, as it is shifted into anagogic high gear, utterly consumes the dualistic world of experience, eliminating the chasm between subject and object, locating all things within a giant human form. All of this recalls Frye's heritage from Blake and Cassirer:

> . . . in the imagination anything goes that can be imagined, and the limit of the imagination is a totally human world. Here we recapture, in full consciousness, that original lost sense of identity with our surroundings, where there is nothing outside the mind of man, or something identical with the mind of man. . . . Literature does not reflect life, but it doesn't escape or withdraw from life either: it swallows it. And the imagination won't stop until it's swallowed everything. . . . If even time, the enemy of all living things, and to poets, at least the most hated and feared of all tyrants, can be broken down by the imagination, anything can be.[40]

For metaphor to function so as to project such a monistic fiction it must (in a traditional sense) cease to be metaphor. It must never "break down"; the terms within the vehicle must devour the tenor; the fixed and the definites of experience must be unloosened, must be made to flow into that universal human body in a spectacular vision of total identity. Frye is explicit about the value he places on apocalyptic metaphor: it is literature's greatest moment when the imagination moves from its wintry, ironic phase into the apocalyptic phase, the serene summer of romance where metaphor no longer tells the sad story that all things cannot be identified, or synthesized in encompassing unity. Exerting anagogic power, apocalyptic metaphor whispers to us lovingly that any distinction between tenor and vehicle is only an illusion; that a monistic principle is immanent in all things—not, as Schelling once supposed, really there, metaphysically there, but there because a certain form of consciousness molds things that way.

> If scientific thought wishes to describe and explain reality it is bound to use its general method, which is that of classification and systematization. Life is divided into separate provinces that are sharply distinguished from each other. The boundaries between the different spheres are not insurmountable barriers; they are fluent and fluctuating. There is no specific difference between the various realms of life. Nothing has a definite, invariable, static shape. By a sudden metamorphosis everything may be turned into everything.

> . . . The feeling of the indestructible unity of life is so strong and unshakable as to deny and to defy the fact of death.[41]

I cite Cassirer's phenomenology of mythic imagination at this point because, like Frye's apocalyptic metaphor, it has common sources in the idea that primitive constructions of the universe are monistically empowered. In the anagogic phase of metaphor, all skeptical consciousness is extinguished and redemptive consciousness reigns alone.

In Frost's version of the supreme fiction, as in Wallace Stevens's version, the existential universe always asserts itself against the fictional universe, invading its residence within the poem itself, halting the monistic thrust of metaphor, reminding us of the stubborn independence of particular things in the world's body—their unwillingness to be anything but what they are, as they assert their ontological autonomy. This impingement of the existential within the aesthetic enclosure of the poem tells of the perilous place of form against the background of hugeness and chaos; isolates more than ever the self's littleness and aloneness in an alien universe, even as the self establishes itself as an Adamic giant within the garden of the poem. No wonder that Frye impatiently dismissed Stevens for his theory of metaphor: the theory was "regrettably unclear" because it seemed to Frye not to give up the meaning of "simile."[42] Since Stevens includes the meaning of simile in his theory of metaphor, his whole desire to annihilate the gulf between subject and object, consciousness and existence, is seriously undermined.

For reasons having to do with their understanding of the genesis of all art, indeed with the genesis of all intellectual activity, Cassirer and Frye cannot grant that some poets *intend* to preserve the alienation and isolation of consciousness, the inhumanness of the other, and the reality of death. As Cassirer has shown, in the monism of the primitive consciousness there is a belief in the indissoluble unity of all life (all empirical appearances to the contrary). Some such notion is the quasi-religious basis of Cassirer, Frye, and a number of modern literary critics who, though far apart on many essential matters, all argue that metaphor is not a mere pointing to the similiarity of two distinct entities, but a revelation of the absolute identity of only apparently dissimilar entities. Both Frost and Stevens, in opposition to this metaphor-worship of modern criticism, offer their crucial dissent to modernism when they insist that somewhere metaphoric identity breaks down (because the overt distinctions insisted upon by simile are built into metaphor as well) and, as it does, the poem reaches back to the confusing and sometimes dangerous real world, which often repulses the creative impulse of our desire to shape out a fully human universe.

The theory that the poem as fictive nature can simultaneously assert and deny its magic world characterizes the doubleness in many of Frost's poems. With remarkable fidelity to the spirit of the *Critique of Judgment* —a fidelity we do not sense in many neo-Kantians—Frost sees the poem performing a strangely double function, a kind of now-you-see-it-now-you-don't aesthetic magic. In the tradition of the supreme fiction the lens of fictive metaphor focuses the world, as Nietzsche put it, as an aesthetic phenomenon. At the same time it allows an aesthetically unconstituted universe to shine in, to impact on the mind unprotected by the molding categories of the "better nature." It was Kant who brought such ironic consciousness initially to poetics because it was Kant who believed that the very "regulative" character of art's better world would demand we carry into aesthetic consciousness the alternative perspectives of ordinary consciousness, the phenomenal reality constituted by Understanding's categories. Willing or not, the duality we have seen at the basis of "fictive metaphor" tends to engender in the reader a duality in his experience of the poem. Kant's description of the aesthetic nature as surpassing actual nature implies the necessity of a dialectical awareness in the auditor: a grasping of the value of that which *surpasses* demands that we be conscious of that which is *surpassed.*

Such dialectical awareness in us, demanded by the dialectic within the poem of fictive and antifictive, establishes the limits of supreme fictions: the gap between the fictive world and the real gives both definition and circumscription to the better world of human desire. It is because of that very gap that the fictive becomes a critique of the shabbier, less-than-ideal facts and ways of nature and human behavior as we know them in our day-to-day living. On the other hand, it is also by virtue of that gap that we bring the norms of the common and the ordinary against the fictive as a corrective and a critique of the sad distortions wrought by the fictive "world elsewhere" when the fictive is projected by the neurotic and the obsessed—those psychically wounded who frequently turn up in Frost's poems. For these reasons the poem as supreme fiction is not the problematic, autonomous and self-sufficient universe—so difficult to relate to the given human world—that it has been made out to be by many post-Kantian critics. It exists in this world as we know it. The poem itself encourages us to recognize that fact—such recognition allows the fiction to function *as fiction*.

Were he to respond to Kant, Frost might have modified his view in much the way that George Santayana did. Santayana, who brought the Kantian aesthetics of the supreme fiction into American philosophy and poetics in 1900 in his *Interpretations of Poetry and Religion*, believed that the poet must disintegrate the world constituted by ordinary consciousness—the "fictions of common perception"—because "the world built up by comon sense and natural science is an inadequate world. . . . The great function of poetry . . . is . . . to repair to the material of experience, seizing hold of the reality of sensation and fancy beneath the surface of conventional ideas, and then out of that living but indefinite material to build new structures, richer, finer, fitter to the primary tendencies of our nature. . . ." Santayana's definition of art as an assimilating of phenomena to the "deeper innate cravings of the mind" is close to the *Critique of Judgment*, where Kant described the aesthetic representation of reality as superior to the world of our everyday experience.[43]

The phenomenal universe constituted by the Kantian Understanding may be conceptually coherent (Frost and Santayana could agree) but, existentially confronted, it is often psychologically threatening; the epistemologically satisfactory universe of rational man is aesthetically wanting and must be transformed. As it both asserts and denies its "better nature," the poem generates an image of the elemental conflict which is the genesis of its being. In Frost's words: as "figure of the will braving alien entanglements," as figure for the creative process itself, the poem asserts its fictive universe—in this way it redeems—and it undermines its redemption when an ironic consciousness insists upon those very entanglements of the existential context which its fictive character would transcend.

There is the madness of Ahab, who in his monomania stares too long into the fires of experience, and there is the madness of the mind swamped in illusions of order and peace, the madness of the Company accountant in *Heart of Darkness*. Frye's apocalyptic metaphor, which burns up the existential in anagogic identification, would seem to be productive of the second kind of madness, and Frost's poetics, though it may seem as well to lean dangerously toward the madness of the second variety, actually avoids both. In his "Letter to *The Amherst Student*" he suggested that the fiction is what is sane and good. In a letter to Louis Untermeyer he saw an "exhalation from some form of reality" as the source of "sanity and energy."[44] But I suspect that he spoke more truly for himself when he told John Bartlett that an "in and out existence" is the best existence.[45] And that is precisely his ideal of the structure of the aesthetic experience —"out" in its transcendence through fictional form; "in" in its breaking down of fictional form.

Perhaps Frost's conception of "monometaphor" defines his position most precisely.[46] Monometaphor is artistic craziness—a kind of monomania, Frost believed—because from its "flint and steel" jump sparks which catch in the lint of the world and touch off the great conflagration. That, I think, characterizes Frye's conception of apocalyptic metaphor, and that, Frost suggested, is the kind of delusion that the humane mind must avoid. Great are Darwin and Marx, he once said, because they originally imposed the metaphor which became a world hypothesis; they had the strength not to accept the fashionable metaphor of the day. Greater still, he might have said, is the poet who imposes the transformative metaphor and simultaneously reveals the thing out there for what it is. This type of figurative language, so far from attracting deluded (and dangerous) men who cannot distinguish between their private "utopian" visions and the world of action, promotes the psychological fitness and proper respect for a pluralistic universe that no other form of discourse can promote.

Frost, therefore, always distinguishes what so much poetry written since Blake generally obscures: the difference between the poet's mind (and the world shaped by his desire) and the rest of reality. In insisting upon that distinction Frost distinguishes his aesthetic from the general idealist aesthetic which has dominated poetry and literary theory since the romantic movement. It ought to go without saying (but it does not in these days of Blake's ascendency) that a belief such as Frost's in the mind's power to shape its world need not imply that Frost wished also to celebrate with Blake, Cassirer, and Frye, the monism of the primitive mind which does not know distinction between subject and object, wish and reality, word and thing.[47] Frost was committed in part to the idealistic celebration of the mind's creative power, but he refused to be a visionary, mythopoeic extremist in his commitment. The difficult paradox that Frost shares with James—that mind is creative within a *real, objective* world—though repugnant to logic, is a richly generative force in his poems and poetics. The lesson urged upon us by Frost, a lesson concentrated in his employment of simile, is that our redemptive thrust to heal the split between subject and object is balanced by a tragic recognition of the irredeemable alienation of consciousness in a world in which the object finally resists being subjectified.

7

We come more formally to the play element in Frost's poetics. The tradition of the aesthetics of play is closely linked to the tradition of the aesthetics of the supreme fiction. Both descend from Kant's view that in its aesthetic function—which he sharply distinguishes from his view, elaborated in the *Critique of Pure Reason*, of the imagination's reproductive function as a faculty of cognition—the imagination is free to exert its energies playfully: that is, for no specific end beyond the activity itself. But imaginative energy must be grounded in an artistic medium, Kant stressed, because pure play is not art.[48] In so grounding its exuberant force in a medium the imagination shapes an aesthetic nature whose essential character is "regulative," a character which affords the self, in the aesthetic experience, a mode of contemplating reality as possessing a kind of harmonious completeness that becomes deeply soothing as the setting within which we must work out our lives. The chief exponent of this aspect of Kantian aesthetic is Schiller and, beyond him, two lesser known theorists of play, Konrad Lange and Karl Groos.

A significant emphasis in Schiller's aesthetic theory derives from Kant's many statements in the *Critique of Judgment* to the effect that the artist manipulates illusions self-consciously—that he "announces a mere play," that he plays "without deceiving by it," that the work of art, as a creation of the play imagination, "does not desire to steal upon and ensnare the understanding."[49] As a Kantian Schiller emphasizes the affective power of art as play: its ability to heal the psychic wound of modernism—the self divided against itself—and to bring about our psychic integration. I quote from Schiller's *Letters on the Aesthetic Education of Man* to establish the link with Frost's theories, particularly as they are expressed in the "Letter to *The Amherst Student*," which strikingly parallels Schiller's view of art and its relationship to the real world:

> As long as man derives sensations from a contact with nature, he is her slave; but as soon as he begins to reflect upon her objects and laws he becomes her lawgiver. Nature, which previously ruled him as a power, now expands before him as an object. What is objective to him can have no power over him, for in order to become objective it has to experience his own power. As far and as long as he impresses a form upon matter, he cannot be injured by its effect; for a spirit can only be injured by that which deprives it of its freedom. Whereas he proves his own freedom by giving a form to the formless; where the mass rules heavily and without shape, and its undefined outlines are forever fluctuating between uncertain boundaries, fear takes up its abode: but man rises above any natural terror as soon as he knows how to mould it, and transform it into an object of his art.[50]

In the aesthetic experience, Schiller wrote, "we attend to the absence of all limits"[51] because "high indifference and freedom of the mind, united with power and elasticity, is the disposition in which a true work of art ought to dismiss us, and there is no better test of true aesthetic excellence."[52]

The plasticity of the world in the creative process, the creative autonomy of aesthetic imagination, the release from necessity and the movement into freedom, the concomitant release from the terror of a formless universe and the movement into the serenity of an ordered aesthetic world—all of these themes in Schiller are themes in Frost—all of this is achieved in the act of making a fictive world in creative play. In Schiller's words again: "a soul that takes pleasure in appearance does not take pleasure in what it receives but in what it makes."[53]

> The instinct of play likes appearance. . . . man has come to distinguish the appearance from the reality. . . .[54]

> . . . man possesses sovereign power only in the world of appearance, in the unsubstantial realm of imagination, only by abstaining from giving being to appearance. . . . It follows that the poet transgresses his proper limits when he attributes being to his ideal, and when he

gives this ideal aim a determined existence. . . . It is only by being frank or disclaiming all reality, that the appearance is aesthetical.[55]

The metaphor of poetry as play is as pervasive in Frost as it is in Schiller.[56] His most suggestive treatment of the idea is his introduction to E. A. Robinson's *King Jasper*. The meaning of play in Frost is generally double-edged, accounting not only for those psychological meanings invested in it by play aestheticians, but also for the idea that poetry is a kind of game and the poet's creative act analogous to the performance of a brilliant athlete. Frost's insistence on performance—on "scoring" as he put it—is at bottom an insistence that the poetic process be always linguistically grounded, that the poet shape the "new word" while working with and against the received conventions and patterns of language. Commenting on Robinson's "Miniver Cheevy" he said, "There is the way the last one turns up by surprise round the corner, the way the shape of the stanza is played with, the easy way the obstacle of verse is turned to advantage."[57]

What do I want to communicate but what a *hell* of a good time I had writing it? The whole thing is performance and prowess and feats of association. Why don't critics talk about those things? What a feat it was to turn that way and what a feat it was to remember that—to be reminded of that by this? Why don't they talk about that? Scoring. You've got to *score*.[58]

I look at a poem as a performance. I look on the poet as a man of prowess, just like an athlete. He's a performer. And the things you can do in a poem are very various. You speak of figures, tones of voice varying all the time. . . . Somebody has said that poetry among other things is the marrow of wit. . . . There's got to be wit. And that's very, very much left out of a lot of this labored stuff. It doesn't sparkle at all.[59]

Frost told John Bartlett in 1919 that he wrote poetry "for the fun of it"—"For the fun of it in the larger sense—for the devil of it."[60] In 1954 he told a reporter for *The Christian Science Monitor* that poetry is "like a wild-game preserve . . . where wild things live. This is the ultimate in poetry."[61] The wild things that live in poems are the poet's witty feats of language. The poem is the poet's preserve: an enclosed linguistic garden, a place where he can define his freedom; a place where he can perform feats of associative prowess outside the limits of ordinary language, creating the new word; even as the hunter, as he steps into the wild game preserve, may step beyond the laws of conservation, limited only by the prowess of his marksmanship. In the "wild free ways of wit and art"[62] the poet has the "greatest freedom of the material to move about in it and to establish relations in it regardless of time and space, previous relation. . . ."[63] "All I would keep for myself is the freedom of my material," Frost wrote, and "the condition of body and mind now and then to summons aptly from the vast chaos of all that I have lived through."[64] Or, returning to the metaphor of poetry as performance and game:

> You excel at tennis, vaulting, tumbling, racing or any kind of ball game because you have the art to put all you've got into it. You're completely alert. You're hotly competitive and yet a good sport. You're having fun, skillfully taking risks, increasing the hazards. Putting up the bar in the high jump, for instance. You deliberately limit yourself by traditional, artificial rules. What you try for is effective and appropriate form. And success is measured by surpassing performance, *including the surpassing of your former self* [italics mine].[65]

Aestheticians since Kant and Schiller, and especially since Bergson, have insisted that creativity and freedom stand in symbiotic relationship. Frost would agree, and would add that the act of creative freedom is located precisely in the poet's organic act of linguistic manipulation. As the poet begins his "surpassing performance" in language he is catapulted into a realm of freedom, beyond the limits of ordinary discourse, beyond even the limits of self. He enters the play world of the poem, a plastic world of appearance where the old self and the old world are transcended in the transformative magic of *as if*; a plastic world where (as in the archetypal Frost play poem, "Going For Water") psychic wholeness is regained as a new self is created, emerges in performance, and a sense of harmony between self and self, and self and nature is felt. Poems, like games, invite the poet-player to locate himself in a context wholly formalized—the lines are literally drawn in sports—invite him to define his freedom within the necessities of conventional enclosures. Paradoxically, those very necessities of conventional form are a freedom from the terrors of the formless universe of our experience, where there is too much freedom; where, as Schiller put it, the mind experiences the terror of indefiniteness. When the outlines of things "are forever fluctuating between uncertain boundaries," then does "fear take up its abode." Frost would agree except that he, with a keen eye for certain metaphors, would never have said that fear takes up its "abode." The self is plunged in fear in Frost's poems precisely because it does not have an abode. It is not having an abode which constitutes those "larger excruciations," and the transcendence of pain lies in the act—the creative act—of enclosing self in the abode, the "room" of the poem, those designed "circles" of form which are so satisfying, as Frost said to Sidney Cox.

But the protective room of the poem is more than just received form. It is, as well, the fictional shape created by the molding force of the poem's metaphoric vision. Nowhere does Frost indicate more incisively than in his "Introduction" to *King Jasper* the psychological necessities of aesthetic play and fiction-making; their intimate, mutually reenforcing relations; their dialectical opposition to the dark "griefs" harbored in the self, and the serenity within their projected enclosures which blocks out the interior pain and the ever-shifting formlessness of the backdrop against which we work out our existence. Frost had a perfect subject in E. A. Robinson, the "prince of heartachers,"[66] as he called him, "whose theme was unhappiness itself, but whose skill was as happy as it was playful."[67] What Frost says of Robinson is even truer of his own theories and poems. It is difficult not to hear a great deal of Frost himself in this description of Robinson; difficult to suppress, at this point, Stevens's couplet from *Esthétique du Mal*:

> Natives of poverty, children of malheur
> The gaiety of language is our seigneur.

Robinson's life, Frost wrote, despite the profundity of his pain, was a "revel in the felicities of language. And not just to no purpose."[68] "Give us immedicable woes—woes that nothing can be done for—woes flat and final. And then to play. The play's the thing. Play's the thing. All virtue in 'as if.' "[69] In the "wild free ways of wit and art," the poet-athlete playfully engages the delights of language, performing those wonderful feats of linkage that create his fictions—the houses of poetry which free the poet (as he makes them) from the necessities of ordinary language and poetic convention, and free him (as he completes them) from the "immedicable woes" and the disorders of self and nature. The theoretical stance suggested by these remarks is difficult and sobering. Frost draws a distinction between the irremediable misery which the authentic poet confronts—what he called a "grief"—and the hell-of-a-good-time he has in writing the poem. A poem's most significant value would lie not in its presumed ability to change the world, or to give us a unique kind of knowledge of human affairs (poets rarely do these sorts of things, the grandiose claims of many modern poets and critics to the contrary), but in the therapeutic import of aesthetic performance. A poem's power for the poet is wholly personal, private in its effects: he makes his self anew. Frost's theory of poetic value may be open to the charge of triviality, but it makes minimal common sense and it is believable—which is more than we can say for the claims of romantics like Walt Whitman and Hart Crane who say that poetry can spur revolutions in consciousness, can give a people a mythology for living.

As Frost enters the house of poetry he enters a realm of appearance where his power is autonomous (but only in that realm); where he is loosed from the overbearing sovereignty of the structure of reality as he exalts the sovereignty of the human imagination over the coercions of the given, empirical order. An important lesson of post-Kantian thought, of Schiller, Nietzsche, William James, George Santayana, and Robert Frost is that we find our humanness, our freedom, as we find our power to transform the world by creatively resisting it. The radical and desperate claim for value of aesthetic theory in the Kantian tradition is that man's freedom, his human wholeness, is born in the aesthetic moment and limited to it. The utopian claims of Herbert Marcuse, that consciousness can become permanently aesthetic, ignores the guarded position of Schiller, who speaks only of the realm of appearance, not being, and ignores the complex counsel of a poet like Frost, who is not afraid to tell us about the distinction between finished art and ragged life.

8

The major themes in Frost's poetics are conveniently summarized by his sense of the pastoral experience. The pastoral scene, and particularly the farm house, came to symbolize for him the psychologically healing fictive world of poetry. He believed that the pastoral scene was an appropriate setting for the poet because, as he told Louis Untermeyer upon purchasing a farm in South Shaftesbury, Vermont, the pastoral world seemed especially pliable before his imagination. "The woods are a little too far from the house. I must bring them nearer by the power of music like Amphion or Orpheus. It is an old occupation with me. The trees have learned that they have to come where I play them to. I enjoy the power I find I have over them. You must see us together, the trees dancing obedience to the poet. . . ."[70] Frost's imagination, needing a loosened, open, flowing reality which would invite it to exert its shaping powers, often found the world beyond the farm far too hostile in its intransigent solidity. This is not to say, as some social critics have said,[71] that Frost's pastoral entrenchment was a retreat from a violent world of action, a withdrawal into those gentler circumstances where his imagination could assert its power effectively. Nor is this to say that Frost's talk about the "larger excruciations" was so much hot air; his dark poems should demonstrate that he meant what he said. As we examine his various statements on the pastoral scene and the imagination's love for it, a little critical mercy will suggest that his version of pastoral is complex, in Leo Marx's sense, and not sentimental-escapist.

The value of the "fictive symbol," or the "better nature," as I have alternately called it, depends directly on its maintaining a structure which both reconstitutes reality by positing it as a unified, metaphoric shape, and, at the same time, lets the antifictive, the existential, peer in—does not let it inside the house of poetry where fatal damage may be done to the psyche, but lets it pound on the door, lets it try to sneak under the door, lets it look in through the windows at night, lets it run crazily on the roof tops. The authenticity of poetry depends on its maintaining this tension of terror and serenity, or so one important part of Frost seems to insist. Once one end of the dialectic is dissolved, and it does not matter which one it is, then you either have the ideal of Frye—the radical transcendence of aesthetic illusion, the catapulting of self into never-never land—or you have sheer chaos, which is not art, and which human beings cannot stand.

Rustic life, Frost said in 1931, is like poetry itself in that it is both "resource and recourse."[72] The boundaries of the farm are sometimes marked by an enclosing fence that marks off the place of resource and all the threats which lay outside of the fenced-off land and make enclosures so necessary:

> Where my imaginary line
> Bends square in woods, an iron spine
> And pile of real rocks have been founded.
> And off this corner in the wild,
> Where these are driven in and piled,

One tree, by being deeply wounded,
Has been impressed as Witness Tree
And made commit to memory
My proof of being not unbounded.
Thus truth's established and borne out,
Though circumstanced with dark and doubt—
Though by a world of doubt surrounded.[73]

Far from dissolving the necessary tension within the structure of poetry, and providing an escape from the way things are, the pastoral scene as metaphor for the poem itself actually increases that tension by starkly outlining the polarity of the fictive and the antifictive.

Epilogue

Epilogue: Versions of Robert Frost

Two lonely cross-roads that themselves cross each other I have walked several times this winter without meeting or overtaking so much as a single person on foot or on runners. The practically unbroken condition of both for several days after a snow or a blow proves that neither is much traveled. Judge then how surprised I was the other evening as I came down one to see a man, who to my own unfamiliar eyes and in the dusk looked for all the world like myself, coming down the other, his approach to the point where our paths must intersect being so timed that unless one of us pulled up we must inevitably collide. I felt as if I was going to meet my own image in a slanting mirror. Or say I felt as we slowly converged on the same point with the same noiseless yet laborious strides as if we were two images about to float together with the uncrossing of someone's eyes. I verily expected to take up or absorb this other self and feel the stronger by the addition for the three-mile journey home. But I didn't go forward to the touch. I stood still in wonderment and let him pass by; and that, too, with the fatal omission of not trying to find out by a comparison of lives and immediate and remote interests what could have brought us by crossing paths to the same point in the wilderness at the same moment of nightfall. (R. F. in a letter 10 February 1912)

The subjects of one's poems are the symbols of one's self. . . .
(Wallace Stevens, *Adagia*)

. . . the person who does not act in reality and only acts in phantasy becomes himself unreal. *The actual 'world' for that person becomes shrunken and impoverished. The 'reality' of the physical world and other persons ceases to be used as a pabulum for the creative exercise of imagination, and hence comes to have less and less significance in*

itself. Phantasy, without being either in some measure embodied in reality, or itself enriched by injections of 'reality' becomes more and more empty and volatilized. The 'self' whose relatedness to reality is already tenuous becomes less and less a reality-self, and more and more phantasticized as it becomes more and more engaged in phantastic relationships with its own phantoms. . . . (R. D. Laing, The Divided Self)

I find this paradox in Frost's aesthetics and poetry: in and through the autonomous poem we are led to the creative energy behind the poem. From an organic theory of poetic creation that issues in an entity whose fictive life is made by and contained within the objective linguistic network, we are given a glimpse of the radically personal and subjective, the life of the poet that is prior to and independent of language, that gives life to the fictions of language. If in my discussions of the poems I have preferred to use the term "persona," or the phrase "self in the poem," rather than "consciousness" (as phenomenological critics would urge) it is because I wanted to make it clear that I believe that the truest way of seeing into the depths of the poet is in and through the objective medium of the poem: the immanence, the immediacy, the subjectivity of person is sensed there, in the language of the poem, or not at all. In disagreement with many recent phenomenological critics, I assume that pure self in itself, consciousness *qua* consciousness—unmediated vision—is unavailable and that we have to seek, as Walter J. Ong suggests,[1] the mediations of consciousness: the fictive worlds which the self chooses to project, in its emotional needs—and by projecting its fiction, revealing what it can of its interiority. The transformative magic of the poet's language that reveals his "supreme fiction" is a linguistic magic motivated by the deepest psychological needs of self, by what James called, in a crucial passage, "practical subjectivity."[2] The selves which we have seen constituted against the dominant objects in Frost's poetic landscape are enveloped by the continuous, guiding consciousness of the poet himself.

When we speak of the intermeshing of consciousness and its object in the poems of Robert Frost we are not speaking so much of "meanings" as we are of "experiences." From a purely formal point of view, we are speaking of the "self in the poem" and what he experiences as he encounters a brook, a farmhouse, or a woods, as he makes his way across the poetic landscape. The objectivist ideology of the New Critics tends to limit our probing to this formal, or aesthetic level of interest. But the organicism of Frost, interpreted from his Jamesian perspective, allows us to move beyond the aesthetic to the existential level. Probing the fixed features in a poetic landscape, and the patterns of consciousness radiated by those "objective" features, we come to grasp the deepest experiences of the poet as we are given a reflected glimpse of his consciousness. From the point of view of Frost's aesthetics of the fiction, the poet's self is revealed when the dominant urge of his consciousness *marks* the recurrent fictions which he *chooses* to project in his emotional needs.

Throughout I have identified the controlling urge of Frost's consciousness as a highly qualified and self-conscious urge to redeem, an urge to resolve tensions between self and the exterior, and to resolve tensions that reside wholly within the self. Many of the examples which I have offered tend to give the impression that Frost's moments of redemptive awareness signal always therapeutic experiences. But the overcoming of tension in Frost signals more than the finding of peace with oneself, with others, and with one's environment. The urge to redeem often results in experiences which are counter-therapeutic. What the aesthetics of organicism in general and the aesthetics of the supreme fiction in particular tend to say psychologically about Robert Frost, in their insistence that metaphors of enclosure and of self-containment best explain the nature of a poem, is his often deep and willful isolation; his disvaluing and contempt of all things beyond the little world of his private ego; at its severist extremity, his sinking into dangerously self-destructive states of an isolated paranoia. (Consider once again the egotism and the incipient paranoia in his definition of the poem as a "figure of the will braving alien entanglements," and in his definition of the existential context of the poet as a place of "excruciations," of "black and utter chaos.")

In the context of a political discussion Frost once told his old friend and former student, John Bartlett, that "one of the best things about the world is its badness."[3] And, in a similar vein, he wrote to Ridgley Torrence, "How am I to tell whether you care whether the world goes to hell or not? I certainly don't. I've got another world."[4] One might say a great deal about such remarks in the light of Frost's well-known political conservatism. My point is that, seen from the perspective of his various poems of enclosure, such remarks are consistent with a characteristic maneuver of his consciousness: to close out everything but me because I know that in a rotten god-forsaken world, where the irrational is king, and which is "unendurably brutal,"[5] I can trust only myself. Predictably, many of Frost's poems of enclosure dramatize the self attempting to "cut and run" by enclosing itself in a private world of its own making.[6] Such a poem as "The Black Cottage" achieves a kind of redemption for the self, to be sure, but at the cost of severing all relations between the me and the not-me, the self and the community. The self seeks comfort from the pain of a human world by removing to an inhuman and human-repelling setting.

Frost delineates this part of himself with cold precision in "The Figure in the Doorway":[7]

> The grade surmounted, we were riding high
> Through level mountains nothing to the eye
> But scrub oak, scrub oak and the lack of earth
> That kept the oaks from getting any girth.
> But as through the monotony we ran,
> We came to where there was a living man.
> His great gaunt figure filled his cabin door,
> And had he fallen inward on the floor,
> He must have measured to the further wall.
> But we who passed were not to see him fall.
> The miles and miles he lived from anywhere
> Were evidently something he could bear.
> He stood unshaken, and if grim and gaunt,
> It was not necessarily from want.
> He had the oaks for heating and for light.
> He had a hen, he had a pig in sight.
> He had a well, he had the rain to catch.
> He had a ten-by-twenty garden patch.
> Nor did he lack for common entertainment.
> That I assume was what our passing train meant.
> He could look at us in our diner eating,
> And if so moved uncurl a hand in greeting.

Locked this deeply in privacy, pleasuring in isolation, keeping "the universe alone," in the words of "The Most of It," the self soon begins to feel the terrible moral burdens of an isolation verging on solipsism and seeks "counter-love, original response."[8] But to no avail.

Sooner or later Frost had to imagine himself old and alone and

> One aged man—one man—can't keep a house. . . .

In "An Old Man's Winter Night"[9] Frost dissects with sympathy and pathos the needs of an enfeebled and senile old man who is approaching death rapidly. Considered within the context of his many poems on enclosure, this is more than a poem about a lonely old man in a lonely old farmhouse. It is a poem about the pain in the "empty rooms" of self. It is a poem about a self so deeply in isolation, so well enclosed that the light of consciousness can illuminate nothing beyond the bounded and frozen world of self, "and then not even that." We have come a long way when we traverse the distance between the early Emerson, who saw man in the woods eternally young and fully integrated within the community of nature, to Robert Frost, who in "An Old Man's Winter Night" evokes a bleak, modern vision of self—old and failing and alienated from a world which is evoked in a barren and inhospitable winter landscape. Ultimately, Frost comes to see that the final burden of enclosure may be too great to bear, may be madness itself: "beating on a box."

> All out-of-doors looked darkly in at him
> Through the thin frost, almost in separate stars,
> That gathers on the pane in empty rooms.
> What kept his eyes from giving back the gaze
> Was the lamp tilted near them in his hand.
> What kept him from remembering what it was
> That brought him to that creaking room was age.
> He stood with barrels round him—at a loss.
> And having scared the cellar under him
> In clomping here, he scared it once again
> In clomping off—and scared the outer night,
> Which has its sounds, familiar, like the roar
> Of trees and crack of branches, common things,
> But nothing so like beating on a box.
> A light he was to no one but himself
> Where now he sat, concerned with he knew what,
> A quiet light, and then not even that.

What is it that drives the ego inward to self-isolating autonomy? One of the answers, for Frost, is the curse of the postromantic self, the painful coming to a self-consciousness which is concomitant, as James suggests in that passage about the utter privacy of personal consciousness, with the fact of alienation, and which is also concomitant with the recognition (generally focused in the image of the woods) of the unmanageable in-

dependence and objectivity of the vast and indifferent world beyond self—
a vastness and indifference which only serves to emphasize the smallness,
the precariousness, and separateness of self. I quote in full "On Going
Unnoticed":[10]

> As vain to raise a voice as a sigh
> In the tumult of free leaves on high.
> What are you, in the shadow of trees
> Engaged up there with the light and breeze?
>
> Less than the coralroot, you know,
> That is content with the daylight low,
> And has no leaves at all of its own;
> Whose spotted flowers hang meanly down.
>
> You grasp the bark by a rugged pleat,
> And look up small from the forest's feet.
> The only leaf it drops goes wide,
> Your name not written on either side.
>
> You linger your little hour and are gone,
> And still the woods sweep leafily on,
> Not even missing the coralroot flower
> You took as a trophy of the hour.

The recognition of "free leaves," of a woods that sweeps "leafily on,"
is the now familiar recognition of an irreparable division between self and
nature. Among Frost's many responses to this modernist dilemma, two
especially stand out. I refer generally to the discussions of his dark wood
poems and, particularly, to "Bereft" and "Stopping By Woods on a
Snowy Evening." In "Stopping By Woods" the suggestion is strong that
the split between self and nature, human and inhuman, may be overcome (but it isn't) by giving in to the death instinct, by yielding up selfhood in a delicious merging with the natural world. In "Bereft" the self
is pushed into another kind of death. With ironic, detached consciousness extinguished, and the world exterior to self projected as a malignantly
hostile force, the self has overcome the split between human and inhuman
but at the cost of ingesting nature into the disturbed recesses of consciousness; at the cost of enclosing itself in a destructive paranoia.

For Frost those dangerous moments of mental imbalance were rare; it
was Jeannie, not Robert, who succumbed psychologically. The example of

Jeannie's pitiful end taught her brother to keep close watch over himself. His ability to objectify those states of mental disturbance in his women, in dialogue poems like "Home Burial," "A Servant to Servants," and "The Witch of Coös," was his way of slaying a self that might have been. His ability to penetrate with irony the minister's closed world in "The Black Cottage"; his ability to smile wryly at the puniness of self in "On Going Unnoticed"—taking home its "trophy" of coralroot; his ability to qualify, to envision alternate possibilities in "Design"; his ability to inject a humorous play on words in the grim "Desert Places" ("I am too absent-spirited to count")—all of these examples (and there are many more) are testimony to his success in keeping himself in hand by checking and limiting a significant drive within the self.

It would hardly be accurate, though, to conclude on a note which suggests a thoroughly unwholesome inner man whose only saving graces are insistent whimsical and ironical attitudes. One need not make excuses for the man—one cannot in honesty do so. Many of my studies of the poems will corroborate the portrait of the historical Frost that is drawn in Lawrance Thompson's formal biography—a portrait of a man mean, petty, and often inhumanly self-centered. If the redeemer, responding to a world sometimes hazardous and baffling, lived often for himself alone and his private redemptions, the testimony of many of his greatest poems —"Mending Wall," "Birches," "West-Running Brook," "Directive"— and the testimony of some of his lovely minor ones—"Going For Water," "The Generations of Men," "Putting in the Seed," "Meeting and Passing," "Devotion," "To Earth-Ward"—suggest a more expansive and capacious consciousness, a more generous self than many of us have been willing to grant: a redeemer who at his best prefers engagement, who seeks the right place for love and the games that two can play together, to twist some lines from "Birches."

"Two Look at Two"[11] embodies one of the supreme moments of wonder in American literature and is, among Frost's major poems, the one that best confirms the more capacious sense of self given to us in the brook poems. We find in "Two Look at Two" that the poet is open, that he wants to put aside self and self-consciousness as the closed self revealed in the house poems cannot. Frost can yield to the moment of wonder, to the moment of integrative vision, and not (at the same time) yield to sentimentality because he has not forgotten to draw the limits of wonder. As his lovers descend from the mountainside, with night near, he lets us understand that they recognize nature's dangers: "how rough it was /

With rock and washout, and unsafe in darkness." There is a touch of ominousness in nature's autonomy: "if a stone / Or earthslide moved at night, it moved itself." When they spot the doe, and then the buck, it is across a barbed-wire wall:

> A doe from round a spruce stood looking at them
> Across the wall, as near the wall as they.
> She saw them in their field, they her in hers.

Then, as if to reemphasize the separateness of the two worlds, of the fields of man and the fields of nature, Frost allows us a glimpse of the couple from the doe's perspective:

> The difficulty of seeing what stood still,
> Like some up-ended boulder split in two,
> Was in her clouded eyes. . . .

After the couple has seen both doe and buck, and both doe and buck have seen the couple, and neither doe nor buck has bolted off in fright, but just "passed unscared along the wall," Frost qualifies the reciprocity of the experience as he ends his poem:

> Still they stood,
> A great wave from it going over them,
> As if the earth in one unlooked-for favor
> Had made them certain earth returned their love.

If we put aside the poet's sobering perspective for a moment, there can be no doubt that from within the perspective of the lovers in the poem the earth *has* returned their love; that nature has opened herself receptively to them, even as they have opened themselves to one another. Love's linkages not only bind self to self, but the two to the earth. And the gentleness of the poet's ironies binds him to his lovers. The poem ends with the "as if." And yet the final image is not one of the lovers moving on down the mountainside, with time flowing again—the final image is of the stillness and of the enchanted moment of vision. It was Frost's choice, after all, to end his poem there, with the magical experience.

Before turning to one last poem, we might recall that though the dominant emphasis in Frost's aesthetics is continuous with the enclosed, contracted, and fearful self of the house poems, a self which looks upon the world as a place that needs to be transformed in order to be borne, it is also true that the aesthetics of supreme fictions cautions against the forging of impenetrable aesthetic worlds; urges, indeed, that the world exterior to self is not always to be taken so grimly as alien, psychologically destructive force. The things of this world which often press the imagination into its fiction-making operation are sometimes as psychically health-giving as the fiction itself. What Frost's poems of the play spirit tell us is that it is precisely the soothing, brighter moods and scenes of nature which encourage the self to release its play energies, and by so doing to open itself to the possibility of mutuality. The world built by the self in its play spirit is a very different world from that built by the self in its paranoid moments when the world is the stuff of nightmare. And, it would follow, the more expansive and open self revealed by play fictions is not to be forgotten or subordinated to the opaque and closed self who, seeing the poem as a "figure of the will braving alien entanglements," projects the fiction in order to free himself (by isolating himself) from a dangerous environment.

So we end where we began, with another poem which in its fragility and in its spirit of union is very reminiscent of "The Pasture," the prologue to *Complete Poems of Robert Frost*. Though a minor poem, "The Telephone"[12] flows from the core self of Robert Frost who in his desire to overcome isolation, and to transform a landscape too often dominated by utter loneliness, reaches out to communicate through the media of redemption: his desire and his imagination. We hear the redeeming poet speak truly and purely through his fictions, those linguistic shapes of desire and imagination. The continuity in Frost's canon, in his poems and aesthetics, is engendered by the mark of self, by the poet who in his best moments can maintain the complex awareness of a world at once hazardous and baffling, lovely and receptive; who can bear the difficult knowledge that redemptions can make life possible, but that, selfishly motivated, can make life impossible, can lock self in deepest isolation, where the self may eventually come to stand at the dangerous edge with the women of the psychological dialogue poems. If the idea of the fiction tends to reveal a man too worried about the mean inhospitality of the world's "hugeness and confusion," its "black and utter chaos"; a man too convinced that he had to construct a private world (a "better nature") in order to redeem, by replacing, his existential situation, then I think we have to modify that view of Frost by appealing again to his poems.

We turn from the particular structure of Frost's experience that is suggested by his poems and aesthetics of enclosure, to the structure of experience embodied by his play poems and love poems—a structure of experience characterized by openness, and by what R. D. Laing describes as that "ontological security" which is the psychological basis of the self's confidence in its place within the dynamics of human relations. "The Telephone," though fantastical, is not pure fantasy—there is the mature, complex recognition, demanded by his aesthetics, that this *is* play: "Well, so I came." But that most mild intrusion of an ironic consciousness does not disturb the core of stillness and tranquility in the play world, with time stopped; nor does it introduce a sense that outside the play world lies a threatening reality. Tonally speaking, the setting of "The Telephone" is consistent with the harmonious sense of integration between self and world that we saw in "A Prayer in Spring" and "The Quest of the Purple-Fringed." "The Telephone" is a "we" poem, consistent with other "we" poems—among them, "Rose Pogonias," "Going For Water," and "Two Look at Two." It is starkly contrastive to "Home Burial," "A Servant to Servants," and "The Hill Wife"—poems which dramatize the tragic inability to say "we" with any confidence; the tragic inability to step out of the prison of our subjectivity and to recognize the reality of another person. The medium of communion for imagination in "The Telephone" is a flower, a real thing in the real world, and always a lovely thing in Frost's world. Flowers, as Frost recognizes in a number of his poems, have an all-too-short stay: but they live, they are beautifully there in nature, and they may encourage a redeeming consciousness, already fueled by desire, to come out of isolation and self-consciousness, to move beyond alienation by seeking contact beyond the self. In "Directive," probably his greatest poem, Frost achieves momentary self-wholeness beyond confusion while staying in close touch with his separate, alienated and ironic existence: "CLOSED to all but me." In "The Telephone," an obscure but perhaps more characteristic expression, Frost finds what he needs, as simple, separate person in mutuality. The dangerously generalized hostility "out there," almost always present in Frost, abates and then disappears. The act of locating his "I" in "We" is an act which confers joy upon the very physiognomy of his landscape.

> "When I was just as far as I could walk
> From here today,
> There was an hour
> All still
> When leaning with my head against a flower
> I heard you talk.

Don't say I didn't, for I heard you say—
You spoke from that flower on the window sill—
Do you remember what it was you said?"

"First tell me what it was you thought you heard."

"Having found the flower and driven a bee away,
I leaned my head,
And holding by the stalk,
I listened and I thought I caught the word—
What was it? Did you call me by my name?
Or did you say—
Someone said 'Come'—I heard it as I bowed."

"I may have thought as much, but not aloud."

"Well, so I came."

Notes

Introduction: *Robert Frost and Modern Poetics*

1. J. H. Van Den Berg, *The Phenomenological Approach to Psychiatry* (Springfield, 1955), p. 32.

2. *The Poetry of Robert Frost*, ed. by Edward Connery Lathem (New York, 1969), p. 332 (hereinafter cited as *PRF*).

3. In the introduction to *Pragmatism and Other Essays* (New York, 1963), p. xv. The historical relations of Robert Frost and William James are traced by Lawrance Thompson in *Robert Frost: The Early Years, 1874–1915* (New York, 1966).

4. William James, *Psychology* (first ed., 1892; New York, 1963), ch. XI.

5. Jean-Paul Sartre, *What is Literature?* trans. Bernard Frechtman (New York, 1965), pp. 32–33.

6. *The Principles of Psychology*, I (first ed., 1890; New York, 1950), 284.

7. Ibid., pp. 287–288.   8. Ibid., p. 363.

9. *Pragmatism and Other Essays*, p. 131.

10. *The Will to Believe and Other Essays in Popular Philosophy* (first ed., 1896; New York, 1956), p. 41.

11. Ibid., p. 42.   12. Ibid., p. 118.

13. For further examples of James's recourse to aesthetic metaphors see: *Pragmatism: A New Way For Some Old Ways of Thinking* (New York, 1907), pp. 61, 64, 65, 247, 256–257, 258; *A Pluralistic Universe* (first ed., 1909; New York, 1942), pp. 9–10. For further examples of James's view of mind as constitutive see: *The Meaning of Truth: A Sequel to 'Pragmatism'* (New York, 1909) pp. 58, 80.

14. *Selected Letters of Robert Frost*, ed. Lawrance Thompson (New York, 1964), p. 361.

15. Ibid., p. 465.   16. *Pragmatism*, p. 64.

17. See: *Selected Letters*, p. 215; *The Letters of Robert Frost to Louis Untermeyer* (New York, 1963), p. 189; *Selected Prose of Robert Frost*, ed. Hyde Cox and Edward Connery Lathem (New York, 1966), pp. 24, 35, 37–38, 39, 40–41, 49–50; Sidney Cox, *A Swinger of Birches: A Portrait of Robert Frost* (New York, 1957), pp. 18–19, 44, 46, 76.

18. *Selected Prose*, p. 41.

19. Lawrance Thompson, *Robert Frost: The Years of Triumph, 1915–1938* (New York, 1970) p. 401.

20. *Selected Prose*, p. 24.   21. *Letters to Untermeyer*, p. 285.

22. Pragmatism, pp. 21–22.

23. *Selected Prose*, pp. 106, 107.   24. Ibid., p. 107.

25. Quoted in *A Swinger of Birches*, p. 121.

26. *Pragmatism and Other Essays*, p. 112.

27. Ibid., pp. 170–171.   28. Ibid., p. 263.

29. Georges Poulet, *The Interior Distance*, trans. Elliott Coleman (Ann Arbor, 1964; paperback ed.), p. vii.

30. *Psychology*, p. 148.   31. *PRF*, p. 251.

32. John Dewey, *Art as Experience* (first ed., 1934; New York, 1958), p. 282.

33. This is, in brief, the central complaint of George Nitchie, *Human Values in the Poetry of Robert Frost* (Durham, 1960).

Chapter 1: Invitations

1. Lawrance Thompson, *Robert Frost: The Early Years, 1874–1915* (New York, 1966), pp. 311–312.

2. *PRF*, p. 1.

3. *Complete Poems of Robert Frost* (New York, 1949), p. vi (from the prefatory essay, "The Figure a Poem Makes").

4. *PRF*, p. 5.

5. A term I borrow from Eliseo Vivas. It carries the idealistic suggestion that the symbol creates the poet's world, that in and through the symbol we gain access to the poet's world.

6. *PRF*, pp. 5–6.

7. *The Collected Poems of W. B. Yeats* (New York, 1966), p. 292.

8. *PRF*, p. 9.   9. *PRF*, pp. 9–10.

10. Gaston Bachelard, *The Poetics of Space*, trans. Maria Jolas (first pub. France, 1958; Boston, 1969), pp. 40–41.

11. *PRF*, pp. 11–12.   12. *PRF*, p. 12.

13. *PRF*, p. 13.

14. Sidney Cox, *A Swinger of Birches: A Portrait of Robert Frost* (New York, 1957), p. 121.

15. *PRF*, p. 17.   16. *PRF*, pp. 22–23.

17. Thompson, pp. 318–320.

18. Reuben Brower, *The Poetry of Robert Frost: Constellations of Intention* (New York, 1963), p. 242.

19. *PRF*, p. 17.   20. *PRF*, p. 18.

Chapter 2: The Brook

1. *PRF*, p. 82.   2. *PRF*, pp. 40–44.

3. *PRF*, pp. 73–81.   4. *PRF*, p. 119.

5. Reuben Brower, *The Poetry of Robert Frost: Constellations of Intention* (New York, 1963), pp. 81–83.

6. *PRF*, p. 231.

7. Leo Marx, *The Machine in the Garden* (New York, 1964).

8. *PRF*, pp. 257–260.

Chapter 3: The House

1. Roy Harvey Pearce, *The Continuity of American Poetry* (Princeton, 1961), pp. 271–283.

2. *PRF*, pp. 34–40.   3. *PRF*, pp. 51–55.

4. PRF, pp. 62–68.   5. PRF, pp. 202–207.
6. PRF, pp. 126–129.
7. Selected Prose of Robert Frost, ed. Hyde Cox and Edward Connery Latham (New York, 1966), p. 107.
8. See Lawrance Thompson, Robert Frost: The Years of Triumph, 1915–1938 (New York, 1970), ch. 9.
9. PRF, p. 102.   10. PRF, p. 223.
11. PRF, p. 255.
12. Wallace Stevens, Opus Posthumous, edited with introduction by Samuel French Morse (London, 1959), pp. 206–207.
13. George Santayana, Interpretations of Poetry and Religion (New York, 1957), p. 245.
14. PRF, pp. 55–59.   15. PRF, pp. 174–176.
16. PRF, pp. 241–242.   17. PRF, p. 108.
18. PRF, pp. 109–110.   19. PRF, pp. 252–253.
20. PRF, pp. 110–117.   21. PRF, pp. 143–156.
22. PRF, pp. 263–264.   23. PRF, pp. 101–102.
24. PRF, pp. 341–342.   25. PRF, p. 264.
26. PRF, p. 315.   27. PRF, pp. 342–343.

Chapter 4: The Woods

1. PRF, pp. 443–444.   2. PRF, p. 148.
3. PRF, p. 245.   4. PRF, p. 250.
5. PRF, pp. 260–261.   6. PRF, pp. 223–224.
7. PRF, pp. 338–339.   8. PRF, p. 261.
9. William James, Pragmatism: A New Name For Some Old Ways of Thinking (New York, 1907), pp. 252–253.
10. PRF, p. 226.   11. PRF, p. 251.
12. PRF, pp. 224–225.   13. PRF, p. 296.
14. PRF, p. 334.

Chapter 5: The Redemptive Imagination

1. PRF, pp. 33–34. For two readings of "Mending Wall" that sometimes touch on points that I make see John C. Broderick, "Frost's 'Mending Wall,'" Explicator, XIV item 24 (1956); Carson Gibbs, "Frost's 'Mending Wall,'" Explicator, XX, item 48 (1962). The fullest context for "Mending Wall" is established by those poems in which Frost explores and attempts to overcome the division between play and work—"Mowing" and "Two Tramps in Mud Time"—and by those poems in which the experience of play is crucial to his vision—"Going For Water," "A Hillside Thaw," and "Directive." In the light of recent reinterpretations of Freud, both Thoreau and Frost would appear to anticipate the views of Herbert Marcuse, in Eros and Civilization, and Norman O. Brown, in Life Against Death, when they insist, against Freud's Civilization and Its Discontents, that the pleasure instinct need not be repressed for the dubious rewards of the reality principle. The revolutionary, even apocalytic implications of Thoreau's analysis of civilization are obvious; that Frost's sociopolitical views, as they are implied in his play poems, may be as revolu-

tionary is not so obvious because of his well-known and often self-styled "conserva-tism" and the hatcheting job done on him in the journals of liberal opinion in the 1930s.

2. *PRF*, pp. 121–122.   3. *PRF*, p. 268.

4. *PRF*, pp. 377–379. For two readings that supply and then debate the theological backgrounds of "Directive" see Robert Peters, "The Truth of Frost's 'Directive,'" *Modern Languages Notes*, LXXV (January, 1960), 29–32 and Margaret M. Blum, "Robert Frost's 'Directive': A Theological Reading," *Modern Language Notes*, LXXVI (June, 1961), 524–525. Other readings that I found suggestive are: Mildred E. Hart-sock, *Explicator*, XXI, item 71 (1963); J. P. Dougherty, "Robert Frost's 'Directive' to the Wilderness," *American Quarterly*, XVIII (Summer, 1966), 209–219; Reuben Brower, *The Poetry of Robert Frost: Constellations of Intention* (New York, 1963), pp. 226–242.

Chapter 6: Organicism and Subjectivity

1. William James, *Psychology* (first ed., 1892; New York, 1963), p. 148.

2. Walter J. Ong, *The Barbarian Within* (New York, 1962). See "A Dialectic of Aural and Objective Correlatives."

3. John Dewey, *Art as Experience* (first ed., 1934; New York, 1958), p. 65.

4. See W. K. Wimsatt and Cleanth Brooks, *Literary Criticism: A Short History* (New York, 1957), pp. 398–399.

5. Benedetto Croce, *Aesthetic*, trans. Douglas Ainslie (first ed., 1909; New York, 1966), p. 111.

6. Ralph Waldo Emerson, *Selected Prose and Poetry*, introduction by Reginald L. Cook (New York, 1966), pp. 26–27.

7. Quoted in Cleanth Brooks, *The Well Wrought Urn: Studies in the Structure of Poetry* (New York, 1947, 1962), pp. 199, 262.

8. Cleanth Brooks, *Modern Poetry and the Tradition* (Chapel Hill, 1939), p. 59.

9. *Selected Letters of Robert Frost*, edited by Lawrance Thompson (New York, 1964), p. 199.

10. Ibid., p. 385.   11. Ibid., p. 141.

12. See *Interviews with Robert Frost*, ed. Edward Connery Latham (New York, 1966), pp. 117, 174, 188, 202.

13. Ibid., p. 117.

14. I refer to Eliseo Vivas, *Creation and Discovery* (first ed., 1955; Chicago, 1965).

15. Ibid., pp. 137–138.

16. I. A. Richards, *Science and Poetry* (London, 1935), p. 43.

17. *Selected Prose of Robert Frost*, ed. Hyde Cox and Edward Connery Latham (New York, 1966) p. 20.

18. Ibid., p. 45.

19. *Interviews with Robert Frost*, p. 202. The term "romantic irrationalism" used above seems to have two slightly different meanings. The first (and, I take it, primary) meaning of the term is most bluntly illustrated by Croce's statement (discussed above) that aesthetic vision cannot be willed. Aesthetic vision is a purely unconscious spiritual act which lies outside of the conscious reason. The second meaning of the term is suggested in the analogy of the poem to an organism. Unlike Frost, the romantics seemed often to mean literally that the poem writes itself. Again, from this point of view, the artist is an unconscious agent whose relationship to his art work is extremely

problematic, since the art work, as a kind of plant would seem to grow into the fullness of its being largely unaided by the artist himself. The artist can only "find" his poem, to use Frost's terms, never "make" it.

20. Ibid., p. 204.

21. I discuss this point in *The Gaiety of Language: An Essay on the Radical Poetics of W. B. Yeats and Wallace Stevens* (Berkeley and Los Angeles, 1968), pp. 35–38.

22. *Selected Prose*, p. 45.

23. *The Well Wrought Urn*, pp. 151–166.

24. Ibid., p. 204.

25. Ibid., p. 205.

26. *Selected Prose*, p. 13.

27. Ibid., p. 18.

28. Ibid., p. 19.

29. Ibid., p. 20.

Chapter 7: The Scope and the Limits of Supreme Fictions

1. The philosophical background of the aesthetic theory that I deal with in this chapter is sketched by Albert William Levi in *Literature, Philosophy, and the Imagination* (Bloomington, 1962), especially ch. II, and by Frank Kermode in *The Sense of an Ending: Studies in the Theory of Fiction* (New York, 1967).

2. Kant is quite clear on this point. Knowledge for him is always the *conceptual* grasp of reality, and the formulation of concepts is *solely* the business of the constitutive principles of Understanding. In the cognitive process, which is the subject of the first *Critique*, the imagination plays the intermediary role of unifying sense data which is then fed into the categories of Understanding, where it is formulated as a concept. In the third *Critique* Kant assigns the imagination an aesthetic function, but in this function the imagination does not, as most neo-Kantians want to suggest about their master's statement on aesthetic imagination, give us a "special kind of knowledge." In its aesthetic phase the imagination is freed from working for the Understanding: there are no concepts adequate to aesthetic imagination's constructions of reality. Aesthetic ideas are thus "fictions" for Kant, not cognitions; as such they have "regulative" status. "Fictions" give pleasure because they present reality as we wish to create it, and not the way our cognitive faculties do create it. Compare *Critique of Pure Reason*, trans. F. Max Muller (New York, 1966), pp. 116–117, with *Critique of Judgment*, trans. J. H. Bernard (New York, 1892), p. 157.

3. I have developed some of the theoretical implications of this metaphor in the Symbolists in *The Gaiety of Language: An Essay on the Radical Poetics of W. B. Yeats and Wallace Stevens* (Berkeley and Los Angeles, 1968), pp. 28–38.

4. For an account of this position and its problematic nature, see Murray Krieger, *The New Apologists for Poetry* (Minneapolis, 1956).

5. Cassirer wrote that science must renounce "its aspiration and its claim to an 'immediate' grasp and communication of reality" because it "realizes that the only objectivization of which it is capable is, and must remain, mediation. And in this insight, another highly significant idealistic consequence is implicit. If the object of knowledge can be defined only through the medium of a particular logical and conceptual structure, we are forced to conclude that a variety of media will correspond to various structures of the object, to various meanings for 'objective' relations. Even in 'nature,' the physical object will not coincide absolutely with the chemical object, nor the chemical with the biological—because physical, chemical, biological knowledge *frame their questions* each from its own particular standpoint and, in accordance with this standpoint, subject the phenomena to a special interpretation and formation." *The Philosophy of Symbolic Forms, I: Language* (New Haven, 1953), p. 76.

6. Eliseo Vivas made the inevitable extension of Cassirer's position into literary aesthetics when he wrote (in essence) that the poem may subject "phenomena to a special interpretation and formation": "What does the poem mean or say? What it means is not a world it reflects or imitates or represents in illusion, in the sense of a world as envisaged by the mind prior to the poetic activity in which it is envisaged in poetry. What the poem says or means is the world it reveals or discloses *in* and *through* itself, a new world whose features, prior to the act of poetic revelation, were concealed from us. . . . The object of the poem is precisely those aspects of the familiar world—its value, its diversity in order, its structure—which we can grasp only *in* and *through* the poetic vision." Eliseo Vivas, *Creation and Discovery* (1955; Chicago, 1965), pp. 132–133.

7. In the "Preface" to *Critique of Judgment*, p. 3, Kant says that he wants to "check the dangerous pretensions of understanding" which, though it had furnished the conditions of knowing, did not thereby confine within its bounds the "possibility of all things in general." The third *Critique*, therefore, has for its subject the affective, rather than the cognitive, side of man.

8. *The Gaiety of Language*, pp. 135–147.

9. Wallace Stevens, *Opus Posthumous*, edited with introduction by Samuel French Morse (London, 1959), p. 192.

10. *Selected Prose of Robert Frost*, ed. Hyde Cox and Edward Connery Latham (New York, 1966), p. 107.

11. See *Critique of Judgment*, pp. 44, 52, 111, 129, 157. I am describing a view of the aesthetic experience which, implicit in Kant, is pervasive in many modern critics, some of whom revere his ideas and others of whom disavow them: T. E. Hulme, Clive Bell, I. A. Richards, John Crowe Ransom, to name the most prominent. For an elaborate and theoretically probing analysis of the idea, to which I am deeply indebted, see Eliseo Vivas, *The Artistic Transaction And Essays on Theory of Literature* (Columbus, 1963), pp. 3–95.

12. Wilhelm Worringer, *Abstraction and Empathy*, trans. Michael Bullock (New York, 1953).

13. *Selected Letters of Robert Frost*, ed. Lawrance Thompson (New York, 1964), p. 361.

14. Ibid., p. 369.   15. Ibid., p. 465.

16. *Selected Prose*, pp. 61–62, 67.

17. *The Letters of Robert Frost to Louis Untermeyer* (New York, 1963), p. 136.

18. Ibid., p. 259.   19. *Selected Prose*, p. 107.

20. William James, *Psychology* (first ed., 1892; New York, 1963), p. 400.

21. PRF, pp. 19–21.   22. *Selected Prose*, p. 106.

23. Ibid., p. 25.

24. Wallace Stevens, *The Necessary Angel: Essays on Reality and the Imagination* (London, 1955), p. 36.

25. *Selected Prose*, p. 24.   26. Ibid., p. 37.

27. Ibid., p. 41.

28. The shaping nature of mind, its metaphoric habit, is a pervasive theme in Frost's writings. See, for example: Sidney Cox, *A Swinger of Birches: A Portrait of Robert Frost* (New York, 1957), pp. 18–19, 44, 46, 76; *Letters to Untermeyer*, p. 189; *Selected Letters*, p. 215; *Selected Prose*, pp. 24, 35, 37, 37–38, 39, 40–41, 49–50.

29. Ernst Cassirer, *Language and Myth*, trans. by Susanne K. Langer (New York, 1946), p. 66; *The Philosophy of Symbolic Forms: II: Mythical Thought* (New Haven, 1955), p. 63.

30. Hans Vaihinger, *The Philosophy of 'As If'*, trans. C. K. Ogden (London, 1924).

31. *Selected Prose*, p. 39.

32. Harry Berger, Jr., "Poetry as Revision: Interpreting Robert Frost," *Criticism* X (Winter, 1968), 1–22.

33. *The Philosophy of 'As If'*, p. 92.

34. *Selected Prose*, p. 18.

35. *The Philosophy of 'As If'*, p. 12.

36. *Selected Prose*, pp. 106–107.

37. *A Swinger of Birches*, p. 121.

38. This discussion of Frye is based on *Anatomy of Criticism* (first ed., 1957; New York, 1967), second and third essays; *Fables of Identity: Studies in Poetic Mythology* (New York, 1963), "The Archetypes of Literature"; *The Educated Imagination* (Bloomington, 1969).

39. *Northrop Frye in Modern Criticism*, ed. with an introductory essay by Murray Krieger (New York, 1966), pp. 11, 19–20. The relationship of Freud and Frye is suggested by Krieger.

40. *The Educated Imagination*, pp. 29, 80.

41. Ernst Cassirer, *An Essay on Man* (New Haven, 1962), pp. 81, 83.

42. *Fables of Identity*, p. 248.

43. George Santayana, *Interpretations of Poetry and Religion* (1900; New York, 1957), pp. 260, 269–270, 272.

44. *Letters to Untermeyer*, p. 92.

45. Margaret Bartlett Anderson, *Robert Frost and John Bartlett: The Record of a Friendship* (New York, 1963), p. 175.

46. *Selected Letters*, p. 466.

47. W. K. Wimsatt's commentary on the romantic way of metaphor may be compared to Frost's modification of the romantic position in his insistence on simile. Wimsatt's comments make it clear that the romantic way of metaphor follows from a profound commitment to a monistic philosophy of some sort. The poet of simile, contrarily, tends to a skeptical and dualistic position: "The theory of imagination elaborated by Coleridge, and less precisely but in substantially the same way, by Wordsworth, was an excellent description of their own best poetry in its formal, structural, and metaphoric aspect. One might redescribe this structure approximately in these terms: It is a structure which makes only a restrained use of the central overstatement of similitude which had been so important in all poetry up to that time. Both tenor and vehicle are wrought in a parallel process out of the same material. The landscape is both the occasion of subjective reflection or transcendental insight and the source of figures by which the reflection or insight is defined. In such a structure, finally, the element of tension in disparity may not be prominent. The interest derives not from our being aware of disparity in stated likeness, but in the opposite activity of our discerning the design and the unity latent in a multiform sensuous picture. This is no doubt a form of 'reconciliation.' " W. K. Wimsatt and Cleanth Brooks, *Literary Criticism: A Short History* (New York, 1957), p. 401.

48. *Critique of Judgment*, pp. 146–147.

49. Ibid., pp. 165, 171, 172.

50. Friedrich Schiller, "Letters on the Aesthetical Education of Man," in *Aesthetical and Philosophical Essays* (New York, 1902), p. 110.

51. Ibid., p. 96.

52. Ibid., p. 97.

53. Ibid., p. 114.

54. Ibid., p. 115.

55. Ibid., p. 116.

56. For examples of the frequency with which Frost reverted to "play" metaphors, see *Interviews with Robert Frost*, ed. Edward Connery Latham (New York, 1966), pp. 103, 140, 161, 167, 177, 203, 235, 247, 268.

57. *Selected Prose*, p. 64.

58. *Interviews with Robert Frost*, p. 234.

59. Ibid., p. 232.
60. *Robert Frost and John Bartlett*, p. 124.
61. *Interviews with Robert Frost*, p. 137.
62. *Selected Prose*, p. 20.
64. Ibid., p. 67.
66. *Selected Prose*, p. 62.
68. Ibid., p. 67.
70. *Selected Letters*, p. 353.

63. Ibid., p. 19.
65. *A Swinger of Birches*, p. 58.
67. Ibid., p. 65.
69. Ibid.

71. See, for example, Malcolm Cowley, "The Case Against Mr. Frost," reprinted in *Robert Frost: A Collection of Critical Essays*, ed. James M. Cox (Englewood Cliffs, 1962), pp. 36–45.
72. *Interviews with Robert Frost*, p. 75.
73. PRF, p. 331.

Epilogue: Versions of Robert Frost

1. Walter J. Ong, *The Barbarian Within* (New York, 1962), p. 60.
2. William James, *The Will to Believe and Other Essays in Popular Philosophy* (first ed., 1896; New York, 1956), p. 117.
3. Quoted in Margaret Bartlett Anderson, *Robert Frost and John Bartlett: A Record of a Friendship* (New York, 1963), p. 183.
4. *Selected Letters of Robert Frost*, ed. Lawrance Thompson (New York, 1964), p. 463.

5. Ibid., p. 247.
7. PRF, p. 292.
9. PRF, p. 108.
11. PRF, pp. 229–230.

6. *Selected Letters*, p. 213.
8. PRF, p. 338.
10. PRF, p. 247.
12. PRF, p. 118.

Indexes

(Compiled by Michael Clark)

Index of Titles of Frost's Works

Index of Names